Art of the Americas

ANCIENT AND HISPANIC

Art of the Americas

ANCIENT AND HISPANIC

with a comparative chapter on the Philippines

PÁL KELEMEN

BONANZA BOOKS • New York

0-517-127199
Copyright © MCMLXIX by Paul Kelemen
Library of Congress Catalog Card Number: 72-87163
This edition is published by Bonanza Books
a division of Crown Publishers, Inc.
by arrangement with Thomas Y. Crowell Company
a b c d e f g h
Manufactured in the United States of America

To the countless unnoticed librarians
of our country, who are carrying on
their cultural work with intelligence and patience.

CONTENTS

By the Same Author

Battlefield of the Gods
ASPECTS OF MEXICAN ART, HISTORY AND EXPLORATION
   [editions in English, German, and Hungarian]

Medieval American Art
MASTERPIECES OF THE NEW WORLD BEFORE COLUMBUS

Baroque and Rococo in Latin America

El Greco Revisited
HIS BYZANTINE HERITAGE
   [editions in English and Spanish]

Pre-Columbian and Colonial Art of Latin America
   [editions in German, Dutch, French, Spanish, and Portuguese]

Art of the Americas
ANCIENT AND HISPANIC
   with a Comparative Chapter on the Philippines

Preface

Every book has its history, its train of past events that explains why and how it was written. This book is no exception. In 1966 Columbia University invited me to lecture at a graduate seminar that the Latin American Institute was offering to selected students—teachers of language, history, literature, social sciences, and so forth. None of them was particularly interested in the art or archaeology of the Americas. Dr. Lewis U. Hanke, then the director of the Institute, thought, however, that talks on the art of the Americas would widen the scope and understanding of the participants, who could influence their colleagues and students, and call attention to these facets of the civilization. When I finished my talks, the applause was rewarding, and more than forty people gathered around me and asked whether there existed a book from which they, as laymen, could learn something more. Soon thereafter, Robert L. Crowell, head of the distinguished publishing house of Thomas Y. Crowell Company, visited me, and the plan for this book was laid out.

Thus, the *why* is answered. The *how* will take a few longer paragraphs. In 1930, en route to Venice for an exhibition and conference, I met an American girl in the Italian Alps, who was living in Europe with her parents, studying music. We sat together on a rainy day, and I told her about my recent trip to Spain and my interest in the Byzantine heritage of El Greco, so little illuminated. I asked her why American millionaires supported the restoration of Versailles and other European sites, but why no money was spent on the American continent to make its ancient civilization better known. At that time I had had some glimpses of the art of the Americas in the British Museum and in Continental collections.

As the rain continued to pour down, I described my trips to several European countries, first with a tutor in my Latin school years and later as a young man, when I was invariably interested in searching out the lesser-known cities and lands. After a visit to Rodin's villa at Meudon Val Fleury near Paris, I had published an essay describing my talk with the great sculptor in connection with his new book *L'Art* (1911). I had also written a study evaluating Max Reinhardt's production in Munich of the *Oresteia,* the Aeschylus trilogy, in the theater of the round decades before other experiments in this field. Finally I spoke of my pleasant associations as a gentleman scholar with the Fine Arts Museum in Budapest.

That September this same American girl, my future bride, came to Budapest with her parents. The Hungarian capital in its blessed autumn splendor was an excellent setting for finding out more about ourselves. At that time, neither the city, the picturesque castles along the Danube, nor the baronial mansion at the end of a chestnut allée had been robbed, burned, and riddled with shot—first by the Nazis and then by the Communists. We were married in Florence, Italy, where my bride's parents were living, and after a few months I went with them on what was planned as a short visit to the United States. Herbert Hoover was then President, and Prohibition was still on the books.

We spent the first weeks in New York City. I went to the New York Public Library to consult publications on Byzantine art. The courtesy and help I received there embarrassed me: in European libraries pedantic treatment, slowness, suspicion are customary; in France, outright rudeness. The different spirit here impressed me deeply. The remaining months we stayed in Boston, where we conscientiously visited all the museums. One windy Indian summer afternoon in 1932 we went to the Peabody Museum of Harvard University. I was overwhelmed by the richness and variety of objects from pre-Columbian America, so soberly gracing the gray-painted shelves. Here was represented a civilization that could contribute much to the universal history of art.

The next day I went around with the director of the museum, urging that a comprehensive illustrated survey of this obscure world should be written from the standpoint of its outstanding and unusual art. And since it was alleged that there was no one else with my background to undertake this pioneer work, I myself was persuaded to carry out the project that I had proposed for an American scholar.

After six months at Harvard, we rolled down to Yucatán in an empty banana boat. The Carnegie Institution of Washington was excavating the Temple of the Warriors and the Group of the Thousand Columns in Chichén Itzá. There was no *turismo.* In April 1933, Maya art had not yet been "discovered" by the public. We slept in hammocks in an Indian hut, ate wild turkey meat. After a day of studying the ruins in their perfect solitude—only wild doves flying about—we gathered in the evenings with the staff of the Institution. There was no electricity there at that time, and the arrival of the first refrigerator, which functioned by kerosene, was hailed with general jubilation. One evening Sylvanus G. Morley, chief archaeologist, took us into the ball-court and played Beethoven's Fifth Symphony on his gramophone to demonstrate the remarkable acoustics. There was a powerful moon in the steel-blue sky and a constellation above our heads different from any we had seen. Once again in Mérida, we carried ice in relays from an ice-cream parlor to the photographer at midnight, to cool water enough to develop our negatives.

Later, on the slow railway trip to the Mexican capital, plagued by dust storms, the stop at Orizaba with its unspoiled colonial charm and its snow-capped volcano is memorable. In Mexico City, small houses were standing along the Avenida de la Reforma, and on Sunday mornings the *charros,* in their broad-brimmed hats, would ride downtown on their silver-bedecked steeds.

I was well received as a European scholar—at that time a rara avis—who showed enthusiasm for the great originality and vitality not only of Mexico's ancient art but also for the Hispanic period, and one who planned to make a study that should bring its culture wide publicity.

My research on El Greco was laid aside. In Greenwich, Connecticut, during the late summer of that year, I started to write my book *Battlefield of the Gods,* a collection of essays on Mexican art and archaeology. I also wanted to see what other cultures in Central and South America had produced—and the more I saw, the more convinced I became that the art of ancient America was worthy of having a separate chapter devoted to it in any universal history of the fine arts.

Five more years, with four crossings of the Atlantic, were spent studying collections here and abroad. Hitler occupied Austria, and Czechoslovakia was next on his program. We left our *villino* in the hills of Florence below San Miniato because, in connection with his slaughter in Ethiopia, Mussolini's anti-Anglo–American propaganda had made our stay uncomfortable. In Central Europe, Nazi and Soviet infiltration had become painfully obvious. In the late spring of 1938, we were in Paris to give a lecture at the Sorbonne on the art and archaeology of the American Southwest. From hotel concierge to university professor, we were assured that the French infantry was the best in the world and that the Maginot Line was impenetrable—and that anyhow Czechoslovakia was far away and not their affair. Then came Munich and "peace in our time"—with Chamberlain, Reynaud, Hitler, and Mussolini posing together for photographs.

By that time I realized that if I wished to complete and publish my survey, originally intended to show the art of pre-Columbian America to Europe, it would have to be done in the United States. We built a house in the foothills of the Berkshires, and all of our belongings—including our photographs and library—from Hungary, Italy, England, and the American Middle West were luckily under one roof when war broke out.

In the subsequent years I had the opportunity on cultural missions to survey the art of the Americas in a dozen Latin American republics, journeying as far as Bolivia, collecting and studying material for publication, which followed quite regularly.

In all these activities I remained conscious that my education had been mainly European. For eight years, I had climbed the stairs of my Latin school, where large dust-covered pictures of the Acropolis and the *Forum Romanum* hung on the walls while, on the landings, "the Dying Gaul" gasped his last breath and the busts of Aristotle and Pericles gazed at me with their blind eyes. My education was the traditional one for Europe. I had, however, also had the luck to see the excavations east of the Danube, on that vast Hungarian plain where the graves of Jazyges, Scythians, Ostrogoths, Huns, Avars, and Magyars had come to light. It was clear that the different arts and crafts of those non-European migratory peoples had exerted a larger influence on Western Europe than those countries were willing to admit. How these observations, gathered over more than four decades of experience in the history of art, affected my attitude toward the artistic production of the Americas is discussed in more detail in this book's appendix.

In 1956, the State Department sent us on a lecture tour to Portugal, Spain, Italy, Greece, and Turkey, amounting to two dozen lectures in thirteen cities, all on the art of the Americas. The chauvinism and self-absorption abroad, especially in the capitals of Europe, seemed little changed by the war. In harbor cities, accustomed to dealing with distant continents, an elasticity of comprehension, even an enthusiastic response, was encountered. But it was not until I spoke at the Turkish National University in Istanbul, where the audience stood deep in the corridors, that my slides evoked excited gasps, betokening a spontaneous response. The next day as we sat talking on the terrace of our host, looking across a bay of the Bosporus with its backdrop of domes and minarets, I realized that these students were studying Persian pottery, the architecture of ancient Iran, Turkish book illumination, the rug patterns of Turkestan. Here I had had an audience for whom the Greco-Roman ideal of beauty occupied only a single chapter in the many-volumed story of art. It was free of West European academism and unhampered by intellectualization and verbalization; it could recognize the beauty of this New World. These students had many other subjects at hand equally as fascinating as, and possibly more illuminating than, the much-thumbed pages of the Gothic and Renaissance. Here I beheld an encouraging trend that the American humanist could follow with great profit.

World War II and the unsettled years that followed closed Europe to the traveling public, and willy-nilly some visited Latin America. Our

Good Neighbor policy—blowing now hot, now cold—brought a beginning to an understanding of the civilization there. The war in the Far East during World War II and later in Korea and Vietnam opened the eyes of many young Americans to the art and architecture of other continents.

This book, as already stated, is first of all for the general reader. Art is above all a visual and emotional experience. Since my two larger volumes on the art of pre-Columbian and colonial Latin America are again in print, it was a pleasure to select unpublished photographs from our archives and to describe sites that have been little touched upon so far. I sometimes have preferred to use old photographs or prints, which convey a more genuine atmosphere than do those modernistic "shots" where a particular angle, the strong play of light and shadow, might produce a more artistic print but one that would confuse the reader unfamiliar with the place.

In our travels since 1932, we have received advice, information, photographs, and books from persons far too numerous to list here. But some must be mentioned, who were especially helpful, and to whom my gratitude is expressed in the acknowledgments on page 377.

Pál Kelemen

Norfolk, Connecticut
May, 1969

The Ancient Epoch

A WORLD APART

The Indians came to the New World as primitive hunters and fishermen. They moved in bands, probably never amounting to a great number at any one time, and certainly not conscious in their quest for fresh grounds that they had stepped across from one continent to another by way of the Bering Strait. Travel on foot would have been possible when this region was covered by the great icecap; even today the distance is only fifty-six miles, broken by islands. Recent evidence indicates that man existed in the New World at least forty thousand years ago. Human bones and arrowheads have been excavated, alongside skeletal parts of the ground sloth and the three-toed horse, animals that have long disappeared from the Western Hemisphere.

The migrations took place over thousands of years. Anthropologically they were composed of diverse peoples. Long skulls, round and medium shapes, have all been found among the remains of early man in this hemisphere. Furthermore, there have been distinguished more than fifty separate and unrelated languages.

In the New World fish, fowl, and wild game were abundant. The wealth of primeval forest and plain offered wild grains, berries, and other edible plants, and toward the south there was a climate well suited to the beginnings of agriculture. Among the vegetable life indigenous to the New World were maize (Indian corn), white and sweet potatoes, tomato, pumpkin, all kinds of squash, peanut, lima and kidney beans, chili pepper, cacao (for chocolate), custard apple, pineapple, strawberry, avocado, manioc (for tapioca), tobacco, coca (for cocaine), cinchona (for quinine), cascara. Bird and animal life were different from those of the Old World. Four members of the camel family existed in South America: the llama, alpaca, guanaco, and vicuña. The turkey, the quetzal, the condor, and some parrots are specifically American, as are the jaguar, mountain goat, puma, American bison, and various types of monkey. There were, however, no large apes, and no beasts of burden, except the llama in the Andean highlands.

The Indian whose art is presented here is the descendant of many generations living in the Western Hemisphere. From the nomadic or migratory state, he has come far, to create large religious centers and populous settlements, powerful and inventive art. His languages are unrelated to any in Asia, and during the long period of isolation, the color of his skin has become red-bronze, in contrast to the yellow-brownish tone of his distant Mongol relatives. His psychology, also, is different, and his art characterized by his own imagination.

While the superficial observer, judging from hasty sketches and retouched or unclear photographs, may find similarities between ancient American (pre-Columbian) art and the sophisticated artistic manifestations of Asia, basic differences will become evident if actual objects of the Old World are compared directly with those of the New. Pottery fragments from the Old and the New World with similar decorations scratched in, punched, scraped, finger-indented, are by no means proof of contact. Decorations of this sort are widespread among primitive peoples. The fact that a number of present-day travelers, drifting across the Pacific Ocean on balsa rafts, have been able to survive the voyage—whether eastward or westward—is not acceptable as proof of mass migration by sea in prehistoric times. There is no evidence that such a movement could have occurred except along the coast or by way of accessible islands, spaced at relatively short distances. The early boats, whether made of wood, hide, or whatever, would have become waterlogged from long use without repair. The lack of knowledge of weather conditions along that hazardous route also precludes any but the most fortuitous crossing. Indeed, there is no record that even Chinese trading vessels, which carried on a busy commerce along the coast, began to ply across the straits as far as the Philippine Islands before the ninth century of our era—by which time the great American cultures had long been in full flower. (This fact is discussed further in the chapter on the Philippines.)

In the last decades various new techniques have been invented that establish the great antiquity of pre-Columbian civilization and clarify the development of its arts. During World War II, in studying the effect of radiation on living organisms, it was found that the radioactive content of any living thing—whether animal or vegetable—gradually diminishes after death. By measurement of the amount of loss of radioactivity in any ancient object which was once alive, the number of years since it ceased to exist can be approximated. This invention, generally known as the carbon-14, or radiocarbon, method of dating, is widely used by American archaeologists today. There is, however, still a latitude of some hundreds of years in the estimated date, and certain anomalies that have occurred in the calculations show that it is not infallible.

2

An earlier method of dating, also made by an American scientist, applies specifically to the Southwest United States. It is known as tree-ring dating, or dendrochronology. Early in this century, in studying the effect of sunspots on the growth of trees, it was found that the growth rings of the native piñon vary in width in wet and dry years, forming a never-repeated pattern that appears in all the trees. Thus, a time sequence of wet and dry years could be established from cross sections of wooden beams taken from the first Spanish mission buildings, the dates of which were recorded, and on these, tree-ring sequences from late prehistoric buildings could be overlapped. In this way, using even charcoal from ancient fires, the tree-ring calendar has been pushed back to nearly the beginning of the Christian era.

It is true that many masterpieces of pre-Columbian art, made of stone, pottery, jade, or metal, are already in museums—lifted out of context as it were. These cannot be dated by either carbon-14 or dendrochronology, though either technique might have been applicable to the sites where they were discovered. Two new methods—thermoluminescent and magnetic dating—are, however, now under study.

Thermoluminescent dating is based on the fact that tiny amounts of radioactive elements are present in all earth materials. Ancient pottery and stone objects that once were heated, when reheated in the laboratory, give off a radioactive glow proportional to the time lapse since the objects were first fired or burned. With the help of a series of complicated computations, their age can be approximated accordingly.

Finally, magnetic dating rounds out the technical possibilities of establishing the period from which an object comes. This method is based on the knowledge that the earth's magnetic force changes direction and magnitude in regular cycles. Materials containing iron oxide, such as natural clay, are magnetized by this force. When the material is subjected to high heat—as, for example, in a fire pit, or when pottery is fired, or a building with clay walls or floors is burned—it loses its original magnetism and is remagnetized according to the direction and force of the earth's magnetic field at that time and place. If such objects or materials have not been disturbed, their approximate dates can be determined by comparing their magnetism with the known earth cycles.

All these methods of dating have so far been applied only to a very small percentage of specimens. Cross-dating and stratigraphy remain the major techniques. For the reader of this book, however, the primary interest of pre-Columbian art lies in the aesthetic pleasure which it has to give to the present-day onlooker.

Art in ancient America reached its height in those centuries roughly contemporaneous to that great period of art in Asia and Europe known as the Middle Ages. The fabric of Old World archaeology and art history is like a vast web and covers styles that extend from the Roman ramparts of Britain to the delicately drawn woodcuts of Japan, from the Byzantine icons of Russia to the sumptuous royal tombs of Egypt. The art that surrounds us today was developed by the cross-fertilization of ideas and technical inventions from other continents. Ancient American art, on the other hand, developed and flowered in isolation—isolation, at least, from those contacts with the Eastern Hemisphere that formed the background for the white man's civilization.

About the time of the birth of Christ, in both the Old and the New World, distinctive artistic developments can be observed. The period in America up to the time of the arrival of the Spaniards could be called "medieval" as it parallels in many ways the Middle Ages in Asia and Europe. Various other designations are in use: pre-Columbian, pre-Conquest, pre-Hispanic, pre-Cortésian. Terminology is, after all, only a matter of convenience.

Although the ancient peoples of America did not advance technologically much beyond the Neolithic, or Stone Age, they constructed architecture on a grand scale and, in some areas, created stunning art. Without the use of the wheel, they moved massive materials incredible distances. They never discovered the smelting of iron, yet their metalwork excited the admiration of Renaissance Europe. Their textiles were highly complicated, though fashioned on primitive looms. And their pottery, manufactured without the potter's wheel, is remarkably varied and sophisticated. There is ample evidence that they were able to imitate nature with fidelity, though their art often expresses a complex ideology in which realism is irrelevant. Now that contemporary painting and sculpture have abandoned the objective and narrative elements, ancient American art has come into fashion. Indeed, many modern sculptors have specifically acknowledged its influence.

The arts of China, Persia, India, Japan flourished even after increasing contact with Christianity. But the ancient American civilization met a violent death with the Spanish Conquest. Between our present contemporary period and the last living manifestation of the culture of ancient America, there is a gap of four hundred years. And there was no Plato to write a philosophy of this art, no Vasari to record the activities of his contemporaries. Pre-Columbian art, therefore, will always remain a torso. The very mystery that surrounds it makes it the more fascinating. It is unique in many points of technique and psychology.

Numerous outspokenly artistic cultures existed in five general areas of pre-Columbian America. Moving from north to south, the first to be discussed is the Southwest United States, comprising the regions roughly covered by the states of Utah, Colorado, Arizona, and New Mexico. The second is the Mexican area, stretching from the Rio Grande south through the states of Veracruz and Oaxaca. The third, the Maya area, covers Yucatán and Chiapas in Mexico, together with British Honduras, Guatemala, and parts of Honduras and El Salvador. (The term Middle America indicates the Mexican and Maya areas combined.) The Interlying area includes the rest of Honduras, El Salvador, Costa Rica, Nicaragua, Panama. And finally the Andean area, the fifth and last, extends along the west of South America, beginning with the Cordillera of Colombia, through Ecuador, the lowlands and highlands of Peru, Bolivia, and some parts of Chile and Argentina.

Pottery, shell and stone carving, and occasional copper work are found outside these areas, but their quality does not warrant inclusion in a short survey. Our knowledge of pre-Columbian commerce is far from complete. But present-day research has shown that there was trade between various regions.

A number of these cultures existed at high altitudes. The elevation of the Southwest ranges between 1500 and 8000 feet. The Mexican high plateau averages about 7500 feet in height. Although in the Maya area Yucatán lies at sea level, and some of the greatest cities throve in the lowlands, evidence is accumulating that the Maya culture first developed in the highlands of Guatemala which reach an altitude of about 7700 feet. Colombia had thriving settlements in the Cordilleras. In the Andean highlands, architectural remains are found over 12,500 feet above sea level.

All these cultures were more or less sedentary. Maize was the staple food, a grain indigenous to America. Various types were grown, adapted to the varying conditions of climate and soil. Where rainfall was sparse or altogether lacking, ingenious systems of artificial irrigation and dry farming were practiced. There is evidence that certain tribes of the Southwest gave up nomadic life and became agriculturists upon the introduction of maize from Mexico.

1 / Architecture

SOUTHWEST UNITED STATES

The Southwest area of the United States is characterized by vast sandstone formations, which the Spaniards called mesas, or tables, and deep eroded canyons. Here a formerly nomadic people began to practice rudimentary agriculture, occupying camps with circular or oval pit houses sunk about three feet into the ground. They fashioned all sorts of basketry and produced a primitive utilitarian pottery. Their weapon was the spear thrower, until the early centuries of the Christian era when they adopted the bow and arrow.

One group of these people called Hohokam are believed to have migrated from the direction of Mexico. They occupied a desert valley in Arizona from about the beginning of the Christian era to the twelfth or thirteenth century, and practiced agriculture with an advanced system of irrigation, drawing water from the Gila River some three miles away. Their dwellings were roundish, sunk about a foot into the ground, with wattled walls supported on posts. A form of ball-court has been uncovered, suggesting that here was a focus of the ritual game played with a rubber ball throughout Middle America.

The Hohokam were expert in basketry and made good pottery, developing and improving their designs. Their outstanding artistic achievement, however, was their invention of a sort of etching on shells brought from the distant ocean. Animal and human forms were outlined and filled with pitch; then the piece was submerged in a mild acid solution, made from the fermented juice of the saguaro cactus, that corroded the surfaces and left a raised design, often quite complex. Frequently represented are the horned toad of the desert and the rattlesnake; hence, the name given to the site: Snaketown. The Hohokam people seem to have amalgamated peacefully with other sedentary groups. It is believed that the present-day Pima Indians are their descendants.

About the ninth century, another people appeared who built their shelters of adobe (sun-dried brick) and wood. They cultivated cotton, domesticated the turkey, and were skilled in the making of pottery. Forced to scatter by marauding tribes, some of them—those now known as the Cliff Dwellers—retired to the mesas. Others drew together on the banks of rivers, where as their communities prospered, a honeycomblike structure developed. Tyúoni Pueblo ruin, Frijoles Canyon, New Mexico, shows the outline of such an early "apartment house," which tree-ring dating places between 1417 and 1505 [1.1]. Ranging from one to three stories in height, the structure sheltered several hundred people. It was built in the shape of a **D** for best security and had only one entrance, with a plaza inside the walls. Neighboring tribes of diverse origin adopted this practical solution.

This culture was given the name of Pueblo by the Spaniards, from their word for village. Around the eleventh century, a new people joined the older inhabitants, bringing with them a better system of building and a different style of pottery. Famous Pueblo sites are those at Pueblo Bonito, Aztec Ruin, New Mexico, and the Gila and the Salt River settlements, all in our Southwest.

The existence of the Cliff Dwellers was not known until the end of the nineteenth century, when some cowboys in southwest Colorado, seeking lost cattle, came upon a hidden canyon and saw the buildings fitted into vast natural caverns high in the rocky walls. The site is now called Mesa Verde ("the green mesa") for its abundance of water and greenery.

The Cliff Dwellers used a buff sandstone for their building material, harder than the cliffs that sheltered them and cut to a size rather thinner and wider than an ordinary brick. For the roofs, branches were laid across heavier timbers, the chinks were filled with twigs and brush, and the whole sealed with clay. Doors and windows were placed asymmetrically. Crevices and dark interiors provided storage space for food. Out-of-door fireplaces are common, and a number of the dwellings have springs nearby. Square and round towers have been found.

Cliff Palace [1.2], dated by tree rings as belonging to the twelfth century, was built into a cavern more than four hundred feet long and eighty feet deep. It contains over a hundred rooms, many of which have indoor fireplaces. Some walls bear traces of painted decoration. Similarly romantically located and strategically placed are the ruins at Canyon de Chelly, Navajo National Monument, and Montezuma Castle, all in Arizona.

The Pueblos had a defined philosophy of life and a quite democratic government. While their neighbors in the Mexican area were practicing human sacrifice, these people avoided unnecessary killing, even of animals. The kiva, a circular subterranean chamber, sometimes thirty or more feet in diameter, was the religious and administrative center of the community.

It seems to have developed from the early pit houses which, as buildings began to be constructed above ground, were deepened and became religious structures—an instance of the conservative nature of religious architecture.

In the thirteenth century, as tree-ring dating has revealed, protracted droughts occurred, one lasting for as long as twenty years. More and more of the Cliff Dwellers were forced to join their relatives on the banks of the larger rivers. A period of general decline and depopulation can be noted in the fourteenth century, also probably connected with diminishing supplies of water and wood, as well as harassment from predatory tribes. When the conquistadores reached the Southwest, many villages were already forsaken.

Even today, however, a few settlements survive that date back to pre-Columbian times. One of these is the Hopi town of Walpi, Arizona, perched on a massive outcropping of rock. The towns of Zuni and Ácoma, New Mexico, are as ancient. Two large terraced "apartment houses" at Taos, also in New Mexico, are still inhabited very much as they were when the Spaniards arrived. The Pueblo peoples continue to preserve various ancient ceremonies, such as their ritual dances, and their pottery and weaving show much vitality.

MEXICAN AREA

The earliest manifestation of high culture in the Mexican area is dominated by the Olmecs, whose heartland lay in the states of Veracruz and Tabasco. Recent excavations at the site of San Lorenzo Tenochtitlán, south Veracruz, suggest occupation as early as the thirteenth century B.C. La Venta, in the state of Tabasco, flourished roughly from 800 to 400 B.C., and Tres Zapotes, Veracruz, from about 600 B.C. Several sites show a period of revived activity around the fifth and the ninth centuries of our era. The region was tropical and well watered, favorable for a sedentary population and the long occupancy of a site.

The Olmec culture had knowledge of the calendar and a form of writing from very early times. As bases for their temples, they amassed large earthen mounds, some of them faced with stone. Their principal god appears to have been the god of rain, manifest in the form of a jaguar. At La Venta a mosaic pavement is laid out in the form of a stylized jaguar mask. Monolithic sarcophagi and a tomb constructed with basalt shafts have been found.

These people are best known from their magnificent carvings of such hard stones as basalt, serpentine, and jade (which will be taken up later in the chapter on sculpture). Rubber is indigenous to the region, and it is thought that it was here that the ritual ball game, important throughout Middle America, originated.

Far-ranging commerce, as well as the migrations of small groups and possibly some conquest, may explain the wide dispersal of the style loosely called Olmec. Its artistic influence is noticeable at Tlatilco and in other very early styles of the Valley of Mexico and Puebla regions, and also, in the development of the three great cultures that came to flowering more or less contemporaneously in three separate regions: the cultures of Teotihuacán on the Mexican high plateau, of the Zapotec in the Valley of Oaxaca, and of the Maya.

Near the present Mexican capital, several archaic cultures have been investigated that throve in the millennium before the Christian era. During this archaic period, a considerable part of the vast Valley of Mexico was under water, and it is believed that some of the sites were then islands. Tlatilco is one of the oldest centers, with evidence of occupation in the mid-fourteenth century B.C. This site—together with Zacatenco, El Arbolillo, Copilco, and Cuicuilco, to name only the better known—seems to have flourished between 900 and 500 B.C. At Cuicuilco, a huge four-tiered circular platform, formed of boulders and clay, that had lain buried under a lava flow since several centuries before Christ, was recently excavated. The characteristic pottery figurines that were unearthed will be discussed in the chapter on pottery.

The city of Teotihuacán, thirty-six miles to the northeast of Mexico City, rose to its zenith when there were still extensive lakes nearby, and the region was far more fertile than seems possible today. In its heyday, the city had a population of over a quarter of a million and covered some thirty-five square miles. An impressive avenue, now known as the Street of the Dead, marked the ceremonial center of the metropolis [1.3]. The sloping terrain drops nearly ninety feet from north to south, and temples and palaces, many still unexcavated, stand on vast terraces in stately array. On the periphery lay the quarters of the many craftsmen who served the theocracy, and the dwellings of "the common people" stretched beyond.

An enormous truncated pyramidal structure, the Temple of the Sun, dominates the site on the east side of the avenue, oriented to the sunset at the equinox. The custom of pre-Columbian peoples from very early times to elevate their temples on artificial mounds is believed by some to indicate that their rites were first performed on hilltops.

It is unfortunate that the term "pyramid" persists in connection with these substructures because of its inevitable association with the pyramids of Egypt. The monuments on the Nile were gigantic tombs, built of great stone blocks to mark the solitary burial pomp of kings. The pyramidal substructures of pre-Columbian America usually consist of adobe or smaller stones on a core of rubble, often faced with stone or painted stucco. Burials have sometimes been found within them, but they constituted the religious center of a living community and served essentially to elevate the temple on top, so that the ceremonies took place in full view of the multitude assembled on the ground. At Teotihuacán, and on the Mexican high plateau in general, the temple buildings proper were constructed of wood, reeds, and other perishable materials, and roofed with thatch.

The "Pyramid" of the Sun at Teotihuacán is constructed of rough-dressed basaltic lava. It rises in slanting tiers to a height of over two hundred feet, a broad stairway leading across the west face. The projecting stones one sees today served to hold in place a thick covering of stucco, once brightly painted. Some place the date around 100 B.C.; others, a century or so later.

The Temple of the Moon stands at right angles to the Temple of the Sun at the upper end of the avenue, which widens to accommodate a plaza with numerous smaller stepped platforms. Though the structure itself is lower, the temple on top stood at the same level as that of the Sun, because of the rising ground.

Another telling monument, the Temple of Quetzalcóatl, the Great Feathered Serpent, the Mexican god of the wind, stands about a mile below the Temple of the Sun, enclosed within low ramparts that have given this section the name of citadel [1.4]. It was the custom of most pre-Columbian peoples in Middle America to enlarge their temples periodically. In the Mexican area, this usually occurred at the end of a cycle of fifty-two years, when the sacred calendar of 260 days coincided with the solar calendar of 365 days, which ran concurrently. Here, inside a larger structure, a substructure of six terraces has been unearthed. Each terrace is framed by cornices, and from the inner panels, carved heads of the grotesque rain-god, Tlaloc, jut forth, alternating with heads of Quetzalcóatl, the plumed serpent, wearing a leafy collar. His fangs are whitened; his eyes glisten with obsidian. His body, with its feathers and rattles, is indicated in relief on the surface of the panels. Conch shells and other marine elements fill the spaces, and serpent heads project from the ramp of the steep stairway.

Evidence is accumulating that Teotihuacán trade routes extended as far as the shores of the Atlantic and Pacific. Sea shells were prized for their symbolic, as well as their decorative, value. The conch, for example, is the symbol of the Feathered Serpent. When cut across, a volute is produced, which, conventionalized into a fret with its many variations is a mark of the god.

Clustered about the temples and occupying nearby suburban areas, the dwellings of the high priests reveal the luxury of their living, with many rooms surrounding numerous courtyards. The Palace of the Quetzal-Butterfly dates from around the third century. It is so called from the intricate relief that covers the walls and square pillars of the entrance patio and was once polychromed and encrusted with glittering obsidian.

Most buildings contain fragments of elaborate murals, generally of a hieratic character, with much complex symbolism. The strange figure of Tlaloc the rain-god, with his hanging tusks and white-rimmed eyes, dominates Teotihuacán, together with depictions of the all-powerful plumed serpent, of jaguars, various types of shells and other symbols of marine life. The walls of one palace are painted with a delightful panorama of Tlaloc's paradise. The figure of the god stands in the center background, flanked by two priests, water dropping from his extended hands. On a hillside beside a lake in the foreground, tiny figures rejoice in the blessings of abundant water—swimming, culling fruit and flowers—while on the opposite wall, a ball game is in progress. Speech scrolls issuing from their mouths (something like the balloons in our comics) are adorned with flowers, indicating song.

Thanks to modern archaeological technique, fragments of murals are now preserved that would have been cast aside in previous times. Three details from this site show three strongly different styles of mural painting. In the case of the rampant jaguar [1.5], the unfilled spaces have been calculated as part of the design and enter into the general effect, reminding one of batik, or even of stencilwork. Some explain the checked pattern as a net covering the animal. Outlines of a feather headdress add to the unrealistic portrayal of this demonic creature. The colors are blue with touches of red.

In the second mural fragment [1.6], from the Atetelco group at the site, there is still strong emphasis on the outlines of the mythical jaguar and coyote, again adorned with feathers. The body of the coyote (right) is washed over with a lighter tone and painted to indicate its hairy pelt. The jaguar's body has the deep red color of the walls and is netted over with a looped pattern. An intertwining serpent motif fills the border. One undulant figure has the hairy coat and the head of the coyote with the haunches and claws of the jaguar; the other carries the jaguar's markings. The composition is skillfully handled, with the feathery strands of the headdresses and the upright tails counterbalancing the speech scrolls that issue from the animals' mouths.

The eyes of the sacred quetzal of Tetitla in the third fragment [1.7] have been designed to form two bird heads—as if the ancient painter had had a premonition of the double-headed Habsburg eagle that would appear on the standards of the white conquerors. The creature is shown with wings and legs spread naturalistically as if alighting. In contrast to the previous examples, it is delineated in solid color.

Parallels to the majestic layout of Teotihuacán can be observed in the great religious centers of the Mexican and Maya areas, in the integration of architecture with the surrounding landscape, the balanced relationship of the buildings one to another. The population of these areas depended on the harvest for their lives; thus, the gods of wind and rain were of utmost importance. Most of these cultures developed their own manner of recording, which included calendrical information—even eventually calculations of the weather and the return of the seasons. Their pottery styles, in many cases, show interconnections.

Around the end of the seventh century, Teotihuacán fell before the Toltecs, a marauding tribe of Nahua-speaking stock. With time, the city seems to have been lost from sight. It is not mentioned either in the Aztec chronicles or in the reports of the conquistadores. The situation on the Mexican high plateau at that time is roughly comparable to that during the Middle Ages of Europe, when wave after wave of "barbarians" swept in to ravage and conquer; some adapted the culture of their new lands and formed the nucleus for modern nations.

The Toltecs rapidly took on civilization. By the middle of the tenth century their capital Tula, described in the legends as Tollan, had become so splendid that for a long time it was thought by scholars to be Teotihuacán itself.

The Toltecs were excellent builders and stone carvers, and they may have introduced the working of metal into the Mexican area. Their special achievement was the enlargement of interior space through the use of pillars and columns. In their capital at Tula, their main temple stood on a broad stepped platform [1.8]. Giant atlantes, nearly eighteen feet high, supported the roof beams. Each pillar was composed of four sections and carved to represent a warrior in plumed headdress, carrying an *atlatl* ("spear thrower"), darts, and a swordlike weapon. All wore elaborate earplugs and breastplates in the form of stylized butterflies, and round targets or shields hung from their backs. Their faces still show traces of paint; the eyes and teeth were probably inlaid.

An ample hall stretched at the base of the temple, its roof supported by a forest of square columns on which elaborately costumed warriors were carved in relief. Some round columns appear to have represented the bodies of huge serpents that guarded the entrances, their heads resting on the ground and their tails with rattles curling around the lintels. On some walls, relief panels are carved with rows of advancing jaguars and coyotes [1.9]. Other panels present eagles devouring the hearts of sacrificial victims. The animals are executed with skill and stark realism.

At least seven ball-courts have been excavated at this site. This ritual game was played in various forms throughout the Mexican and Maya areas. Some ball-courts—believed by some to be the earlier form—have gently sloping sides, suggesting tiers of seats for spectators. In Central Mexico and at a later period in Yucatán, stone rings were set up high on vertical side walls, and it was considered a special triumph to strike the ball through one of these. Many carved stones depict various phases of the ball game.

In the middle of the twelfth century, Tula, in turn, was overcome and burned by new invaders, the Chichimecs. Remnants of the defeated Toltecs emigrated to Yucatán, where they became dominant in a number of Maya cities and spread their heritage.

In the early fourteenth century another Nahua-speaking people, the Aztecs, subdued the region and settled on a marshy island in Lake Texcoco, known as Tenochtitlán, now the site of Mexico City. Their houses were built on piles. They traded fish, game birds, and reptiles with the folk on the mainland for stone, beams, and other building material. Protected by the surrounding waters, they throve, increased, and began to expand. In time, they established hegemony over the other peoples of the area. At first, they were ruled by chieftains, but by the end of the century, a dynasty had been founded whose descendants held sway until the city was conquered by Cortés.

Of the two lakes in the Valley of Mexico, one was fresh, the other brackish. Several massive causeways with stone ramps led into the city, which because of its many canals, the Spaniards compared to Venice. Two pipelines were constructed of masonry to carry drinking water to the inhabitants—one to take over when the other needed cleaning. At its height, the city's famous market offered a rich assortment of goods, some drawn from tribute paid by subjugated tribes. There was pottery of varied shapes and decoration, gold and silver ornaments, skeins of cotton dyed in many colors, fruits, vegetables, game of all sorts cooked and uncooked. There were booths for furniture and tools, and a court for the regulation of weights and measures. Circumscribed as it was, the city grew somewhat crowded, especially when compared to the suave spaciousness of Teotihuacán.

The ruins of a typical Aztec temple have been found at Tenayuca, six miles north of Mexico City. The conquistadores mention this place in their reports, for there was fighting nearby when the Spaniards cut off the water supply to the Aztec capital. The temple base there is a massive structure. Faced with stone laid in mortar and then covered with plaster, it was painted in brilliant designs and studded with the projecting heads of serpents. Twin stairways led up to two temples, standing side by side on top. A row of 156 coiled snakes surrounds the structure; their heads, carved from solid stone, projecting beyond the edge of the low platform around the base. Their bodies, modeled of small stones and mortar and covered with stucco, were originally painted according to their orientation: blue predominating on the south and east, black on the north and west.

Inside this structure, a second temple base from the late thirteenth century, the period of Chichimec dominance, has been uncovered, and further excavations have revealed buildings of six previous periods within these two, including Toltec work.

Xochicalco, a large ancient site, occupies a superb position on a terraced height near Cuernavaca. Four roads lead from the principal plaza in the four cardinal points of the compass. The approach must have been magnificent. Among the many ruined temples, palaces, and lesser dwellings, still largely unexcavated, an early form of ball-court has been found. Outstanding in its linear grace and plasticity is the temple base—or rather, temple platform—said to date from mid-tenth or early eleventh century [1.10]. It is constructed of dressed stones of even size. A bold overhanging cornice tops the sharply slanted foundation, which is covered with the undulant bodies of eight huge plumed serpents in low relief. In the spaces created by their fretlike curves, seated human figures in their ceremonial paraphernalia alternate with glyphs. Such figures are rare as sculptural ornament in the Mexican area and suggest the late Maya. The glyphs, reminiscent of the Zapotec-Mixtec, are said to refer to the kindling of the new fire at the beginning of each fifty-two-year cycle. A stairway of fourteen steps leads up the west side to the platform on top, where there are traces of a masonry temple, one of the very few found up to now in the Mexican area.

Apparently the carving was done before the stones were set in place, and the work was touched up afterward. Like most architecture in Middle America, the temple base was painted, the colors that remain being chiefly red and green.

Malinalco, in the southwest corner of the state of Mexico, is one of the rare pre-Columbian sites where buildings were hewn directly out of the living rock. Pottery finds date it in the fourteenth or fifteenth century. Its most notable temple faces a small plaza on the brink of a deep gorge. Fourteen steep steps, carved from the ledge itself, lead up to it as if across a temple base.

The entrance to the temple appears to have been carved from a single slab, which is deeply incised to represent the yawning jaws of an immense serpent. Its forked tongue forms a low dais, extending nearly to the first step of the approach. Within is a circular chamber some sixteen feet in diameter, which was probably roofed with beams and thatch. An eagle altar, naturalistically carved, occupies the center of the room, the wings half spread along the floor, the head raised, the fierce curving beak facing the entrance.

Calixtlahuaca, a Matlatzincan site on a hill near Toluca, has another of the infrequent round structures, dating from the fifteenth century. Stone snake heads have been exposed, protruding from the sloping walls of an earlier temple. This site was apparently abandoned after its conquest by the Aztecs, who founded a town on the adjacent plain.

The royal bath of Netzacoyotl, the Texcoco king, at Texcotzingo nearer the Mexican capital, presents another instance of the use of living rock. It is approached by a long stairway hewn in the precipitous ledge. Water was brought some distance from a mountain appropriately called Tlaloc, and guided through a succession of cascades into two plaster-lined pools. Chroniclers report a garden with sculpture roundabout. José M. Velasco (1840–1912), unsurpassed as a painter of the many majestic landscapes in his native land, has left us a picture in which the red rocks, the soft greens and yellows of the shrubbery, and the shining blues of the distance transmit the magic of this place.

On the Gulf Coast of Mexico, three separate cultural regions are outstanding: the Huastec, the Tajín-Totonac, and the Olmec, already mentioned. Each had its own religious tenets and recognizably individual art style.

Apparently, the Huastecs occupied the northern portion from as early as 800 B.C. until the Spanish Conquest. A nation of warriors, they belonged to Maya stock. They never fell under Mexican sway, and throughout their existence, they seem to have resisted strong influences from the high plateau. The figure of Quetzalcóatl, the Feathered Serpent, preeminent among the gods of Middle America, is believed by some to have been of Huastec origin. These people are notable for their pottery and their shell carving.

Maize, cocoa, and vanilla thrive in the central section of the coast, a semitropical region in what is now the state of Veracruz. The early culture, dating roughly from the seventh century, shows connections with Teotihuacán. The best-known site is an extensive ruin, near the town of Papantla, known as El Tajín, after which the culture is sometimes named.

The Temple of the Niches is one of four artificial mounds grouped around a plaza [1.11]. This striking structure with its single stairway rises in seven receding terraces to a height of some seventy feet. The clean-cut, accurately fitted stone slabs of the edifice show even in decay an excellent quality of workmanship—a strong contrast to the rougher masonry of the same period found in the Mexican Valley. Each terrace is completed by a cornice, projecting obliquely, and the seven tiers of niches—apparently ninety on each of the four sides—are symmetrically arranged. Corresponding as this number does to the days in a regular calendar year, it reflects knowledge of an accurate count of the days and suggests that the recesses may have been used as day shrines, perhaps filled with idols, incense burners, or offerings.

In the section known as Tajín Chico (Little Tajín), a substructure of similar form has the blind niches filled with uniform *grecques* ("Greek frets") in stone mosaic.

Some corbeled arches have been found. It appears that all the buildings were originally covered with a coating of painted stucco, to brilliant effect. Later, about the eleventh century, the Totonacs took over the region, and interchange is evident with the conquering tribes in the Mexican high plateau.

Mexico is the lucky nation where the construction of a subway system or the construction of a new highway can bring important new archaeological specimens to light. The builders of the subway in Mexico City encountered pottery, stone objects, and remnants of wooden piles from the pre-Columbian period when the Aztec city was transversed by several canals. They also found the remains of a colonial aqueduct and pottery of early Hispanic-American manufacture.

The construction of the highway between the capital and Puebla revealed a settlement at Tlapacoya, which has been roughly dated as existing in 22,000 B.C. Still farther south, excavations around Cholula, have brought an unexpected extension to the estimated size and age of the pre-Columbian settlements there. Finally, at Tehuacán, seventy-two miles southeast of Puebla, an unbroken record, spanning some nine thousand years and covering most aspects of man's life in the region, has been established among the millennia-old litter from hunting parties. The presence of an early type of corn and even of its wild predecessor marks the first evidences of budding civilization. The revelations of these regions are expected to clarify the development of the Mixtec people who appeared so decisively later in the Valley of Oaxaca, in southern Mexico.

Legend has it that the Valley of Oaxaca was once a lake—a similarity with the ambience of the Aztec capital. One of the most extensive and majestic ruins of the entire Mexican area lies seven miles to the southwest of the thriving state capital, Oaxaca. Called Monte Albán ("the White Mountain") by the Spaniards, the vast dead city of the Zapotec and later of the Mixtec peoples is situated on a promontory about four hundred feet above the valley floor, at the convergence of three valleys and framed by the imposing peaks of the Sierra Madre del Sur. The fertile fields below provided the settlement with food, and the steep slopes minimized the danger of attack.

Monte Albán, however, seems to have been a religious center rather than a fortress. Its history falls into five periods, the first four of which are connected with the Zapotecs, the fifth with the Mixtecs who infiltrated the region around A.D. 1000. Excavations show a considerable culture there as early as 700 B.C. The inhabitants had a form of writing, a knowledge of

In all these regions, the rise of civilization was based on the development of a stable agriculture. Religion was closely allied to the crops. The Maya custom of burning off and replanting a succession of fields was ingenious enough, considering the primitive quality of their tools and the terrific vitality of the jungle in which they lived. But the method tended to exhaust the soil, and each settlement needed a broad surrounding terrain to sustain it. Precise calculation of the seasons was vital, for the fields had to be planted before the rains began. This might be one reason that the Maya calendar was so highly developed.

The Maya, also, elevated their temples on pyramidal bases, which were usually oriented to the cardinal points of the compass, and laid out their palaces on broad artificial platforms. From the limestone that abounded throughout the area, they produced excellent stucco, cement, and lime mortar. Thus, in contrast to the Mexican area, many temple buildings and palaces have been preserved with roofs that are partially extant, with high stucco reliefs still visible on some façades, and even with recognizable interior murals.

These people solved the problem of roofing with a type of corbeled vaulting, placing flat, dressed stones so that each course overlapped the one below it and the sides gradually approached each other. Thanks to the use of excellent cement, the masonry became essentially monolithic. Variations of the corbeled vault were developed. Palenque produced a spectacular trefoil arch; bottle shapes are common at Tulum and other Yucatecan east coast sites, and rounded forms at Labná and Chichén Itzá. The great height of the vaults from the spring line conditioned the appearance of the outside of the building, producing an extensive upper zone that invited lavish decoration.

The vaulted chambers within were high and narrow. Very thick walls were evidently deemed necessary to support the enormous weight of the monolithic roof, to which at some sites (notably Tikal and Palenque) a highly decorative roof comb was added, a veritable headdress of masonry. Often the back of the roof comb seems to descend in a line with the rear wall of the building, and in some cases, as if to emphasize this, the substructure falls away beneath it at a steeper angle than in the front. At other sites (Labná, Sabacche, Chichén Itzá), it takes the form of a sheer wall on a line with the front of the building—a "flying façade."

The jungle produced such hard wood that its use for crossbeams and lintels was feasible. Many traverses are still intact in ruined temples more than a thousand years old, despite the immense weight they bear.

The great Maya cities, though politically independent of one another, seem to have collaborated in intellectual exchange, notably in the correlation of the calendar which they carried far back in time. They were, also, evidently acquainted with the advanced cultural achievements of contemporary Teotihuacán, and they traded with their neighbors. Apparently, they did not fight among themselves, but were strong enough to hold off intruders until the influx of the Toltecs.

A number of the great sites now lie in the depths of almost impenetrable jungle. Chicle hunters, tapping the forest for the raw material for chewing gum, rendered pioneer service by reporting many a ruin. Their trails are still used by archaeologists in places where a small plane cannot land.

Kaminaljuyú, now in a suburb of Guatemala City, has lost most of its architectural remains because of its proximity to the capital, from where digging and looting have gone on in comfort for centuries. Undisturbed tombs have been found, however, that offer evidence of a pre-Maya culture showing parallels with Teotihuacán. Its history extends far back into the centuries before Christ. There are no signs that Maya vaulting was used there, though the city continued, with diminishing importance, well into the first millennium.

The beginning of the greatest florescence (the birth of the so-called Classic period) of Maya art is marked by three important features: the construction of temple buildings of stone with corbeled vaults; the erection of carved stone shafts, or stelae, with glyphs that record calendrical data and possibly historical events; and the fashioning of polychrome pottery. All of these appeared at Uaxactún at almost the same time, in the early fourth century.

This large site, which lies north of Lake Flores, Petén, Guatemala, has stela sequences ranging in date from 327 to 889. As in Mexico, there is evidence of frequent alteration and rebuilding. In one case, five superimposed substructures all reveal the fundamentals of Maya construction, that is, they were built over a loose fill of rubble which was covered with concrete, then faced with cut stone. All bore a smooth surface of stucco.

One of the earliest edifices, found almost intact under later buildings, consists of a series of low receding platforms with heavy projecting cornices [1.16]. Huge grotesque masks, once brightly colored, adorn the abutments, and wide stairways with balustrades lead up on all four sides. The stairway as a decorative factor and the gigantic stucco masks also characterize later Maya architecture.

Smooth wide roads connected the Maya settlements, although there were no beasts of burden or wheeled vehicles and all travel was by foot or palanquin. Such roads lead out of Uaxactún. Considerable engineering skill and tremendous labor were necessary for their construction and upkeep.

Tikal, in northeastern Guatemala, was the most recent of spectacular Maya sites to be excavated, and the study under scientific conditions of its tombs, many stelae, and carved round "altars" has established the long occupancy and the sustained importance of this community. Floor levels and pottery fragments prove that it was inhabited as early as 600 B.C. At its height a thousand years later (A.D. 600–900), the center of the city covered nearly seven square miles with some three thousand structures, while the limits of habitation are lost in the surrounding forest. The populace lived in thatch-roofed huts of wood and withes, such as are pictured on the façades of certain buildings and in the murals of a later period. Like other ancient Maya cities of importance, its plan is characterized by a number of large courts or plazas, within which various buildings were grouped and numerous stelae and altars set up.

The pyramidal bases here are considerably steeper than those of other Maya sites, and show architectural finesse with inset corners and offset panels. In each case, there is only one entrance to the temple, which usually contains three vaulted chambers connected by beamed passageways.

The aerial view of the Great Plaza at Tikal gives an idea of the extension and imposing character of the site [1.17]. Temple I (center), partly reconstructed, stands 145 feet high, the equal of a fourteen-story building. A wide stairway, once smooth with plaster, leads to the summit. An amazingly tall roof comb crowns the structure. The impression is one of soaring lightness.

At this site, the evolution of the roof comb can be traced, from massive walls on more or less solid foundations through a series of experiments aimed to lighten the weight. From here, it is only a step to the lattice-work roof combs in Yaxchilán, Piedras Negras, and Palenque.

Superimposed stories are rare in Maya architecture, doubtless because of the great weight of masonry involved. A two-story effect was sometimes achieved by "stepping back" the second tier and placing it over a solid core or by filling in the chambers over which it was to rise. In Tikal, however, two and even three stories have been found standing directly one above the other.

The use of wood is a characteristic of the site. Beams of the extremely hard *chico-sapote* were employed at the springline of the narrow Maya vaults and as lintels, sometimes placed side by side to cover the span between the massive walls. Much of the exposed surfaces was elaborately carved in low relief and painted. Laboratory investigations have been started to determine why many such lintels, often carrying tremendous weight, are still in relatively good condition after a thousand years, despite the termites that infest the surrounding jungle. It is believed that the red paint, which is obtained from mercury, contained a deterrent.

While Tikal is outstanding for its vast expanse, the massive grouping of its structures, and the stunning effect of their staggered heights, Palenque, though quite small in comparison, holds an extraordinary position for the variety and high artistry manifest in its buildings. It lies at the mouth of a deep gorge in Chiapas, the southernmost state of Mexico, some hundred and fifty miles from Tikal. The region is tropical, damp, and heavily forested. The entire terrain is graded and terraced. A mountain stream, running through the narrow valley where the city stands, was directed into a vaulted culvert, apparently large enough to carry off the swollen waters of the rainy season.

In 1787, Captain Antonio del Rio "explored" Palenque with several companies of Spanish soldiery, on orders from the king of Spain. Two hundred Indian laborers were set to work, clearing the ruins with axes and billhooks. The eighteenth-century colonial soldiers made themselves comfortable in the wilderness, removing stones to make fireplaces, driving hooks into the fragile stucco of the walls to hang up their armament and hammocks, stabling horses where roofs could be found to shelter them. According to del Rio: "There remained neither a window nor a doorway blocked up, nor a room, corridor, court, tower, in which excavations were not affected from two to three yards in depth." It is a testimony to the quality of Maya masons that anything at all remains.

The chief buildings of Palenque consist of a palace complex and five temples, connected by open courts, stairways, and terraces [1.18]. Again in contrast to Tikal, doorways are many, and the wall spaces between them are so reduced that they seem rather like squarish pillars. Thin slabs of a fine-grained limestone face some façades, carved in very low relief with great fluency of line. Delicate reliefs in stucco are found, unequaled in their elegance of composition. Black, white, blue, yellow, green, and two shades of red paint are visible, both inside and outside, and traces of colored geometric designs remain on some of the inner walls.

A three-story tower stands more or less at the center of the palace group, one of the most remarkable constructions in pre-Columbian architecture. Each story consists of a narrow gallery built around a massive central pier, which encloses a stone stairway only about twenty inches wide.

The temples of the Sun, the Cross, and the Foliated Cross, small gems of Maya architecture, face a court across the ravine from the palace group, on relatively low substructures. Wall surfaces and the sloping frieze sections are covered with decorative stucco reliefs. The elaborate roof combs form only a trellis, a foundation for stucco ornamentation. Inside, set into the walls of an inner sanctuary, the magnificent tablets of limestone were found which give the temples their names, each carved with a different central symbol, surrounded by officiating priests and columns of glyphs. It has been remarked that at Palenque most glyphs are not calendrical but unfold a text.

In 1949, the Temple of the Inscriptions, standing somewhat apart, came into prominence. A large stone in the floor of this temple was discovered to open upon a filled-in staircase, leading deep into the body of the substructure. The skeletons of six sacrificial human victims lay at the foot, as if to guard a crypt beyond. Inside this was a large slab, carved with the graceful figure of a young man, elaborately dressed and bejeweled, reclining on the symbol of a terrestrial monster. In the sarcophagus beneath lay the remains of a high priest, surrounded by offerings. His face was covered with a jade mask, and a pectoral, earrings, wristlets, and anklets of jade adorned his body. From the point of view of beauty, perhaps the most remarkable of the finds in that crowded airless chamber were the stucco heads of two young men, with the noble features of the ruling class and gorgeous plumed headdresses [see 2.20]. The hieroglyphs date the tomb in the last decade of the seventh century.

Graves have been found inside temple bases in Teotihuacán and Tikal, as well as at Palenque and other parts of the Mexican and Maya areas. It has been suggested, on the basis of these instances, that the temples were built to contain the tombs. Few if any of these buildings can, however, be classified as primarily mortuary structures. Early Christian churches were always built over the bones of a martyr, and important personages are still buried within holy confines. This still does not cancel out the primary purpose of the building, that is, as a place of worship.

In 1839, President Martin Van Buren commissioned John L. Stephens to survey the possibilities of a canal across Nicaragua to connect the Atlantic and Pacific oceans. Though civil warfare, then prevalent in Central America, hindered Stephens in that task, he succeeded in journeying nearly three thousand miles through the strife-torn interior, visiting eight ruined cities. He has described his experiences with brilliant perception and accuracy in his famous book, *Incidents of Travel in Central America, Chiapas, and Yucatan,* which was illustrated by the English artist Frederick Catherwood, who shared his adventures. Stephens was so impressed by the charm of Copán, Honduras, that he bought the site for fifty dollars but, in the end, could not transport the massive stones out of the jungle to the United States.

In Copán, as in most Maya cities, the layout was clearly influenced by the character of the terrain. There was apparently little concern over the matter of defense. An immense artificial platform at the edge of a river accommodates a number of buildings linked by staircases and broad terraces, so that all blend into one body of architecture. Giant ceiba trees have gained firm foothold to the very top of the structures, and floods have cut into the mound, revealing the manner of construction. The site is characterized by the use of fine greenish-gray limestone, with intricate sculptured detail. Some carving is in very high relief; some, in the round.

Outstanding is the Hieroglyphic Stairway [1.19], adjacent to the great mound, which ascends at a characteristic steep angle; it is twenty-six feet wide and has some eighty steps, each about a foot high. The risers are carved with glyphs, executed with great beauty and precise detail, and so arranged as to be read in lines across each step—not, as was usual, in columns. Human, animal, and monster heads in their shieldlike frames represent elements of the Maya time count, with dots and bars standing for numerals. About every twelve steps, a life-size statue of a magnificently arrayed priest or dignitary was placed, each with his head framed in a monster's jaws. The carving comes to its fullest effect as the sun crosses the zenith.

The glyphs have never been fully deciphered. Some are dates, ranging between 540 and 746, the period of the city's greatest prosperity; some may recount the history of the site or record astronomical observations. This longest of Maya inscriptions could be paralleled today only in a church, with lines from the Bible carved on the entrance stair, or in some public building, with verses from a patriotic poem or the commemoration of some historical event.

The stela facing an altar at the base of the Hieroglyphic Stairway sets its date as around the middle of the eighth century. The structure overlooks a ball-court, dating from the same period, which is constructed with slanting sides and has two gigantic parrot heads in stone as decoration. Two previous ball-courts have been uncovered beneath its flagstone pavement. Significantly, two stairways with glyphs carved on the risers were discovered near Seibal, Petén, Guatemala, both flanked by panels depicting Maya dignitaries in the panoply of the ceremonial ball game.

Piedras Negras, another impressive site, lies in a region of precipitous gorges on the Usumacinta River, which separates Mexico from Guatemala and was probably much used for trade and travel in ancient times. The city itself is not large, but some of the finest stone carvings of the Maya have been found there. They are primarily rather shallow reliefs with revealing details of ceremony and costume. Again, there is evidence of much rebuilding. From the earliest period there are no traces of masonry vaulting. The terraced substructures of later phases are elaborate in plan, with rounded and inset corners, raised panels, projecting buttresses, and coffered sections. Fragments of gigantic masks testify to the type of ornamentation. There are a number of buildings set on low platforms that have been identified as sweat baths, where rites of purification may have been held. Each consists of a single large room with a low vaulted chamber at the back, provided with a hearth and benches on which the bathers reclined.

Here Zaculeu should be mentioned, a site in the northwest corner of Guatemala near the state capital, Huehuetenango. This was the ceremonial center of the Mam-speaking people who are believed to have migrated into the region at the time of Toltec expansion in the north. Neglected, crumbling, overgrown with vegetation, its greatness could be realized only with difficulty by the connoisseur. Today a number of the buildings have been restored, and they have already acquired a patina in the nearly two decades since the reconstruction work was finished.

The site shows a steady progression of culture, from the first rude constructions of boulders set in clay to the dignified edifices using roughly dressed slabs and a facing of stucco. Some temples are elevated on as many as eight or nine receding terraces; others stand on relatively low daises. Narrow galleries with one open colonnaded side are notable. A ball-court with slanting side walls has been restored, and more than a hundred tombs have been excavated. First inhabited about the sixth century, the city was at its height between the eighth and eleventh centuries.* Although its buildings are perhaps earlier than those of the Chichén Itzá in Yucatán, certain similarities in type and construction can be observed with that Maya site, so distant in time and space.

The conquistadores fought bloody battles around Zaculeu and finally succeeded in subjugating the population. But the place apparently continued to be used for religious rites. Nineteenth-century reports tell of pagan ceremonies still being held there.

Had the Spaniards not followed up with fire and iron every pagan rite and forced the Indians into degraded peonage, many more records of ancient Maya life would have been preserved. Recent research suggests that the great centers of pre-Columbian culture were not so completely abandoned before the Conquest as early chroniclers would have us believe. Disease, crop failure, warfare, so often repeated as causes of depopulation and degeneration, are contradicted by the data now being collected. It seems clear that many centers and towns were flourishing with active commerce until the Conquest put its iron hand on the life of the Indians. It was the Spaniard who drove the Indian from his land and used him in back-breaking labor, whether in the field or the mines. It was in the first hundred years after the Conquest that new diseases and cruel exploitation decimated those Indians who had not escaped to the less accessible parts of their ancestral lands—into the jungle or the high altitudes of their mountains.

A case in point is the site of Dzibilchaltún, an enormous ancient city situated a few miles north of Mérida, the present capital of Yucatán. Signs of habitation cover at least thirty square miles; there are hundreds of ruined dwellings, the bases of huge temples and palaces—some of which were vaulted—and, also, a number of cenotes (sink holes in the natural lime-

* R. B. Woodbury and A. S. Trik, *The Ruins of Zaculeu, Guatemala.* Richmond: United Fruit Company, 1953.

stone formation, which provided the water supply for many Maya cities in this region).

Dzibilchaltún is believed to have been inhabited as early as 100 B.C. and flourished as a city through the first millennium of our own era, surviving many later vicissitudes into colonial times. Traces of stucco ornamentation testify to its former splendor. A causeway connected the city proper with the sites where more tangible remains exist. Small wonder that it is in such a deplorable state, for it served throughout the entire colonial epoch and up to a few years ago as a quarry for nearby haciendas. Even the roads were mended with material taken from here. With heartbreak, the visitor observes carved stones used in the walls of huts and even in the enclosures of pigsties. That Mérida, the colonial capital, was founded so near this great Maya center is another proof of the vast resources that stood at the disposal of the conquistadores, of which they took ample advantage as they did at Tenochtitlán, establishing upon its ruins their Mexican colonial capital.

The intensive archaeological work at Dzibilchaltún has invalidated an earlier theory that Yucatán was populated late by the Maya. Thus, a new perspective has been gained on the styles of this region, where better preserved ruins of a later date have long been known and studied.

Excavations in Yucatán reveal several periods, in some places traces of prehistoric settlements. Outspoken Maya characteristics appear around the fourth century. Between the seventh and tenth centuries, an architecture developed, quite different from that described previously. Elements which had been functional came to serve as ornament. Technical difficulties were overcome, and the talent of the builder turned toward new possibilities and problems.

By the tenth century, Mexico to the west was seething with warring tribes and factions. Groups of invaders spilled over the borders. The theocratic rule of the major cities was shaken, and the warrior caste— whether native or usurpers from the north—grew dominant. Maya culture entered a new period of flowering, centered in the northernmost part of the Yucatán Peninsula. The Toltecs, pressed by invasions in the north, were moving from the high plateau of Mexico, and their influence becomes evident. New decorative motifs were introduced. The city plan grew more diffuse. Thinner walls and more spacious interiors were achieved with the introduction of the column.

The buildings of Yucatán were often very large, with many rooms arranged on several levels. Stairs were dramatically placed; from first to last, the imposing stairway remains one of the most characteristic features of Maya architecture. Portal arches came into use, and stone lintels sometimes replaced wooden ones. On the façades, monster masks, chiefly of the rain-god with his projecting hooked snout, rise in tiers on walls, jut from corners, or decorate the panels above entrances. The free-flowing curve of earlier Maya work is occasionally seen, but more often the designs are angular. Atlantes appear, holding cornices or altar tables. The general custom of erecting stelae stopped with the year 889, giving way perhaps to records in the form of manuscripts.

A new style can be recognized in a structure at Rio Bec, on the border between the states of Campeche and Quintana Roo. It is of the palace type with rather spacious vaulted rooms. On the roof, stone trellises, side by side, comprise a decorative screen. Two towers, fifty-five feet high, flank the façade. Each represents, with little reduction in scale, the traditional tall substructure with a temple on top, complete with sculptured frieze and roof comb. But here the towers are purely decorative. There are no chambers within; the doorway is blind; and the stairs are so steep that even a Maya Indian with his wild-cat tread would be unable to scale them. Ruins at Hormiguero and Xpuhil in northern Campeche indicate a similar scheme. Some of the portals are carved to represent a serpent's gaping jaws.

Various other regions developed individuality. Notable are the "Chenes style," in which the entire façade—sometimes the entire building —is covered with over-all decoration, and the "Puuc style," in which an elaborately ornamented frieze is placed above plain lower walls. In some sites, both of these styles are found.

The ruins at Sayil in northern Yucatán are an excellent example of the style of building known as Puuc—a name taken from the range of limestone hills where it reached its highest development. The palace type of structure is predominant in this region. Decoration consists of a sort of mosaic, made up of separately carved elements fitted together in varied patterns. Human figures, appearing as adjuncts, are generally modeled in stucco.

The vast palace, with its close to a hundred rooms, comprises three tiers, each in turn set back and resting on a solid core [1.20]. A broad stairway leads across the front of the building to the top of the third story. Some of the rooms are nearly sixteen feet wide, the maximum for a Maya vault. Here the use of the column affords unusually wide doorways; engaged, it breaks the intervening wall surfaces and enlivens the frieze, giving the massive façade an open, almost airy touch. The absence of complete symmetry in all these structures lends elasticity and vigor to the total effect. Sayil is judged to have flourished in the ninth century.

Kabáh, with a date from the late ninth century, is interesting for the splendid application of the mask as a decorative feature [1.21]. Six tiers of rain-god masks in stone mosaic—one in the foundation, three in the middle wall, and two in the frieze—make up the walls of one building there, which is estimated to have been over one hundred and fifty feet long. Their curling snouts jut far beyond the façade; the mouths are hollow, with jagged teeth sharpened by the shadows behind them. Conical stones set into the cavities for eyeballs give the faces an eerie animation. Near an altar standing before the palace, an underground cistern was discovered into which rain water drained from the roof.

Virtuoso stucco work appears on a section of wall at Acancéh, in northern Yucatán, which dates from about a century earlier [1.22]. The space is divided into panels, framed by bands and containing a fantastic assemblage of masked figures in relief. Bats, serpents, squirrels in human pose, can be recognized. Besides the excellent craftsmanship, which is partly responsible for its preservation, the surface was protected, when discovered, by a covering of bright paint.

The Great Palace of Labná [1.23], with its columnettes and masks, shows a certain similarity to Sayil, with which it is more or less contemporaneous, but even more to Uxmal (a description of which follows). It consisted of several stories set on a dais about twenty feet high, facing a vast plaza. Engaged columns, masks, and frets make up the decoration. Intertwined serpents appear—a new interpretation.

Above this structure, the sharp profile of another building demonstrates more clearly than any description can the meaning of the term "flying façade." The highly decorative unsupported wall, rising here to some thirty feet, was once covered with colossal figures and designs in stucco. Other notable flying façades are seen in the Red House at Chichén Itzá, at Sabacche, and at the Nunnery at Uxmal.

A paved way leads to another group of buildings some two hundred yards south of this palace. Here, in the great archway that served as portal between one building complex and another, the structure of the Maya corbeled vault is clearly revealed [1.24]. This illustration presents the side facing the court. The spring line of the vault can be seen on a level with the lower edge of the frieze, and the eye follows the curving line of stones to the top, where a broad, relatively thin slab bridges the gap. The span is about thirteen feet. The latticework, scalloped zigzag motif, and stepped elements in the upper molding are frequently met with at other Yucatecan sites. Above each doorway is a small reproduction of the huts in which the populace lived, even to the thatched roof, the ridgepole, and the tuft above it. A roof comb topped the central arch, flanked by a separate, lower one at each side, all probably carrying stucco ornamentation.

A number of cities in Yucatán were fortified—the result of warlike conditions. Tulum is notable for its striking situation at the edge of the Caribbean Sea, on a forty-foot cliff that forms a natural barrier along one side. A stone wall some twenty feet wide and twenty feet high encloses the other three sides.

Although a stela dated as mid-sixth century was found at Tulum, excavations indicate that the city reached its height in the thirteenth and fourteenth centuries. The wall was erected early in that period, and the city was still inhabited at the time of the Conquest. Toltec influence is seen in the use of columns to enlarge the interior space, in the style of some of the mural paintings, and in the entrance columns which represent rattlesnakes, with heads recumbent and tails supporting the lintel and cornice. Fragments of such columns exist at Tula, and they are an outstanding feature of Chichén Itzá.

Tulum used bottle-shaped corbeled vaulting, common to some other east coast sites. The figure of the diving, or descending, god is characteristic of the place, and pottery figurines were found set in recessed panels, as at Monte Albán.

Various stylistic periods are preserved in the architecture of Uxmal and Chichén Itzá, in the extreme northern section of Yucatán. They are the two most-visited Maya sites, as since the beginning of interest in the field, they have been more easily accessible. At Uxmal, a vast temple base, called the House of the Dwarf or *Adivino* ("Soothsayer"), is striking for its elliptical shape [1.25]. Some of the smooth slabs are still in place which faced the rounded corners. Five rebuildings have been revealed so far. An enormous mask of the rain-god decorated the façade of the third temple, with the open mouth as entrance. The final temple was raised above the others, and a stairway at the "back" of the substructure was built to reach it.

From the summit, the contours of artificial mounds, bristling with undergrowth, indicate the great extent of the city. Uxmal had no cenotes. To provide water for the large population, depressions in the ground were coated with lime to prevent leakage, and *chultuns* ("cisterns") were constructed to conserve the water of the rainy season.

Across a small court from the tall substructure lie four separate buildings of the palace type, grouped into a quadrangle [1.26]. The Spaniards called this "the House of the Nuns," perhaps because of its cell-like chambers—ninety in all. The entire complex stands on an artificial platform about fifteen feet high. Each building is again raised on its own dais, so that at a distance the flying façade of the north structure merges with the comparatively low building opposite, to form a splendid display.

The Nunnery at Uxmal is of Puuc style with plain wall surfaces and ornament lavished on the projecting upper zone. Each of the buildings is quite different in ornamentation. Small models of houses are set into some friezes, as already encountered at Labná. Great serpents, carved in the round, wind across the entire length of one façade, bringing animation to a geometric design. Stone latticework runs around all four sides of another building. A tier of rain-god masks crowns the center entrance, and at the corners, the great hooked nose of the deity projects in striking profile.

Uxmal has the tradition of considerable antiquity, but all existing dates on the site point to its reaching its height between the seventh and eleventh centuries. The Xiú dynasty, the last ruling family there, claimed Toltec descent, but Toltec influences so evident in Chichén Itzá are little apparent at Uxmal. The city's final period is clouded by struggles between ruling families.

The name Chichén Itzá means "the mouth of the wells of the Itzá"—the Itzá being one of Yucatán's ruling families—and it refers to two cenotes within the confines of the settlement, which made the site exceptionally livable. Chichén Itzá was a great pilgrim center. One of its cenotes was held sacred to the rain-god, and tribes from far and near sent emissaries to plead for crops. In the first decade of the twentieth century, divers brought up copal incense, jade, turquoise mosaics, copper bells, and gold objects of various proveniences, which had been flung into the pool as offerings. Human skeletons of those who had apparently been sacrificed as messengers to the deity were found there, also. Since then, various attempts have been made to discover what the cenote still had to divulge; the year 1967 produced a stone jaguar, a wooden bench, and above all, pottery on which animals and humans are designed with amazing detail and liveliness.

The Nunnery, the Red House, and the House of the Three Lintels belong to the early period and are related to the Puuc style just discussed. From the late tenth to the thirteenth centuries, many edifices show Mexican influence. The Nunnery is generally accepted as one of the oldest buildings [1.28]. Its substructure consists of a huge solid block, 228 feet across the front and 32 feet high. It was enlarged at least twice, and the monumental stairway was continued across the face of the original structure to a new edifice on top.

The Caracol, rising from two irregular platforms, is one of the rare round buildings of the Maya area and dates from the Mexican period of the city [1.27 center foreground]. It was probably dedicated to Kukulcán, the wind-god, just as the round structures of Mexico are associated with his Mexican counterpart, Quetzalcóatl. It may, also, have served as an observatory. Inside lies the spiraling ascent that gives the building its name —"snail shell," or "winding stairway." Openings in the walls of the small chamber on top indicate the cardinal points of the compass and mark the line along which the sun sets at the vernal and autumnal equinoxes. When the city was still living, incense burners in the shape of human heads with hollow eyes and mouths stood along the upper coping, aglow with burning copal.

A great ball-court with vertical walls forms an impressive stadium, 274 feet long and 120 wide (just visible at the far left in the illustration). The related temple, overlooking the arena, presents a profile quite different from that regarded as typically Maya. The walls have a batter reminiscent of Mitla. Two massive serpent columns that divide the wide entrance were once brightly painted, their deep-set eyes inlaid, perhaps with obsidian. A fine carved frieze of jaguars alternating with jaguar-pelt shields extends all the way around the building. One is reminded of the serpent columns found at Tula and the procession of sacred animals, including the jaguar, that decorates a wall there.

From certain points of view, the Temple of the Warriors is even more reminiscent of the Toltec capital (right of the Caracol). Serpent columns appear here, also. The inner halls are spacious. Small atlantes uphold one altar table. At the foot of the substructure spreads the vast "Group of a Thousand Columns," its many square pillars faced with carvings of Toltec warriors elaborately accoutered. A brightly colored bas-relief at Chichén Itzá graphically depicts the conquest of the city by the Toltecs, the opponents clearly differentiated by costume and features. Reliefs of jaguars and eagles devouring human hearts and a platform carved with skulls are reminders of the Mexican practice of human sacrifice.

The Temple of Kukulcán, called El Castillo by the Spaniards, faces the lane that leads to the Sacred Well (left of the Caracol). Nine receding terraces make up the substructure, some seventy-five feet high, which is oriented to the cardinal points of the compass, and four stairways lead up to the temple building on top.

Though the early Maya temple base at Uaxactún and the Toltec-Maya El Castillo are approximately a millennium apart—among the first and the last instances of a continuously developing style—in both, stairways mount the four sides of their pyramidal substructures. As the opening motif of a symphony returns in the finale, here at the end of Maya greatness the early theme appears in an impressive restatement.

About 1200, Chichén Itzá lost its political power, though it long remained a place of pilgrimage because of the Sacred Well. Mayapán rose to dominance. Founded in mid- or late tenth century, Mayapán reached its height at the beginning of the thirteenth, when it became the religious and administrative center of a league in which power was centralized under a single chieftain. It comprised residences as well as ceremonial buildings and was surrounded by a wall five and a half miles long. The city was practically destroyed in the struggles that ended its period of domination in 1461.

About the same time, in the Guatemala highlands, a similar type of federation came into being at Utatlán. Like the Xiú and the Itzá families of Yucatán, the leaders there boasted descent from the Toltecs. But with militaristic rule, the arts were in decline.

Seldom has the discovery of one site added so much to the knowledge of the Maya as that of Bonampak, Mexico, which lies in Chiapas, not far from Yaxchilán and Piedras Negras. How splendidly attired were the Indian chieftains who had the misfortune to face the conquistadores is known from Spanish reports. Scenes of Maya life and ceremonies are glimpsed in painted pottery, and in stone panels and stucco fragments that have survived the corrosive effects of centuries. At Bonampak, a group of Lacandon Indians of Maya stock reluctantly showed an explorer a cluster of ruined buildings. Figures in stucco could be made out on the entablature sections of some structures, exquisitely executed in free and lively pose. Stone stelae and sculpture of fine quality were found buried in jungle growth. One of the buildings harbored the murals for which the site was named "the painted walls"—a revelation of Maya ceremonial pomp and Maya artistic achievement.

The three painted rooms at Bonampak tell an epic tale, starting at the left of the entrance and going around the walls, as in a panorama. The first presents a dance with musical accompaniment before a group of high personages [1.29]. The dancers are garbed as terrestrial gods: one appears as an alligator; another wears the mask and claws of a crab, deity of earth and fertility. A musician at the extreme left is blowing a whistle or pottery ocarina. The long trumpets give a sense of sound; they are thought to have been made of wood and clay. Beyond the group of dancers, who are relaxed and intermingling as if just preparing to perform, musicians beat on turtle shells with the antlers of deer. There is a large upright drum with hide bound over the top—familiar from numerous Maya and Mexican representations. A group with decorated rattles in both hands seems to lead the procession forward. Though these instruments could not find a place in a modern orchestra, this writer has witnessed in a village church in the high Andes the blowing of a conch trumpet at the elevation of the Host during Mass. Parasols are depicted in Bonampak with artistic freedom, breaking through the upper frame of the panel into a band of glyphs.

In the second room, captives are being taken in a raid and brought before high dignitaries. Finally, in the third, a festival is recorded, the dancers wearing immense flowing headdresses of green quetzal feathers. Glyphs are a definite addition to the decorative effect. Those set in panels beside the various personages probably give their names and stations.

The murals were apparently first outlined, then painted on the dry wall surface. They give not only a graphic picture of life and ceremony but a display of talent and artistic skill. Broken lines, with groups of excited figures and criss-crossing spears, suggest the noise and confusion of the raid. The chiefs, set high above all at the top of a flight of stairs, are each individually garbed and given ample space, bringing out their dignity, even hauteur. Their opponents are represented in darker tones with stringy unkempt hair and ruder features. One prone figure, dead or unconscious, is delineated in sweeping brushstrokes that reveal the hand of a master painter, with even a suggestion of foreshortening. The participants are represented from the front, in three-quarter and side view. One does not notice at first that all the heads appear in profile.

A mural buried within the Temple of the Warriors at Chichén Itzá presents a peaceful village at the water's edge [1.32]. Women can be seen cooking out-of-doors; a figure kneels on the shore; men are starting off with burdens on their backs. A crane wings over, and animals hide in the forest. Three canoes move across the water, carrying men in warriors' dress, and fish swim through the waves. It is like an illustration of a fairytale from another planet.

The higher cultures of Middle America had some form of writing on sheets made of plant fiber, tree bark, or animal hide coated with white. As much as can be judged from the few remaining examples, they folded like a screen and opened horizontally into a long line of glued-together pages.

Some Mexican codices have been more or less deciphered, and a number are under study. Some refer to the time count; others relate legendary and historical events; genealogies are proffered. Strange as they seem to us, it is clear that each culture had an established form of picture writing with a long past. Unable to fathom the meaning of these books, and fired by the zeal which saw the workings of evil and the devil in everything that ancient America produced, the Spanish missionaries destroyed all of them that came into their hands. Of the hundreds of Maya written works, three remain: the Madrid, Paris, and Dresden codices. The last is regarded by many as the most artistic.

The strangely attired personages illustrated here [1.30] have calendrical significance. They are delineated by a sweeping outline that reminds one of a modern cartoon. Each is enough differentiated to make its individuality clear to the initiate. The glyphic characters are fluent. Above the figures is a sample of the digit count, in which the dot stands for one and the bar for five.

The second example [1.31] is painted in a different manner. In the upper section, a seated high priest is writing; below him, a warrior brandishes arrows. Each elaborately dressed figure is placed against a panel of solid color, precisely framed. In each case, the headdress is constructed around an animal mask. The warrior's loincloth shows the lively pattern of Maya textiles, and a jade pectoral is depicted on his chest. His face streaked with war paint has an expression of ferocity, while that of the scribe is serene. Strong color contrasts are used, and there is an animation that attracts even the casual viewer. Here again the dot and bar system for the lower digits can be observed.

The tribute rolls of the Aztec ruler Montezuma were so informative that the Spaniards used them in ferreting out the rich regions where gold, dyes, fine textiles, and other products were to be had. Pictographic writing, this non-European way of expressing ideas by glyphs, survived into the colonial era. The topography of large areas was reproduced in small scale— as a sort of map—on cotton sheets. Volcanoes, towns, lakes, all were marked with their special glyphs; roads were indicated by footprints. Later, when land disputes arose in Mexico, such *lienzos* were called in as testimony, and those of remote villages are prized even today as records of the community's history.

INTERLYING AREA

The present political boundaries of the Central American countries do not coincide with the prehistoric confines of their native peoples. In the republics of Honduras and El Salvador, the influence of the Maya and of migrants from southern Mexico, generally called the Pipils, can be seen, notably in their pottery and jade. In Nicaragua, Costa Rica, and Panama, the proximity to South America made the art of these regions susceptible to influences from the south. No architectural remains of high artistic quality have been found in these Isthmian countries, nor were any mentioned by the conquistadores. The artistic flair of the inhabitants, however, is evident in the great variety of pottery and in the sophistication of the metalwork.

ANDEAN AREA

In northern Colombia, in a region that lies actually northeast of the Isthmus of Panama, is a high plateau, more than three thousand feet in altitude, known as Tairona. There the ruins of an isolated culture have been found—the outlines of streets, the foundations of houses built of small stone slabs, and circular ceremonial platforms with stairways. Bones, ancient pottery, *metates* ("grinding stones"), and other objects worked in stone have been unearthed. Indians of lesser culture live there now, practicing rudimentary agriculture.

San Agustín lies in southwest Colombia, near the upper reaches of the Magdalena River. About thirty major monuments have been investigated. These consist largely of subterranean chambers, which served as tombs or shrines, covered by earthen mounds. Large stone slabs, sometimes painted with geometric patterns, make up the walls and roof. Monumental stone figures abound at the site, used as tomb markers, sometimes as tomb covers, and as caryatides [1.33]. The representations vary widely—from what seem to be chieftains to demonic figures, probably tribal deities. The bedrock in nearby streams has been carved, causing the water to flow in patterns.

Judging from the different types of burial and the conventions of the sculpture, three phases of culture at San Agustín have been postulated: the first beginning more than five centuries before Christ and extending to about A.D. 500, the second from the sixth to the twelfth centuries; and the third, a final indefinite one. The use of plain stone shafts reminds one of some Olmec constructions, notably at La Venta, Mexico, and the grinning figure holding up a child is strikingly similar in pose to those found in Olmec jades, such as the one illustrated in the next chapter [see 2.3].

Situated somewhat north of San Agustín, on the mountain range that separates the Magdalena River Valley from that of its tributary, the Cauca, the site of Tierradentro bespeaks a remarkable culture, believed to be somewhat later in date and to have lasted a shorter duration. There a number of unique sepulchral chambers lie buried, with no mounds or exterior signs to indicate their existence. They are circular or oval in shape, cut into soft rock to depths of as much as twenty feet, and are accessible by steep spiral staircases. Pillar-like shafts brace the sloping roof [1.34]. One such tomb measures some sixteen feet in length, eight feet in width, and six feet at its greatest height; hollowed-out recesses like small side chapels give it a complex form. Walls and ceilings of the chambers are painted with geometric designs in black, white, red, and yellow. In some cases, large shield-shaped human faces appear; in others, human figures are incised on the walls and decorated with painted designs. Bones have been found in large pottery urns and in shallow pits dug in the floor, indicating cremation.

The principal ancient ruins of the Andean area lie mainly in Peru, but they also extend into Ecuador on the north and Bolivia on the south. The cultural panorama revealed is highly complex, and the chronology has not yet been fully established.

The Andes, a southward continuation of the Cordilleras of Colombia, comprise a series of mountain ranges interspersed with high valleys. Winding rivers drain these, which though they rise close to the shores of the Pacific, flow north and east and finally join the Amazon. The Andean highlands harbored a number of pre-Columbian cultures.

The Chavín culture in the north is recognizable as early as the tenth century B.C. Wari, in the central highlands near the site of the present-day city of Ayacucho, is believed to have been the political center of the so-called Tiahuanaco culture, which spread its powerful influence not only into Bolivia but also to various coastal settlements. Considerably later, the Incas rose to dominance in the broad rich valley around Cuzco, which is nearly twelve thousand feet in altitude.

A narrow, sandy coastal zone some forty to a hundred miles wide borders the Pacific Ocean. Numerous rivers, fed by rain in the highlands and melted snow from the Andes, cut their way westward to the sea, forming strips of fertile valley. These valleys constituted the nucleus for a variety of cultures based on elaborate systems of irrigation and isolated one from the other by stretches of desert and rocky outcroppings [see 4.1].

On the northern coast of Peru, one of the oldest cultures appears to have been the Cupisnique, recognizable after 900 B.C. The Mochica occupied the same valley probably from a century or so after Christ to around A.D. 900. Then the Coast Tiahuanaco, or Coast Wari, culture makes its appearance, followed by the Chimú who reached their height between 1200 and 1300. On the central coast, the site of Cerro Sechín dates from the ninth century P.C. Somewhat farther south, the Ancón culture was dominant for some two thousand years, giving way to the Chancay about A.D. 1300. On the south coast, Paracas (from roughly about 600 or 700 B.C.), Nazca (A.D. 1 to 800), and Ica (from about 1200) are outstanding.

Differences in style and structure show how many tribes were working their way toward a higher stage of civilization. In the coastal regions, where there was much sand and clay, great edifices were constructed of adobe and clay blocks, with some use of stone. In general, the south coast used small square adobe bricks; in the north, the adobes were large and flat. Logs were used for lintels and to strengthen the walls. In the mountains, stone was the chief building material; it was cut and laid with precision, and in certain regions, without the use of mortar. Terraced substructures appear on the coast; in the highlands, temples and palaces rise from the ground. Formidable citadels, placed strategically, are found both in the highlands and on the coast. Defense walls are familiar features, as are fortified community dwellings. The common people lived in huts of wood, reeds, and adobe on the coast, and of rough stone bound with clay in the mountains; adobe and sod may have also been used there, though all traces of these have disappeared. The roofs seem to have been thatched, and the crest was often decorated with protective symbols.

These cultures and sites will be discussed, as were those of Middle America, in geographical sequence, in this case proceeding from the coast to the High Andes.

To begin with the northern coast of Peru, the Cupisnique are known chiefly through their pottery, which was dark in color and generally made with incised designs in a variety of shapes, some representing animals and deities. The Moche Valley was the seat of the Mochica who followed them—a warlike people judging from the scenes on their painted pottery.

They were organized into social classes, even with distinctive forms of dress.

A huge temple structure of adobe, nearly 130 feet high—the Huaca ("Tumulus") del Sol—stands on a level space on the left bank of the Moche River. As at Copán, a side of the substructure has been washed away, revealing layer upon layer of flat adobes [1.35]. Five terraces make up the sloping substructure. From the platform on top rises a pyramid of seven steps, and a ramp gives access on the north. Another structure, called the Mound of the Moon, stands about a quarter of a mile away. In between lay the town itself, a settlement of clay and reed huts.

The surrounding plain is covered with graves, long since plundered, and a cemetery of a much later period (A.D. 900–1200) was found on the platform of the Huaca del Sol. From the top of the temple, one sees the cultivated fields stretching toward the mountains. On the other side, the plain extends to the sea, with the modern city of Trujillo in view and the ruined walls of Chan-Chan, the capital of the succeeding pre-Columbian kingdom of the Chimú.

Chan-Chan covered some six square miles, with clearly defined suburbs. The mass of architecture, even today in its desolate state, reveals its monumentality. There were streets with rows of dwellings, large pyramidal bases, terraces, ramps and stairways, irrigation canals, reservoirs, and extensive gardens. A lofty aqueduct carried the water from far up the Moche River. Some writers number the population at a quarter of a million. The buildings were constructed of adobe, a material that attained an almost concretelike hardness in the arid climate. The roofs were probably of thatch or reeds carried on long wooden beams. Walls were stuccoed and painted or decorated with patterns in relief [1.36].

A Chimú design has much individuality. Geometric elements are enlivened by conventionalized birds, fish, and abstract motifs. The flowing character of the decoration shows advanced technique. On a section of decorated terrace at the nearby ruins of Esmeralda, one can see the meticulous layout of a basket-weave pattern and a frieze of birds with their curling tails [1.37].

A somewhat similar kind of construction was used throughout coastal Peru. Because these Peruvian sites were among the easiest of the ancient ruins to reach, over the centuries they have been dug up and tunneled into for treasure. Only through the writings of sixteenth- and seventeenth-century chroniclers can one now get an impression of their original expanse and organization.

At the southern end of Chimú territory, La Fortaleza ("The Fortress") at Paramonga, dating between 1200 and 1450, closes off a coastal strip. Constructed throughout of adobe brick, it rises in terraces following the natural contours of a hill—nine hundred feet at its greatest length. Each terrace is surrounded by a solid wall, and four sturdy bastions stand guard at the corners. Military engineers say that the plan would be effective today, if carried out in more durable material. Only when the besieging Incas cut off the water supply of the fort, did the region fall to invaders.

Pachacámac, not far from present-day Lima on the central coast, was a city probably as large as Chan-Chan. It rose somewhat earlier, but even at the time of the Conquest, the place was still a famous religious center. Pizarro sent an expedition to seize its fabled gold, but most of the treasure had been spirited away and was never found. Notable there are the remains of a huge temple base dedicated to the god Pachacámac. Some of the earliest examples of interlocking designs on the coast have been found on the ruined walls—a series of fishes, reminiscent of textile patterns. Strong characteristics of the Coast Tiahuanaco cultural style are evident.

La Centinela, in the Chincha Valley on the southern coast, was an urban center of the Ica or Late Nazca people. Conquered by the Incas sooner than the northern coast regions, it has buildings from both the pre-Inca and Inca periods. Palaces set on platforms of varying heights surround a terraced temple base. Some were furnished with running water within their walls. La Centinela was plundered not only for possible treasure but also for its ancient adobe bricks, which are much harder than modern ones and command ten times the price.

Stone sculpture is rare in the coastal regions. At Cerro Sechín, however—a site dating between 900 and 400 B.C.—figures incised on a row of unshaped slabs remind one of the *danzantes* from the early period of Monte Albán [1.40]. Upright warriors or chiefs are represented carrying clubs or staffs, and a series of smaller stones set in between them shows heads in profile with closed eyes, probably indicating death. The shapes are angular and give the impression that the tools used were adequate for only a simple design. Despite technical limitations, the expressions, poses, and gestures are strikingly effective.

At Huaylas, northeast of Chimbote, two rough slabs with pre-Columbian carvings were discovered in 1960, serving as benches outside the town library. One of these shows an animal mask; the other, a human head with a suggestion of fangs. The technique resembles the early incised carving at Cerro Sechín. Such discoveries reveal how much more there is to investigate before sequences and styles can be established.

In the centuries before Christ and even perhaps for some time afterward, the Chavín culture exerted widespread influence, comparable to that of the Olmecs in the Mexican and Maya areas. The cult of the feline deity can be traced to Chavín tradition. It persists, as a jaguar in the lowlands and a puma in the mountains, in the pottery and weaving at a number of sites for many centuries. The Chavín culture seems to have resulted from an amalgamation of influences and may have constituted a powerful early religious movement.

The style takes its name from the site, Chavín de Huántar, which consists of a settlement and a group of temples on the banks of a tributary of the Río Marañon. The river has cut away the end of one structure, as at Copán and Moche, revealing rough material and poor construction where it was not intended they be seen. From the various groups of buildings, the contents of graves, and the refuse from different periods, it is clear that this was a place of pilgrimage that had been laid out according to plan and was growing as time went by. Fanged masks and life-size stone heads of old men protrude from the showy and quite well-preserved walls of one building, carved fully in the round, with more skill than those at Cerro Sechín.

Unusual are the round columns, some seven or eight feet high, each shaft a single stone, incised with symbols [1.39]. The work is skilled; the design is smoothly adapted to the cylindrical shape. In some sections the background has been cut away, leaving raised motifs. Masks of a feline creature are recognizable, with abstractions drawn from its elements—fangs, eyes, and snarling lips. The involved character of the all-over design accords with the Chavín style, found also on pottery and even influencing textile patterns.

Until recently, archaeological work was concentrated mainly on the coastal sections of Peru. Less difficulties were encountered there climatically, and the promise of treasure from the graves—gold, textiles, and intact pottery—was an incentive for digging. In the highlands, the railroads connecting the mineral-rich regions with the lower levels could take archaeologists only a certain distance. The problem was to reach the ruins beyond the end of the line, where the expedition with its equipment had to proceed on foot or by mule. Thus, the gorge of the Marañon River and the course of its tributaries have yielded a number of surprises. This great river rises in the central highlands, bears northward taking on numerous smaller streams, then turns abruptly east, and empties into the Amazon. Water was, therefore, more abundant than in the coastal regions. Agriculture, home industry, and trade were all pursued here, also; but the different character of the population produced differences in art and architecture.

An early culture of pre-ceramic horizon has been found inland from Chavín, on a tributary of the Marañon. Further investigation of this site, Kotosh, three miles from the town of Huánuco, may go far to substantiate the theory that at least some of the highland civilization evolved from cultures on the tropical eastern slopes of the Andes.

The practice of interring important dead in *chulpas,* or burial towers, occurs in a wide range on the high plateaux of the Andes, and dates from pre-Inca times. Many legends perpetuate the lives of the rulers whose remains these structures once harbored. The chulpas of the south are mostly round, with a low narrow entrance opening into a vaulted chamber that sometimes has another room above it. Built without mortar, of smooth even blocks, they measure as much as thirty-nine feet in height and sixteen in diameter. In the north, the chulpas are usually rectangular. Some are large structures of several stories and numerous chambers, leading one to believe that they may have served for other purposes than burial.

The chulpa at the Chocta ruins, something less than one hundred and fifty miles north of the city of Cajamarca, is an example of the northern type [1.38]. Like the buildings of the nearby site, it is constructed of large flat stones, bound with a mortar apparently made of ground stone and clay, and roofed with stone slabs. The chulpas here are mostly two-storied. Some have entrances to both upper and lower chambers from the steeply sloping mountain side. In several, depressions in the floor contained human bones.

The Chocta ruins stretch for nearly a mile along a sharp ridge at an altitude of 10,600 feet. Eastward, the ground falls rapidly to a glen overlooking the great canyon of the Río Marañon and commanding a magnificent view. There are a number of houses with several rooms and roofs of stone in a remarkable state of preservation. A temple group is recognizable, a round tower as well as the numerous chulpas, and a citadel. This was apparently a fortified town.

Southeast of the Chocta ruins, on the eastern slope of the Cordillera San Martín, tropical forest covers the rain-rich mountains and valleys. There, along the banks of the Huallaga River, which finally flows into the Marañon, a number of villages found ample space to develop. At the end of the eighteenth century, one settlement counted over two thousand inhabitants. Today these villages are approachable only by air or mule train from the town of Juanjui, where the last small airfield connects with the world. Near the village of Pachiza, the pre-Columbian ruins of Gran Pajatén are found at an altitude of over nine thousand feet. The slopes along the way show the outlines of ancient structures, covered with heavy verdure. Agricultural terraces abound, for the region is healthful and immensely rich, and could have provided for thousands.

All the buildings so far uncovered at Gran Pajatén are round and generally two stories high, amazingly well preserved despite the overgrowth. They are constructed of cut slabs of slate laid in orderly arrangement, embedded in mud mortar, with small stones inserted between the larger ones to even the courses. Slate slabs, with carved sections of red sandstone tenoned in, produce mosaiclike friezes of flowers and geometric motifs, human figures in radiating headdresses, and a series of eagles or condors with spread wings. Some pre-Inca pottery was found here in preliminary excavations. A typical Inca copper knife, however, taken from a higher—that is, a later—stratum, bears witness to widespread commercial connections with the Incas or even to Inca occupation, for the Incas later subjugated this important region when they expanded their rule far beyond, into what we know as Ecuador today.

Sections of pre-Columbian aqueducts can be seen near the present city of Cajamarca, a number of which are still called by their ancient Indian names. Some seven or eight miles above the city, the course of the Cumbe Mayo can be followed to its source by way of an ancient path. It leads across shoulders of greenish limestone studded with fantastic out-croppings, skirts an ancient fortification, and passes a cave with carvings on walls and floor. Footholds are cut into the rock where the going is difficult. The water apparently originates in a spring high in the mountains. The course of the waterway is sometimes a mere depression in the grassy slope, then turns into a channel carved out of the rock [1.42]. Averaging twenty to twenty-five inches in width, it rounds corners, passes through tunnels. It is astonishing to realize that this efficient work was carried out without hard metal tools. There are signs of ruined structures near the spring, and various carvings mark the rock side all along the course.

The Incas were not outsiders, as were the Aztecs in the Valley of Mexico, but belonged to one of the highland tribes living along the Urubamba River on the well-watered eastern slope of the Andes. They cultivated maize and potatoes as staple foods and tended flocks of llamas. Their principal seat was Cuzco, which lies in a fertile valley at an altitude of over eleven thousand feet. These people became progressively more power-ful in the last three centuries before the Conquest and consolidated their empire around the middle of the fifteenth century.

At its height, the Inca Empire comprised not only what is today Peru and Ecuador, but Bolivia, parts of Chile, and a fraction of the Argentine. The various regional cultures were held together under a highly organized theocratic government, at the head of which stood the ruling Inca, a benevolent but absolute monarch. Tribute was exacted from subject peo-ples, but their leaders were generally allowed to retain their local authority. The children of powerful families, however, were educated in the Inca capital where, while practically hostages, they were taught the values of the existing system. (This same method of intermingling and intermarriage among members of ruling families was practiced by the Habsburgs to produce cohesion in their multilingual empire.)

Owing to the complications of administering so vast a territory, a second capital was later established at Quito, in northern Ecuador. It was there that the last fortunate ruler—the eleventh Inca—died about 1525. His two sons were engaged in a fratricidal war over the succession, while the Spaniards were exploring the coast of Peru. As Cortés took advantage of the inimical relations between the Tlaxcalans and the Aztecs in the conquest of Mexico, Pizarro used the divided empire to further his own victory. In 1533, his march into Cuzco marked the end of Inca power.

The South American peoples had no form of writing, but some kept arithmetical records, such as of crops harvested, the size of llama herds, a count of the population. Boards with boxlike divisions probably served as a sort of abacus for calculation, using beans or pebbles as counters. Totals were recorded and transmitted by means of the *quipú*. This consisted of a thick cord to which a series of smaller cords was attached. Knots on these cords represented the decimal units, while different colors were used to denote different categories. The Inca calendar was based on the solar year; lunar phases do not seem to have been marked.

The Inca people were outstanding in their transmission of legends and history by word of mouth, possessing a truly phenomenal memory. For some time after the Conquest, entire historical plays and legends from this oral tradition were recorded by Spanish-writing Indian and mestizo scribes. The language is sonorous; the poetry has majesty and dramatic impact. Some two decades ago, this writer attended an evening of music and declamation, held in a former chapel of the University of Cuzco. Parts of the heroic epic "Ollantaytambo" were recited. The dignity of elocution and the poise of the performers—undernourished and ragged as they were—was an experience that everyone in the small invited audience will remember for the rest of his life.

Inca structures are strong and imposing. They are built of expertly dressed stones, often varying in size, fitted together without mortar. Bonded and locked joints are the rule. In some places, a sort of interior lock was achieved by means of a groove in one block which fitted exactly over a corresponding protuberance in another. Some lesser buildings and terrace walls were built of random boulders in a rougher but no less efficient polygonal masonry. These methods are especially effective in an earthquake region, as is the absence of mortar, and may account for the astonishing state of preservation in many of the ruins today. Colonial Cuzco was devastated by a temblor in 1650, and so was the modern city exactly three hundred years later, in 1950. Both times the centuries-old Inca masonry stood unmoved, while the edifices of colonial and modern times tumbled to ruins.

The ancient Inca capital was laid out on a geometric plan, with straight narrow streets. The austere stone walls of temple and palace are said to have been sometimes embellished with fine textiles and sheathed with gold and silver. Gold was regarded by the pre-Columbian peoples not as currency but as a gift of the gods, a symbol of the beneficent light of the sun.

The fortress of Sachsahuamán guards the city from a promontory at the edge of the shallow valley. Almost twelve hundred feet long, it rises in three irregular terraces, constructed of enormous stones of uneven size and shape, one of which measures thirty-eight feet long by eighteen feet wide and six in depth. There are indications that the fortress was started in pre-Inca times. The stones were quarried several miles away from the site, carried across streams and ravines, and hoisted many feet. How they were shaped, transported, and fitted without the use of iron tools, pulleys, wheeled vehicles, or beasts of burden remains a matter for wonder and admiration.

Some thirty miles northwest of Cuzco is Ollantaytambo, one of the fortresses that protected "the sacred valley" from attack by aggressive tribes from the north. This site is characterized by the pale greenish tint of its stone and the elegance of its use in a sort of stone paneling. As the garrisons of such Inca strongholds had to be self-supporting, the ground around and above the citadel is graded and terraced for agriculture. A living village lies at the foot of the ruin, and abundant water still courses through ancient channels.

Pisac, in a dramatic setting in the Urubamba Valley, is strategically located on steep mountain slopes overlooking the river [1.41]. The disposition of the groups of dwellings, the garrison, the pinnacle with its temples, the endless terraced fields, bespeak the development of generations. A single huge slab forms the lintel of a portal which is characteristically wider at the base [1.44]. Though the masonry at Pisac is not so cyclopean as at some other sites, the smooth even work gives the place prominence.

The spectacular fortress city of Machu Picchu lies at an altitude of over eight thousand feet on one of the mountain shoulders carved out by the Urubamba River. It is situated two thousand feet above the river bed, on a saddle between two peaks. Aqueducts, bathhouses, smoothly rounded walls, picturesque flights of stairs, all of granite, furnish superb examples of Inca construction. Natural boulders and ledge were incorporated into the masonry. The ground around the buildings is terraced for agriculture.

The ceremonial center stands on a height overlooking the entire settlement, enclosed within walls but open to the sky [1.43]. There the summit of living ledge was carved into a sort of altar topped by a shaft. This is said to be a sundial or *intihuatana* ("place where the sun is tied up"). Some believe that such monuments were used for astronomical observations—a supposition all the more plausible since it is held that the great circular group of monoliths at Stonehenge in England had a similar purpose. The impact of this monument is intensified by its setting, against the snow-covered range known as the Sangre de Cristo. The association of the blood of Christ with the resplendent glow of the snow-covered peaks at sunrise and sunset also occurs in our own Southwest and elsewhere in the Americas.

Some archaeologists would date Machu Picchu from pre-Inca times, some from around the ninth century; others feel that it was built not much before the Conquest. There is also a tradition that it formed the last refuge of the Incas after Cuzco had fallen to the Spaniards. Hidden away on its tremendous bluff and covered with subtropical vegetation, it remained undiscovered until 1911, when dynamite opened a passage through the river's gorge for a narrow-gauge railroad.

As the Inca empire expanded, the uniform style of its stone masonry spread into many areas. Typical Inca settlements can be found as far away as Ecuador, notably at the site of Ingapirca. Broad roads and well-based causeways covered the country in a systematic network. Bridges were built and kept in repair. *Tampus* ("wayside shelters") were kept up, one day's journey from one another, where the traveler could find lodging and food. So smooth were communications, that relay runners regularly carried fresh fish up from the Pacific for the table of the Inca at Cuzco. As the Roman roads were used in a number of instances during the Renaissance, so the conquistadores, and later the Spanish colonial administrators, used those of the Incas. Long sections have been traced that are still in a comparatively good state of preservation.

Recent excavations at Huánuco, a town northeast of Cajamarca in the central highlands, have thrown new light on the Inca control of its provinces. An impressive group of buildings there in typical Inca style apparently served as administration and ceremonial center. On a hill nearby stood warehouses where tribute was stored. It appears that tribute pottery and textiles were fashioned according to strict requirements. On the other hand, the dwellings and the household wares of the local common people seem to have been little influenced by Inca style—a conclusion that is corroborated by the study of late coastal textiles.

Tiahuanaco had perhaps a more profound effect on contemporaneous art styles, except, strangely enough, on that of the neighboring Incas. As already mentioned, this culture is believed to have centered around Wari, a very large site near the present town of Ayacucho in the central highlands, and to have flourished between 600 and 900 of our own era. The nature of its expansion—whether by conquest or by religious penetration—is uncertain. Both pottery and textiles, notably of the coastal districts, record its distinctive motifs. As time went on, however, these influences were absorbed, and the character of the various groups re-emerged with considerable individuality.

The site of Tiahuanaco in Bolivia, south of Lake Titicaca, is believed to have been the religious center of this culture, an important place of pilgrimage, built up over a considerable period of time. The masonry there is highly skilled and complex. Even in its early phases, stones were often bolted together with copper cramps.

Four great rectangular earthen platforms containing the remnants of buildings characterize the site. A slight natural rise was built out, possibly as a fortress, with a reservoir. The most conspicuous and artistically important of the ruins is a great monolith known as the Gateway of the Sun [1.46]. Cut from a single piece of extremely hard trachyte, darkened by the years, it stands over seven feet high, thirteen feet wide, and only eighteen inches thick. An elaborate carving in low relief decorates the upper part, while the wall space below is plain except for two shallow niches. The principal figure on the frieze represents Viracocha, the creator-god. A radiant headdress surrounds his large square head, and teardrops, probably designating rain, are among the incised symbols on his masked face. He stands on a platform, with snakes curling at the foot, and wears an elaborate tunic with a girdle embellished with puma heads. In one hand, he holds a spear thrower; in the other, a quiver containing darts. Forty-eight personages of smaller stature attend the god. These are winged men, bearing staffs or spears, who look as if they were running—possibly genuflecting. In the middle row, personified birds appear, wearing cloaks. A considerable amount of other sculpture is found at the site: friezes in low relief, tenoned-in heads of human beings and of animals, and tall stone shafts carved into human shape. During the colonial centuries, much material was, however, dragged away and used for civil and ecclesiastic structures. The church that is visible through the archway in the illustration was largely built of ancient stones.

Tiahuanaco style is characterized by rectangular drawing. Geometric motifs abound. The several figures on the Gateway of the Sun, together with stylized pumas and condors, persist throughout all the Tiahuanaco arts, often in abstract form.

The southwest sector of Peru is the best explored in the Andean highlands. Upon the arrival of the Spaniards, a mule-train route was established, connecting silver-rich Potosí with the Pacific coast. Some mines were worked there centuries before the Conquest.

The region near Vizcachani on the Peruvian-Bolivian border, somewhat north of Lake Titicaca, is still a gold-mining area. Not far from a landscape torn by placer mining, one comes upon the awesome plain fifteen thousand feet above sea level. Even on clear days, a black cloud hangs over the glaciers of Mount Queuo that make a telling background for a herd of guanacos grazing on the tundralike plateau [1.45]. Their wool has been highly prized since ancient times. Vicuña, whose pelts are still more precious, abound in the region. Small brown lizards and shy Peruvian hares (*vizcachas*) dart among the crags, their evanescent lives a contrast to the permanence of the massif.

1.1] Týúoni Pueblo Monument. Frijoles Canyon, New Mexico.

1.2] Cliff Palace. Mesa Verde, Colorado.

[1.3] Teotihuacán, Mexico.

[1.4] Detail, Quetzalcóatl Temple. Teotihuacán.

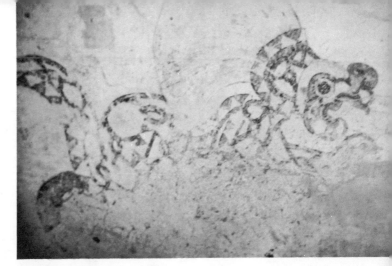

[1.5] Jaguar mural. Teotihuacán.

[1.6] Mythical animals, mural. Teotihuacán.

[1.7] Sacred quetzal, mural. Teotihuacán.

[1.12] Monte Albán. Oaxaca, Mexico.

[1.13] *Danzantes*. Monte Albán.

14] Palace of the Tombs. Mitla, Mexico.

15] Palace of the Columns. Mitla.

[1.16] Uaxactún, Guatemala.

[1.17] Tikal.

[1.18] El Palacio and Temple of the Tomb. Palenque, Mexico.

[1.19] Hieroglyphic Stairway. Copán, Honduras.

[1.20] Sayil, Yucatán, Mexico.

[1.21] Kabáh, Yucatán.

[1.22] Acancéh, Yucatán.

[1.23] Flying façade. Labná, Yucatán, Mexico.

[1.24] Maya archway (after Stephens). Labná.

[1.25] Temple of the Magician. Uxmal, Yucatán, Mexico.

[1.26] Nunnery. Uxmal.

27] Chichén Itzá, Yucatán, Mexico.

28] Nunnery. Chichén Itzá.

[1.29] Fresco detail. Bonampak, Mexico.

[1.30] Detail from Maya Dresden codex.   [1.31] Detail from Maya Dresden codex.

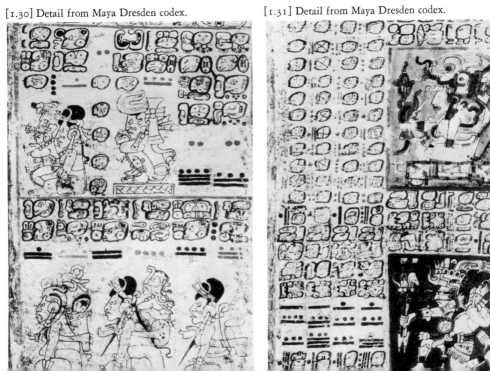

[1.32] Mural. Chichén Itzá.

[1.33] Tomb. San Agustín, Colombia.

[1.34] Tomb chamber. Tierradentro.

1.35] Temple base. Moche, Peru.

[1.37] Adobe reliefs. Huaca la Esmeralda.

[1.36] Adobe reliefs. Chan-Chan.

[1.39] Carved columns. Chavín de Huántar.

[1.38] Chulpa. Chocta, Peru.

[1.40] Monoliths. Cerro Sechín.

[1.41] Pisac, Peru.

[1.42] Aqueduct. Cumbe Mayo.

[1.43] Intihuatana. Machu Picchu, Peru.

[1.44] Stair and lintel. Pisac.

[1.45] Landscape near Vizcachani, Peru.

[1.46] Gateway of the Sun. Tiahuanaco, Bolivia.

2/Sculpture

Sculpture in the round is generally considered to be the high point of plastic art. The peoples of pre-Columbian America approached this peak in different locations, at different periods, and to very different effects. Some very early pieces show a strong feeling for the three-dimensional, while others are done only in incised outline. In some cultures, one can observe how relief carving was developing more and more toward the round; others seem to have been content with the elaboration of design on a rather flat surface.

It is difficult to take the full measure of pre-Columbian sculpture, since much of it functioned as ornament and most of what we see today is stripped from out of its setting. In many cases, the provenience can be judged only from the style. As in many early civilizations, color was lavishly used in both sculpture and architecture—a fact that must be kept in mind in any attempt to visualize how the art originally looked.

The pre-Columbian sculptor had great feeling for his material. The Aztec carver used trachyte, serpentine, and other rugged stones of the region. For the Maya, limestone was at hand, which was tractable when quarried and hardened on exposure to the air; it also provided the material for stuccowork. Carvings in jade, bone, wood, and even shell testify to the plastic talent of these peoples.

The tools and techniques of the pre-Columbian sculptor were highly ingenious. Tubular and solid drills were used, rotated on bowstrings, to define circles or parts of circles, or to start a pierced or hollowed-out section. Deep cutting and grooving were done with hard stone and even hardwood tools, with the use of various abrasives, and the fine incising was accomplished with implements of jade, quartz, flint, and possibly obsidian.

MEXICAN AREA

The Olmecs left, nearly exclusively, three-dimensional work. A number of gigantic heads discovered at the Olmec site of San Lorenzo Tenochtitlán, in the state of Veracruz, are dated at least as early as 800 B.C. One of them measures nine and a half feet in height and weighs over thirty tons. Apparently, at some unknown date, these heads were thrown down from ancient temple mounds and became buried in jungle debris. All represent the same type of man, with the full round face, thick lips, and squat nose of the dweller in tropical lands [2.1]. All wear a helmetlike headdress. The eyes are focused; some even have the iris indicated, framed with a double line. The huge basalt stones for these monumental works had to be transported from as much as seventy-five miles from where they were quarried —probably, they were floated down the river on rafts. The skill with which the Olmec sculptor chipped, cut, rounded, and polished the hard stone with his primitive tools until it had form is no more remarkable than the artistic assurance with which he kept his concept in mind, without sketch or model, through months, perhaps even years, of execution to achieve such clarity and proportion.

Another favorite material of the Olmecs was that known to the pre-Columbian peoples as "greenstone" and valued above gold throughout Middle America. This comprised several types of hard greenish stone, such as jadeite, nephrite, serpentine, as well as true jade, all of which were associated with the green of abundant life. Early writers termed it all "jade," and we shall, also, use the collective term. The colors vary from light buttery green to veined, dark hemlock green. True jade, though with a slightly different chemical composition from Chinese jade, is found *in situ* in Alaska and in some of the Rocky Mountain states of the United States, as well as in Mexico and Guatemala. The stone of the blue of a star sapphire, which is much favored in Olmec carving, is so common in pieces from El Salvador as to suggest that land as one source of its provenience. There has been little organized research in this matter. Investigation in other regions might discover other sources.

In 1965, at Las Limas, a village not far from San Lorenzo Tenochtitlán, a father saw his children cracking nuts on a stone of unusual shape. It turned out to be a greenstone statuette, nearly a foot tall, representing a man seated cross-legged and holding a child. The man has the characteristic Olmec features while the child has a grotesque, angular, tigerlike snout familiar from other Olmec carvings. There were lines incised on the man's face, knees, and shoulders, and glyphs on the body of the child. The statue was cleaned and placed on an improvised altar by the village population, with hangings of linen and lace. Garlands of artificial flowers were looped from the baldachin above it and down the sides of the shrine. More flowers in vases, candles, tapers, and other paraphernalia surrounded it. Indian and mestizo villagers who are without a priest are wont to decorate their churches in this way for festive occasions. When the authorities finally heard about the find and claimed it for the museum, they were confronted with the indignation of the villagers, who insisted that the statue, having been found on a feast day of the Virgin, was a new appearance of the Mother and Child.

A close parallel is found in another jade statuette, eight and five eighths inches high [2.3], though here the man is standing. His ears and nose have been pierced for ornaments, perhaps of gold. The figures are completely nude. Only the heads are elaborated. Irises are indicated in the hollowed-out eyes. The child—some say, dwarf—wears a close-fitting head-dress and has slanting eyes and an animal-like mouth, without fangs. This is interpreted as a "were-jaguar," a combination of infant and animal, the jaguar, among the Olmecs, being connected with water. The fact that such figures appear more than once shows that we are dealing with an established iconography. A similarity with a sculpture at San Agustín, Colombia, has already been mentioned [see 1.33]. Other Olmec characteristics in such sculpture include over-all incised lines like tattooing, coxcomb or flamelike designs above the eyes, drooping lips, the incorporation of accessory "hidden" faces in a piece, the "crying baby" figure, part feline, part infant, sometimes with a cleft head.

Numerous small jade heads exist without definite provenience, in which apparently the whole stone—perhaps a waterground pebble some two or three inches high—was utilized. In the piece illustrated [2.4], attention has been given to the artificial elongation of the skull, practiced by various peoples of pre-Columbian America. The ears are mere lugs or handles at the side. No eyeballs are indicated; the hollowed-out eyes may have been inlaid, but the shadow gives them expression. Heavy grooves between the eyes are sculpturally effective. The swollen lips have an Olmec droop, and the bald head, also, is in keeping with that style. The undecorated surfaces are just as effective as the features. The sculptor knew exactly what he wanted to achieve.

Pieces with Olmec characteristics are amazingly widely dispersed, and in some regions turn up as an isolated specimen. A seated nude figurine [2.2] was found at La Lima, a farm near Cortés, Honduras, not far from the Ulua Valley, which is famous for its carved "marble" vases. The flattened forehead, blunt nose, and thick lips are Olmec traits, but in its whole effect, the style of this piece is baffling. Unlike the small jade head just described, the mouth lacks the typical Olmec turn, and the nose is not connected with the curling lip. A beard and fringe of moustache make it still more unusual. The piece has a forward thrust that commands attention. When we realize that it is only three and a half inches high, its air of monumentality is remarkable.

Olmec influences can be found, also, in some of the pottery pieces. The head from Tlatilco near Mexico City [2.5] belongs to the archaic type that pioneer archaeologists called "baby face." Besides the characteristic facial features, the finely incised lines designating hair appear in outspoken Olmec work.

Notable from Teotihuacán and the Mexican high plateau are numerous "masks," approximately life size and carved in stone of various kinds and colors. They depict a human face without hair or ornamentation, but nevertheless pervaded with a certain realism. The eye sockets are hollow, perhaps for inlay; sometimes they are pieced clear through the stone. The ears sometimes protrude like lugs; sometimes they are carved at the sides of the head. The mouths are usually slack, implying death. Some of the masks have small holes at the sides, suggesting that they may have been worn for decoration, as breastplates or as trophy heads, hung from a belt.

The western states of Mexico, notably Guerrero, though little investigated, have produced stone sculpture showing much skill and power that often has Olmec traits.

The Totonac people flourished between the eleventh and the thirteenth centuries in the semitropical regions of the Gulf Coast of Mexico. Their capital was Zempoala, north of Veracruz. Among the most fascinating of their carvings are the so-called *hachas,* wedge-shaped ceremonial "axes." One such piece depicts an acrobat [2.6]. His upturned body in its back-breaking pose follows the traditional shape of the "axe." The straining ribs and the patterned loincloth are brought out with rare economy. Other ornament is sparse. The hands and feet are merely indicated. The eyes may have been inlaid. Utilizing the shape of the stone, the unrealistically curved body of a snake towers over the figure. Its head with curling snout and the feathers along its back are clearly defined. Even the perforations have their artistic value.

In another wedge-shaped stone, showing the head of an old man wearing a bird mask [2.7], nearly half of the surface has been left without decoration, which serves to concentrate attention on the face with its light linear marking, representing either teardrops or tattoo. A row of glyphs beneath the helmet breaks the starkness of the piece. When these are deciphered, they may cast some light on the enigmatic personage portrayed. He looks like an accursed magician in some fantastic play.

Another widely-known type of sculpture found only in this region is the *palma* [2.8]. These slender carvings, which range between nine and twenty-four inches in height and look like the fronds of a palm tree, also had a ceremonial purpose. The main subject is usually a standing figure or an animal set against an oval background. The angular intertwined frets are a characteristic feature.

This people polished greenish jadelike stones into massive yokes, apparently connected with their version of the ball game [2.9]. As with the *palma,* the subject matter varies widely, and its adaptation to the unusual and restricted form of the yoke makes an absorbing study. A fragment [2.10] shows strongly different facial features from those in other heads illustrated on the same page.

Miniatures of all three of these forms have been recently found in graves in this region, emphasizing the significance of such objects in the life of the Totonac people.

A carved head of unknown provenience, though related to examples previously discussed, is more complex in concept and finer in execution [2.11]. It is estimated to have been about six and a half inches wide when whole. A rich jade green in color, it is carved in very high relief, giving a nearly three-dimensional effect. The nose is narrow, the septum pierced for the insertion of an ornament. The heavy grooving intensifies the expression of the eyes with their slight cast which was considered a mark of beauty among some pre-Columbian peoples. The ears with their round earplugs are indicated on the flat surfaces at the sides of the plaque. Glyphs appear at the extreme left, and may also have been incised on the other side, which is broken off. Though the piece has a number of Maya characteristics, the glyphs are not Mayan. The carved pupils, the heavy down-curved lips, point toward the Olmec. Though such elegantly sculptured hair is rare in Olmec plaques, it does occur in pottery and on jade heads from the region, as we have seen.

The stone head from La Venta, Tabasco, Mexico [2.13], illustrated just below, shows the manner of rendering hair. Here less subtlety has been used in tracing the locks. The great divergence in the eyes and mouths of the two pieces demonstrates that neighboring cultures had their own plastic expression.

Some writers have little praise for Aztec art, because the iconography had some starkly horrifying concepts: a god dressed in the flayed skin of a sacrificial victim, a deity whose body is composed of writhing serpents. In the seated Indian warrior [2.12], there is no such shock or coarseness. A young person is represented with amazingly few sculptural tricks, watching, half relaxed but also intent. Detail is sparse. The piece is compact and can be viewed with satisfaction from all sides.

The same directness of approach can be seen in Aztec carvings of snakes, toads, and mythical creatures. The Aztecs had a special facility for portraying a mythical figure in such a way that it seems to have been observed from life, to belong to reality. The coiled serpent, on the opposite page [2.16], believed to have come from Central Mexico, is in size compressed, but it has considerable elaboration of detail. The head with its long drooping fangs has characteristics of Tlaloc, the rain-god. Curving lines and loops depict symbolic feathers—with a sweeping brush of them at the end of the rattles. Its various stylistic elements make it difficult to assign to any one culture.

The *danzante* figures at Monte Albán [see 1.13] date from at least 700–300 B.C. The name "dancer" derives from their contorted poses, outlined on irregular stone slabs. Deeper and shallower incision gives them a certain plasticity. Differences in style indicate that they were fashioned over a long period. The presence of glyphs indicates the development of writing and calendrical observation at a very early stage.

MAYA AREA

A pendant of brilliant green jade, about five and a half inches high, said to be from Nebaj, Guatemala, shows a typical Maya jade carving [2.14]. A seated Maya dignitary is presented in profile, with loincloth, earplugs, pectoral bar, arm and leg bands carefully delineated. Although the piece was broken and small sections are missing, one gets an idea of how the sculptor had to visualize his composition, even before he started, to make full use of the uneven piece of precious material. The figure is given plenty of room within a curving frame. A demon mask at the right side and symbols in the lower section enhance the composition and suggest a complex meaning. Here the skilled use of tubular drills can be observed in the circles, semicircles, and curves.

In a group of jades of various styles and various cultures, a celt is typical of work from Nicoya, Costa Rica [2.15]. As conventionalized as it is, one can make out a figure standing with folded arms. He wears a headdress of intertwining serpent scrolls and a breast ornament suggesting a jaguar head. The many drilled indentations not only reveal the painstaking methods by which such carvings were achieved, but also suggest inlay.

In two small jade pendants [2.17 and 2.18], each somewhat over three inches in height, the clever use of a minute piece of stone can be observed. A full figure has been composed in the first without cramping—complete with feathered headdress, folded arms, crossed legs. In the second, the grotesque face is emphasized in an entirely different concept. Body and ornaments appear in a sort of shorthand. A tiny hand (bottom center) closes the composition. Note the difference in the representation of the eyes.

Certain concepts run through Middle American art, such as the Feathered Serpent, various anthropomorphic figures—combinations of man and animal—animal masks, often worn as headdresses. Yet in the way they are presented, there are great stylistic differences. The Mexicans had a predilection for mass in their sculpture, as in their architecture. The Maya dealt less with solid form than with subtle composition and balance of detail. They perfected the relief in many aspects and reached an apogee in their three-dimensional statuary. From earliest times, they cut stone and modeled stucco to ornament their structures. Doorways were crowned with sculptured lintels in wood or stone; busts and masks were tenoned into walls; tablets and panels had a place both inside and outside of the building.

Palenque's abundance of sculpture in stone and stucco reveals complete mastery, in the sophistication of its line and the command of deep- and shallow-cut detail. The figure seated on a jaguar throne [2.19] shows what highly delicate nuances can be achieved in relief, and gives an impressive idea of the quality of work in which the Maya sculptor was able to transmit a sense of dignity, of ceremonial, almost hieratic pomp, and of physical grace.

The stucco head, apparently broken from a larger piece [2.20], was discovered in the hidden burial chamber in the Temple of the Inscriptions, already mentioned. Here is a simpler treatment of the surface than in relief, though no less effective. This piece, executed fully in the round, presents the classic Maya aristocrat, with flattened forehead, somewhat receding chin, a sharp nose, high cheekbones, and elongated ears. The headdress is carefully detailed. A fringe of tassel represents hair. A garland of water-lily buds is surmounted by a bush of feathers, suggesting leaves of the maize.

The stela—a vertical shaft of stone that sometimes reached thirty-five feet in height and weighed more than fifty tons—was an integral part of a Maya center, serving as monument and, also, as a lasting time marker. Though much of the text remains undeciphered, the dates recorded, ranging from A.D. 328 to 889, furnish invaluable contributions not only to our knowledge of the various sites, but also to the study of style. Altars were frequently connected with the stelae, fashioned of huge natural boulders and often carved, as at Quiriguá, with reliefs related to the earth deity.

The sculptors of various sites and periods found innumerable ways to differentiate a concept that was, at the core, limited. In general, a figure or figures occupy the center of the composition—a priest or chieftain, a deity or some abstract, symbolic conception. He may stand with body turned to the front, the feet pointing outward, the head in profile or fullface, arms bent, often carrying an ornate ceremonial bar. At Tikal, some of the sculpture is in incised flat relief, cut so that its intricate detail overflows into the frame. In the dark-red sandstone at Quiriguá, very high relief, almost three dimensionality, was achieved. At Copán, the outline of some of the figures extends around the sides of the slab. The sculpture at Piedras Negras is outstanding for its depiction of ceremonies and events with a number of figures expertly composed, and at Yaxchilán, extraordinary finish in detail can be observed.

In later sculpture, Maya dress grows more and more ornate. The headdress is in itself a study of artistically flowing feathers or intricately bound hair. Earplugs and nose ornaments, collars, belts of jade, and loincloths or aprons of patterned textiles are well defined—even sometimes distracting in their abundance of detail. Sandals—a sign of distinction—evolve from the plain sole held by a band to ornate footwear with bow ties, leaves, ribbons, jade beads, and even small masks. The glyphs are placed in different ways, with stylistic variety.

On a stela from Ixkun, Guatemala, that dates from the end of the eighth century, the edges of the slab have been carved to form a frame for the composition [2.21]. Two dignitaries stand facing each other on the same level. From their waving headdresses down to their decorated sandals, they appear in full regalia, with enough differences to make it clear that the chiefs of two separate clans are meeting. The older one stands somewhat taller, on the left. As if to emphasize the dignitaries' importance by the apportionment of space, two nude crouching captives, with loose hanging hair, are crowded into the two small panels below. These crouching figures are quite different in feature, even from one another. Their foreshortened legs and bent bodies are delineated with skill. Bands of glyphs enclose them as if in prison walls. Although the whole surface has been used to its fullest extent, the composition is not cramped. Human beings are represented; a real scene is being enacted.

Whether in painting or sculpture, the most difficult task is to design and execute a storytelling or figural composition within a circle; in the Italian art of the Quattrocento, the tondo was accounted the test of an artist's virtuosity. On a ball-court marker from Copán, twenty-five inches in diameter, which is dated around the beginning of the seventh century, two kneeling figures face each other across a panel of glyphs [2.22]. The one on the left is apparently a ball player clad in the protective armor of the game. The other, in tights of jaguar skin with masks attached to his belt, might be an officiating priest or chieftain. Dense as the composition is, it fits with ease into the limited space of a quatrefoil. Interest is held by the variety in sculptural lines and shapes.

How much pre-Columbian iconography and tradition survived into the Spanish colonial period is still a matter for lively discussion. In a former Franciscan monastery, at Zinacantepec, in the state of Mexico, stands a large stone baptismal font carved with round medallions. One such tondo shows the Annunciation. Another presents the Baptism of Christ [2.23]. The font was carved in 1581, evidently by an Indian sculptor by order of a friar named Martín de Aguire, according to a text in Nahuatl (Aztec) language around the edge of the font. This composition in tondo form would not be especially noteworthy were it not so similar to the pre-Columbian carving just previously discussed. Furthermore it is Tlaloc, the rain-god, the dispenser of life-giving water, who appears in full panoply between the circular medallions, as in pre-Columbian codices, sculpture, and pottery. The Maya relief was carved in fine-grained limestone; the Aztec, in a harder and rougher volcanic material.

The maize-god from Copán [2.24] is a masterpiece of sculpture in the round. The bust was tenoned into the wall of Temple 22 at Copán, a small but imposing building, the entrance to which is framed with figures from the complex Maya pantheon. The youthful god has all the characteristics of the Maya princeling from Palenque [see 2.20], but the features seem softened and humanized. There is rhythm in the unsymmetrical fall of the hair, the slight disbalance of the heavy jade necklace with its clearly detailed mask as pectoral. The soft round shoulders and significant gesture pulsate with life. Like its neighboring Hieroglyphic Stairway [see 1.19], this figure is seen at its best as the sun crosses the zenith—when lighted from above, the half-closed eyes and parted lips give a sense of incantation.

A rubbing, artistically executed, singles out a detail from the lid of the Palenque sarcophagus already described [2.25]. Because it has been removed from the original's intricate composition of glyphs and symbols, the ease and grace—one might say, the elegance—of the main figure comes to full effect. The contrast in the work from the two sites is clear. Here the Maya aristocrat is depicted with sensitive nuance in very low relief. Feather headdress, earrings, jade beads, and wristlets, such as were actually found inside the coffin, are depicted in detail. The huge breastplate represents a turtle—an earth deity—with a demon head. The effective movement, floating or falling, is skillfully caught: hands and upturned face as if in a dance, the lips parted perhaps in song.

Connoisseurs of pre-Columbian art have sometimes been reproached for giving so much space to Maya art. From the illustrations reproduced in this volume, perhaps the reasons for their enthusiasm will be evident.

The seated wood figure, about two feet high [2.26], is a rarity, not only because of its size and its excellent state of preservation, but also because it is entirely in the round, effective from all angles. Some priest or functionary has been masterfully brought to life. In facial characteristics, he is completely different from the aristocrats of Palenque and Copán. The heavy "moustache" may represent the writhing body of a snake used in Maya rituals, as depicted in a demon figure at Copán. Cloak or scarf, kilt of patterned textile, and elaborate jewelry of heavy jade are detailed with finesse. Nobility of rank radiates from the carving. In its exquisite decoration and the superb delineation of physical vigor, this piece can only be compared with some of the best scenes painted on vases and found occasionally in murals of the assembled hierarchy. Here, no surrounding details support the figure, but its effect is immediate.

A diminutive figure, only two and three-quarters inches high, representing a Maya warrior or dignitary, has been carved from the femur of a jaguar [2.27]. It may have served as the top of a ceremonial staff. The little warrior's unbending stance and stoic expression are emphasized by his arms akimbo. The helmetlike casque covers his head, with a hole in front for an inlay of jade or turquoise that has been lost. Long quetzal feathers cascade across his shoulders. The figure is clothed in the skin of a jaguar with the tail hanging down behind, and the detail in the elaborate sandals is carefully delineated even in this tiny piece. Remnants of red paint are still visible. Glyphs adorn the base of the statuette. Its provenience is unknown, but it is considered to be about sixth century in date and to have come from Yucatán or southern Veracruz.

The department of Esquintla, in the western part of Guatemala, is believed to have never been occupied by a Maya people, although some monuments reflect the influence of that great culture. A large upright jaguar at El Baúl shows a certain relationship to Mexico [2.28]. Carved in the round, compact and uncluttered, it has the playful pose of a domesticated animal. The bulging eyes, the well-defined jaw, with fangs and slavering tongue, are well executed and can be accepted as quite realistic. But the creature's position and frilled collar suggest that this is a representation of some deity.

In 1964, near the same location, a stela was discovered carved with two figures masked with animal heads, one standing over the other as if in conquest. Both hold balls, indicating some connection with the traditional game. A frieze across the bottom contains seated figures, all alike, and some glyphs. Neither humans nor glyphs are Maya in style. Yet from the upper left corner, a dignitary, strongly Maya in profile and accouterment, reaches out of the sky toward the standing "victor," extending what appears to be a heavy necklace of jade beads, tied with a ribbon. This work is a rare example of how the iconography from different cultures has been adopted and blended.

A large puma of clay [2.29] from Pungurí, on the coast of Peru, affords us the opportunity to compare two pieces of sculpture in the round from two separate cultures. From the eyes alone, the onlooker can observe the difference—one pair being finely worked out with irises; the other, merely empty holes in the skull. In the Guatemalan piece, the claws are in full three dimensions; in the Peruvian, they are done in a sort of shorthand, evidence of how early conventionalization appears in the Chavín style.

The quality of the stuccowork of the Maya sculptor, its solidity both technically and artistically, can be judged from examples still extant on the walls, the roof combs, the entablature sections at Palenque, Comalcalco, Bonampak, and other sites, and from the many masks, heads, even whole figures, that have been carried away. A mask from Chiapas [2.30], where

Mexican and Maya influence crossed, shows assurance in modeling, even in its present fragmentary state. It has the same facial characteristics as those of the seated figure in wood discussed previously, with slanted eyes, bulging forehead, and blunt nose. Contrast is achieved through the use of varied geometric shapes in the headband and earplugs, the forward-sweeping uppermost detail in the former suggesting feathers or a plume of maize leaves.

A stone *hacha,* or ceremonial axe [2.31], believed to have come from the Maya area, represents a skull being picked at by a vulture. This motif also occurs in Peruvian pottery, showing how similar mythological concepts existed in widely distant areas of ancient America. Here, again, relatively few sculptural details achieve an arresting effect.

Two fragments, both from Maya sites, demonstrate that the same plastic vocabulary was used over a wide area. The wattles of the stone turkey from Copán [2.32] and the feathers of the parrot head—perhaps a ball-court decoration—from La Jula, Obrajes, Honduras [2.33] are executed in the same manner, yet a different effect is brought out.

A large collection of stone shafts in the shape of human beings, animals, and fantastic creatures stands behind the walls of a religious establishment in Granada, Nicaragua [2.34]. Though lacking the refinement of its northern neighbors, the carving even if damaged is expressive in its directness, reminding one of the stone shafts at San Agustín, Colombia [see 1.33].

Similar talent in stonework can be observed in the sculpture from the rest of the Interlying area. In Costa Rica, boldly executed statues of human beings, sometimes combined with animal features, have been cut from the rough volcanic stone of the region. The metates, used for grinding corn, often represent conventionalized pumas or jaguars. The alligator is a frequent subject. Low stone chairs, almost footstools, come from the same area, supported on pedestals shaped in the form of animals or crouching human beings.

The sculpture of the Andean area—some of which has already been seen in the illustrations for the preceding chapter—is strongly conventionalized, powerful in its angularity. A statue from Moscopán, Colombia, now in the courtyard of the University of Popayán [2.35] shows a close relationship to the work at San Agustín. It is carved from a pillar-like shaft, four and a half feet high. The limbs are kept close to the body, only the ears and block-like headdress stand out. The pectoral, in the shape of the so-called "ceremonial knife," will be seen in the chapter on metalwork [see 5.16].

The Gateway of the Sun at Tiahuanaco, Bolivia [see 1.46], and the stelalike statues found there are representative of the stone sculpture of the southern Andean highlands. Tiny figurines of llamas and men, fashioned by the Incas in turquoise and various other colored stones, prove that these highland people were, also, able to carve effectively in the round.

[2.1] Olmec giant stone head. San Lorenzo Tenochtitlán, Veracruz, Mexico.

.2] Jade figurine. Cortés, Honduras.

.4] Jade head. Mexico.

[2.3] Olmec jade figurine. Mexico.

[2.5] Olmec pottery head. Tlatilco, Mexico.

[2.6] *Hacha.* Acrobat. Papantla, Mexico.

[2.7] Huastec(?) *hacha.* Old Man. Mexico.

[2.8] Totonac *palma*. Mexico.

[2.9] Totonac yoke. Mexico.

[2.10] Relief from a yoke. Mexico.

[2.11] Olmec jade plaque. Mexico.

[2.12] Aztec warrior. Mexico.

[2.13] Stone head. Tabasco, Mexico.

[2.14] Maya jade pendant. Nebaj, Guatemala.

[2.15] Jade celt. Nicoya, Costa Rica.

[2.17] Small jade pendant. Oaxaca(?), Mexico.

[2.16] Aztec(?) serpent. Mexico.

[2.18] Small Maya jade pendant. Zacualpa, Guatemala.

[2.19] Maya stone relief. Palenque, Mexico.

20] Maya stucco head. Palenque, Mexico.

[2.22] Maya ball-court marker. Copán, Honduras.

[2.23] Detail of stone baptismal font. Aztec work. Zinacantepec, Mexico.

2.21] Maya stela. Ixkun, Guatemala.

[2.24] Maya maize-god. Copán, Honduras.

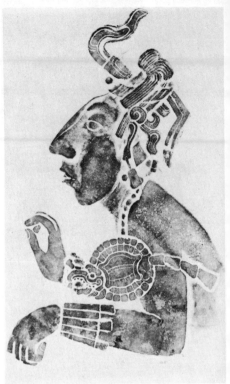

[2.25] Figure from Maya sarcophagus (rubbing) Palenque, Mexico.

.26] Seated Maya figure in wood.

[2.27] Maya warrior. Jaguar bone. Yucatán, Mexico.

[2.28] Stone jaguar. El Baúl, Guatemala.

[2.29] Puma in clay. Pungurí, near Chimbote, Peru.

[2.30] Stucco head. Chiapas, Mexico.

[2.31] Maya ceremonial *hacha*.

[2.33] Maya stone parrot head. La Jula, Honduras.

[2.35] Stela. Moscopán, Colombia.

[2.32] Maya turkey in stone. Copán, Honduras.

[2.34] Stela. Zapatera Island, Nicaragua.

3/Pottery

The people of ancient America never knew the use of the potter's wheel. Their rich and varied production must be judged with this in mind. The objects were built up from coils or strips of clay, smoothed with the hand or with some small implement like a bit of wood or broken pot; they were sometimes formed by pressing into molds or by the paddle and anvil method, that is, by supporting the inner surface of the clay with a stone or some other hard material.

Pottery has been found at one site in Colombia that dates back to about 3000 B.C., and it can be expected that similar early dates will be established elsewhere, also. All five of the areas discussed offer distinctive examples of this art in an amazing variety, from basket-weave imitations to the inimitable fresco vases. Bowls, jars, pitchers, and platters have been found, and there are countless variations in handles, rims, necks, and legs. The pots may be painted, carved, or stamped by a mold, or molded into human, animal, or plant shape—sometimes life size—or into fantastic mythical creatures. Glazing is rare. In some places, a durable polish was produced by burnishing or by applying a wax preparation. The choice in pre-Columbian ceramics would be even larger had it not been for the common practice of "killing" a piece to release its spirit before it was placed in a burial or, among the Mexicans, destroyed at the end of the fifty-two-year cycle. It is interesting to note the share that women had in this craft.

SOUTHWEST UNITED STATES

In the Southwest, and in some other regions, the early utensils were baskets, which were sometimes daubed with clay to make them watertight. Basket-weave patterns persisted even after pottery became an independent art.

The pitcher from Anasazi, New Mexico [3.1], has a counterpart in the European beer mug. In contrast to its unpretentious form, the decoration painted on the surface reveals skill and considerable imagination. Note the handle. (Handles came late to Europe by way of the people of the Migration Period, who were riding nomads and had to fix their small utensils to their belts and saddles. Though the Chinese potter had produced the most elegant shapes and sophisticated decorations for millennia, he added the handle to his cup only for export ware, as requested by European traders of the eighteenth century.)

An ancient Pueblo people flourished in the Mimbres River Valley in southern New Mexico, isolated from east and west by two mountain ranges. Their architecture differed little from that of their neighbors, but in their pottery, they display a talent for observation and a delightful imagination. Turkeys, quail, parrots, cranes, deer, antelope, rabbits, even bear and various kinds of fish, appear in silhouette on the mat surface of Mimbres food bowls. Some of them are drawn realistically; some are highly conventionalized, but they are always recognizable. A swarm of mosquitoes that fairly seem to buzz offers eloquent testimony that the Mimbres people, also, knew what it was to endure such a plague. Human beings are depicted only occasionally, often in connection with mythical monsters, suggesting some ceremony or a scene from a legend.

On a Mimbres bowl [3.2], the somewhat rare motif of a bat is reproduced. The pattern is negative, making use of the buff color of the base for the main design. The two hooks at the shoulders represent claws. An obliquely placed rectangle on the body and asymmetrical frets and angles on the wings give the feeling of the animal's erratic flight.

Distinctive pottery styles were developed in many Pueblo villages. The ingenuity with which the people of the Southwest adapted highly complex geometric patterns to the rounded surfaces of their bowls and jars has seldom been surpassed.

MEXICAN AREA

A tripod jar of polished blackware [3.3], with a lid and deftly turned knob on top, shows the mature proportions, the dignity characteristic of Teotihuacán ceramics. Like the murals from that site, the decoration is usually hieratic and stylized. It is sometimes incised, and in the so-called fresco vases, it was often applied in bands and broad sections of color, giving the effect of enamel. Modeled figures are rare.

Continuing the discussion of rounded shapes, a small Mixtec pitcher, illustrated on the opposite page [3.8], comes from near Puebla, which in both pre- and post-Columbian times was renowned for the variety of its ceramicware. Its charm lies in the contrast of the colorful butterfly frieze with the chocolate brown of the body.

In another piece from Cholula, about eight inches high [3.9], a free approach to pottery can be seen, different from that of the Old World. The body of a coiled serpent is indicated largely by paint, and the head, accentuated by its coloring, protrudes like a tenoned stone from a temple base, forming a sort of lug or handle for the jar. A spiraling lighter line makes the reptile seem undulant and alive. The colors—clear red and orange yellow—and the repeated small diamond motif are characteristically Mixtec. Though the glyphs are in the style of Mixtec manuscripts, they are purely decorative.

The painted tripod was a favorite form of the Mixtec potter, whose mastery of his craft is evident in the complex representation of a human figure [3.10]. A dignitary wearing a bird mask is depicted sitting on a serpent throne; with extended arm, he displays a trophy head. The decoration on the rim of this piece, also, calls to mind Mixtec codices. A number of excellent Mixtec pottery pieces have been found at Teotihuacán; and the recent discovery of a Zapotec urn there offers tangible proof that there was an exchange of wares among the higher artistic cultures.

Turning to modeled figures, succinct and diverse pottery figurines were picked up from pits of clay by workmen at a brick kiln at Tlatilco, a suburb of Mexico City, who offered to sell these delightful finds to anyone who came by for less than a penny. The fame of this informal "dig" spread fast, and some twenty years ago the Mexican government closed the area for archaeological excavation. More than two hundred graves were opened, and the place was recognized as the key site of a very early culture, extending well into the centuries before Christ. Literally thousands of figurines were collected, many of them representing women—some busy with household tasks, some with children, some painted and bejeweled like small fetishes.

These little Tlatilco figures, usually not more than four or five inches in height, are modeled with great skill in an established aesthetic canon. The mother with her child shown here [3.6] displays the characteristic emphasis on the head and the arrangement of the hair, with two plaits hanging down in front. There seems to have been no intention of more than suggesting the rest of the body; the legs are mere round stumps. The piece, nevertheless, has balance and piquant charm.

In a stirrup vessel from the Huastec region on the Gulf Coast of Mexico [3.7], a certain air of bonhomie has been achieved not only through the modeling—from headdress to squat legs—but also in the fluency of the large painted design. The rather unusual depiction of the eyes adds to the doll-like friendliness of the piece.

Very different in both approach and technique is a slender figure of a warrior priest from the island of Jaina [3.4]. Only eleven and a half inches tall, he has a majestic stance. Both of his hands hold weapons, clearly symbols of rank. Jade is probably represented in the small mask on his breast and in the feathers on the upper part of the casquelike headdress. Many fine coils of clay were used to fashion the details of this piece, and the result is light and lively. Similar figures, though seldom so perfectly preserved, were unearthed, one by one, many years ago at Palenque and more recently from Tabasco and other inner regions of the Maya area.

The island of Jaina lies offshore from Campeche, Yucatán, looking from the air like the leaf of a tropical flower. The place seems to have been a large burial site with a concomitant ceremonial center. A recent expedition has identified tombs from two separate periods at Jaina: the earlier lying nearly ten feet deep; the later, about three. All are stocked with the well-known Jaina figurines. Some of those from the later period, taken from the ground under scientific conditions and, thus, known to be authentic, are especially animated; they represent ball players, people gesturing as if declaiming, chieftains seated on circular "thrones," women weaving, and other genre compositions. Jaina pottery ware includes dishes and vases—some in black plumbate ware, some polychromed—and large mortuary jars. There were, also, some personal ornaments of jade. To the connoisseur and collector of ancient American art, the names Tlatilco and Jaina are well known, and objects ostensibly from these sites are much sought after —though in some cases their authenticity may be open to doubt.

Differing in size, in subject, and in the manner of execution, the pottery of western Mexico tells as lively and convincing a story as any discussed previously. A musician from the Colima culture, around seventeen inches in height, waves a rattle in one hand and plays on a drum with the other [3.5]. The drum is realistically depicted, with an opening on the side to strengthen the reverberation, like those pictured in codices. Traces of paint can be seen on the man's body, and there are holes pierced for earrings. Innumerable pottery figures come from this region, depicting various aspects of tribal life, often full of action—dancers, acrobats, ball players. Pottery toys, also, have been found, vegetables and fruits of all sorts, naturalistic in approach and well worked out in detail. Favorite among collectors are the fat Colima dogs, often modeled life-size, curled up asleep, or playing together, or gazing expectantly at the onlooker. Two dogs dancing together [3.12] present a less realistic aspect. One seems to be alive, in contrast to the other which, gaunt and skeletal, apparently symbolizes death. All the Colima figurines are burnished to a pleasant sheen. Gestures and expressions have been caught with admirable economy yet convey a sense of vibrant life.

Nayarit pottery, also from western Mexico, portrays a number of incidents from ancient life in a very different style. Judging from its elaborate paint, a tripod figurine [3.11], almost two feet in height, represents a warrior or chieftain. Here naturalism gives way to a strong conventionalization that will appeal to the modern eye. What immediately strikes the attention, however, is the contrast in the painted pattern. The bowed legs are striped like the body. Disks appear on the shoulders. The painting of the face and the helmetlike headgear places emphasis on the head. The hands are merely suggested, holding a ceremonial staff across the chest.

Another Nayarit piece, about fifteen inches in length, shows a funerary procession [3.13], with some twenty-eight figures in all. In the front row, five persons carry the funeral meats in round containers on their heads. Rows of similarly dressed mourners follow, surrounding the flat bier which has three bearers on each side. All wear striped cloaks and turbanlike headdresses. The dead dignitary is somewhat related to the figurine of the warrior just presented. He is larger than the others and differently clothed, apparently to bring out his importance. Though no particular attention has been paid to realism or to differentiation among the large group, the piece has the slow forward movement of a procession and the attraction of a quaint story-telling scene.

Pottery whistles in human and animal shape are numerous, but the one in the form of two girls on a swing is remarkable in more ways than one [3.14]. The black patches on the lower half of the faces identify the piece as coming from the neighborhood of Veracruz. Each of the youthful figures, about six inches high, has individuality. Their hairdresses are well differentiated and so is the decoration on their bodies and the pattern of their wraparound skirts. The ears are pierced with large holes for heavy earplugs. The short legs, fitted separately, move as the figures swing. The picture of these two so evidently having fun gives a rare glimpse into the pleasures of a long sunken, ancient world.

Discovered three decades ago in a shed behind the Oaxaca Regional Museum and first photographed by this writer and his wife, the seated pottery figure, nearly three feet in height, is now one of the treasures in the new Anthropological Museum in Mexico City [3.15]. Probably, it represents a dancer or the celebrant in some religious ceremony. The body is mature and powerful, the pose elastic. The proud carriage of the head bears out the haughty expression on the mask he wears. A necklace of large beads, wristlets and anklets are done in detail, and masks in beaded frames cover the upper arms. The style is somewhat puzzling. The fact that it has few characteristics of the region where it was found leads to speculation about what will come to light in the highland section between Oaxaca and the Gulf Coast, a region that is only now becoming accessible.

That there is a relationship between this figure and a clay mask [3.16] of uncertain provenience may be accepted. The mask has the same exaggerated upturned nose, the same hooded eyes, with a somewhat more open mouth. Striking is the painted decoration, with lines that arch across the forehead and stripe the cheeks, while the lower third of the face is empty except for a scroll on the jaw and curves around the mouth. This writer has photographed two small jades with such "harlequin" noses, one from El Salvador and the other from the Guatemala highland. Large pottery figures are rare, especially those in good condition. Similarly nearly life-size ball players of pottery have recently come to light, showing the paraphernalia in detail. They are said to have come from the Totonac region.

Pottery from the first periods of Monte Albán, dating from the seventh century B.C., is already varied and assured. At the time of its greatest flower-ing, which covers roughly the first millennium of the Christian era, Monte Albán pottery shows stimulus from adjacent cultures without any loss in individuality. Most Oaxaca pottery comes from the innumerable tombs that from earliest time were furnished with incense burners, the figures of gods and demigods, and elaborate receptacles for the remains in a secondary burial. There are even groups arranged as if attending a funerary ceremony. Many of the figures are seated in a conventionalized pose, cross-legged with the hands resting on the knees. Emphasis is placed on the head, the head-dress, and ornaments, which sometimes can be used to identify the repre-sentation; the more important the person, the more elaborate the depiction. The common man appears—when he is shown at all—as a small undistin-guished creature, rather reminiscent of those in the Nayarit funerary pro-cession [see 3.13]. The three-dimensional is remarkably well brought out. Presented here are four rather unusual subjects, recently discovered, which are somewhat different from the widely-known types.

The Zapotec jaguar-god has his front feet with their powerful paws spread as if to spring [3.17]. In the oversized head, the glaring eyes and snarling fanged jaws add ferocity. As a god, the figure wears a flamboyant headdress, with what seems to be a monster's mask, and a heavy necklace ending in two curved plaques suggesting bells. The piece is an urn, sixteen inches high, and held a secondary burial, apparently of some personage associated with the god.

The "idol of Yogana," which probably dates from the early centuries of our era, is fifteen inches tall [3.18]. His nude body is undecorated except for a glyph on the loincloth which trails behind, making the figure into a tripod. His beaklike headdress, also, is plain. He wears, however, large earplugs and a necklace of beads. The unusual pose of the hands is said to identify him as a runner—a messenger. He carries an open baglike con-tainer on his back, and, like much of the ware from this region, actually is an urn.

Illustrated directly below [3.20], we see the statue of an old man, identified as the fire-god, from the best period of Monte Albán. Though he is seated cross-legged with hands on knees, like the usual Zapotec funerary figure, he is distinguished by the absence of flamboyant headdress, by the fringe of beard, and by his heavy jewelry. The exaggerated wrinkles, the eager expression of eyes and mouth, give an impression of personality unusual in Oaxaca statuary.

In the great span of this culture, many leaders, priests, and chieftains were honored with burial under and around the ever-multiplying temple bases, and in time they became legendary figures, semideified. In the final centuries, pottery urns were turned out by the hundreds. Craftsmanship declined; conventionalized formulae came into use; and sometimes molds were used to shape the pieces. The work of even the late period, however, has sufficient character to be identifiable as to provenience.

Excavation is just now in progress in the Mixteca Alta in the northern part of the state of Oaxaca, where Mixtec clans still survive. A Mixtec burial urn [3.19] came to light recently in a tomb at Huajuapan. Although it has certain standard features, showing a human figure with complex head-dress and elaborate jewelry, it is very different in concept and execution; it has considerably more vitality than much of the better-known Zapotec work. A jaguar pelt makes up part of the headdress, the paws flanking the face. The personage holds a glyph with an animal head and numerals— doubtless, his identification.

MAYA AREA

A lidded jar from the southern Maya area [3.21] shows a ball player, sculptured in deeply incised relief. He wears a heavy padded belt, ending in a parrot head. He is turning toward an altar, partly visible, and a speech scroll emanates from his mouth. The headdress extends into the upper rim; in the lower, space was opened for the outward-thrust foot in its heavily decorated sandal. Other figures can be seen on the ornate surface, engaged in some ceremony. The work is free and assured.

The sturdy little hunchback [3.22], eight inches high, comes from Uaxactún, and can be dated between A.D. 500 and 600. The piece is actually an urn, the upper body above the waist forming the lid. Ingenious slits in the back of the head allow light to shine through the hollow eye sockets, giving the face a mischievous boyish expression, slightly cross-eyed. White has been rubbed into the incised decorations on the polished black surface, and there are holes for nose- and ear-rings. The figure may have held some object in the circle of his hands. Hunchbacks were held in reverence by a number of pre-Columbian peoples, and many representations of them have been found, especially in pottery and jade.

A unique piece, cylindrical in shape and nearly twelve inches high, is said to come from Ataco, El Salvador, the southern limits of Maya culture [3.23]. The little figures relate somewhat to the carved vase just described [3.21]. Their arrangement in two double rows of separate miniature niches makes one think of the temple of Tajín [see 1.11]. The various glyphs are not Maya. All the decoration is blended into a flowing pattern by interlacing bands that add to the inherent grace of the piece.

In ancient American pottery, the shape itself may be simple, but what covers the surface is all the more remarkable. Four seated persons are incised on a vase from Copán [3.24]. All are in ceremonial dress; all wear elaborate nose plugs; two have jade masks on their breasts. On the side illustrated, a man works on a mask—jade or clay?—held in his left hand. His bowed head and pursed lips express his concentration. The working hand, with its tool and beaded wristlet, is a masterpiece of concise drawing. Surrounding details of ceremonial and symbolic content are incised with the same flair. Through paint, which has partly disappeared, a full effect was achieved.

For one type of pottery, the craftsman had only to fashion an evenly rounded cylindrical shape, which was covered with a slip of fine stucco and then turned over to the painter. As has already been mentioned, such "fresco" vases of very high quality exist from the Teotihuacán culture. The Maya developed them, however, to a still higher expression. There are six human figures and forty-four glyphs on a vessel about ten inches high from Altar de los Sacrificios, Guatemala [3.25]. The colors used are brown, red, black, and orange on a cream ground. All six figures seem to be involved in a ceremony, which the glyphs illuminate. One panel shows a heavy-set elderly man, bald, and naked to the waist, wearing snakeskin tights with a bushy tail attached. His head is thrown back; his mouth is open, possibly chanting; his eyes are closed as if in ecstasy. A huge snake arches above his head, and his hand holding an inscribed pot thrusts into the upper band of glyphs.

The youthful figure in another panel [3.25] wears fringed trousers of jaguar skin, the head of a jaguar as a headdress, and jaguar paws as mittens. His graceful dancing step is unique in Maya painted pottery. The ease with which the right foot is lifted and counterbalanced by the raised arms is in itself a masterly solution of how to fill space and at the same time communicate swift movement. The placement of the figure in relation to the glyphs is a fine example of the Maya artist's freedom in design. This piece is both decorative and symbolic. Luckily, it was found recently during a scientifically conducted excavation and can be accurately dated as belonging to the mid-eighth century. The analysis of its elements has thrown new light on vessels of this type—indeed, on much of the funerary offerings found in abundance in Maya and Zapotec-Mixtec burial sites. In this case, the grave was that of a young woman, apparently of the highest caste, within a tomb that contained pottery from several different parts of the Maya area. All the figures on the painted vase have to do with deities and symbols of the earth and of death. The jaguar-dancer might even represent an actual personage, dressed as the jaguar lord of the night and the underworld, in some funerary rite. It has been pointed out that one "Bird Jaguar," lord of nearby Yaxchilán, came to power in 752, two years before the date inscribed on the rim of this vessel.*

A shallow bowl from Yucatán, a little over thirteen inches in diameter, presents a single subject, a flamingo in tones of reddish brown and grayish brown on a center field of orange [3.26]. Groups of bars crossing the simple frame at the edge lead the eye to the center. Keen observation is evident in the delineation of the bird within the limitations of a tondo. The webbed feet, the extended neck with its heavy curving bill, the frozen eye, have all been captured. The characteristic double outline of the beak and the tuft on the head are brought out by the use of two colors. A few loose feathers, separated from the massive body, give balance and life to the composition. All this for a piece of pottery that apparently has no special significance. It must have been made in that section of Yucatán where these birds congregate.

A bowl in plant form—perhaps a gourd—also comes from Yucatán [3.27]. The smooth fine-textured surface is realistically shaped; the delicately incised glyphs lend the piece significance.

Still greater skill is displayed in a bowl from Mayapán, Yucatán [3.28]. It is decorated by two lozenge-shaped medallions placed on opposite sides, and in between are panels with glyphs. Both medallions have a human figure in relief as their central subject enclosed in a well-defined double frame. On the side illustrated, a priest or dignitary, resting on a cushioned seat, points significantly to the vessel or brazier placed beneath a column of glyphs. The plant shapes around his figure have been identified as cocoa pods. At first glance one does not realize the technical virtuosity involved: this ingratiatingly curving vessel must have been comparatively soft before firing, and all the plastic decoration had to be applied by a hand swift and sure enough not to distort its shape.

A pizote, modeled in the round, makes up part of a double vessel with handle and spout [3.30]. The pizote is a member of the raccoon family, about twice the size of a squirrel. It lives mainly in Central America, and is not difficult to domesticate. The fact that it walks on the soles of its feet like a bear gives it a comical gait. In this piece, its body is conventionalized. Both front and back legs are only indicated, yet the little animal seems quite naturalistic, holding its snout in its paws. The double vessel, constructed to make a whistling sound when liquid is poured from it, is a form that frequently occurs in the pottery of coastal Peru. This piece, however, was excavated at Kaminaljuyú, Guatemala, and was modeled from local clay.

* Richard E. W. Adams, *The Ceramic Sequence at Altar de los Sacrificios, Guatemala.* Cambridge: Harvard University Press (in press).

A pottery serpent's head [3.29] comes from Conacatepeque, El Salvador, an ancient Indian site, apparently once a center of commerce. Stylized as the piece is, the characteristic features give an amazingly lifelike impression, to which the flash of its obsidian eye adds considerably. Turquoise-blue and brown paint are still visible.

In El Salvador there is interesting evidence of the interplay between artistic influences. The strongest trend is still from the north, from the Maya and their neighbors. A small flask from that country, about three inches high, carries a scene in relief on each of its two flat sides, which may have been made in a mold [3.31]. On both circular panels, two dignitaries dressed in ceremonial garb with sweeping headdress are seated facing each other, divided by a column of glyphs. Traces of cinnabar and of mercury have been found in similar small flasks, materials highly prized in ancient America. Cinnabar was used for red paint; mercury for magic and perhaps in the working of metal. Despite its diminutive size, the piece is carefully modeled; the rim on top is smoothed, so that a stopper of wood or rubber would keep safe the substance inside.

Costa Rica was so called from the gold found there during the Conquest. The pottery vessel illustrated here is an outstanding example of complex iconography [3.33], from the Chorotega tribe, in the northwest part of the country. At first glance, one sees a birdlike figure incised on the surface in outline and enhanced by painted sections. Closer inspection shows that this is actually a masked winged being with arms and legs that end in claws. The head consists of two bird profiles facing in opposite directions; the "headdress" between is made up of double serpents' heads, complete with fangs and hooded eyes. The iconography is similar to that of the sacred quetzal in the Teotihuacán mural, bringing to mind the powerful and widespread influence of that early culture [see 1.7].

Completely different in style is a tripod vessel, also from Costa Rica [3.32]. On each slender leg, a realistic lizard—a chameleon?—crawls upward, its head fully three-dimensional. The piece was once painted, which must have brought out still more clearly the creature's pivoting eyes and scaly body. The Costa Rican potter also applied a batiklike negative painting to pottery. In this process, the pattern is covered with a protective layer and the rest of the surface is painted, so that upon removal of the covering, the design stands out in the natural color of the base.

Archaeological objects usually come to light through either illegal digging or institutional excavation. A shallow tripod dish from Nindiri, Nicaragua [3.34], has a more unusual story. In the 1920's, the Rockefeller Foundation started a pilot project there for better rural sanitation. In digging wells and ditches for drainage and sewage, numerous graves were found and many striking objects were unearthed. The local postmaster, being on the scene, was able to assemble a rare collection.

Though south of what is usually considered the Maya area, the decorative painted design on this piece shows Mixtec as well as Maya echoes. A mythical figure with a bird mask occupies the center. The monster heads forming the legs of the piece are hollow and contain clay balls or pebbles that rattle. Although these two painted pieces were found only a few hundred miles apart, the difference in shape and decorative language is worth attention.

INTERLYING AREA

The tribes of the Isthmian regions of Panama may not have produced monumental architecture, but in their pottery and in their gold work, as will be seen later, they show themselves to be masters of their art. A stingray—they are spotted when young—is realistically represented in a platter on a cylindrical base from Veraguas, a province of Panama [3.35]. The wavy nervous shape of the creature and its leering "face" are clearly recognizable, while other features have been turned into a fluid decorative design.

A bowl from Coclé, Panama, represents an alligator, highly abstracted [3.36]. Its bent legs are indicated in a winglike design; the eyes are placed at the sides of the head; and the huge toothy jaws are shown in profile. The rendition of the body and the strong scaly tail, in brown and black, not only divides and stabilizes the pattern, but gives the impression of a powerful creature in repose. This piece could well be called a forerunner of abstract expressionism had not the term become so misused of late.

ANDEAN AREA

In the same way that the tropical landscape changes in the altitudes of the Cordillera of South America, the pottery, also, takes on other characteristics. One sees many reproductions of the ceramic work of Middle America and Peru, but very little from those other countries that lie between. The Chibcha tribe of Colombia had an individual style in their pottery, as well as in their goldwork. The large urn, nearly three feet high, in the shape of a seated figure is conventionalized as far as the body is concerned [3.40]. Attention focuses on the bandoleerlike decoration crossing the chest, which may represent a necklace of bone or of stylized birds in gold—jewelry of both sorts has been found in the region. The sharply modeled features, also, call metalwork to mind. Contrasting linear designs decorate the flaring headdress and the broad mouth mask, with its bird at opposite corners. Compare the Nayarit figurine [3.11]. Numerous funerary jars for secondary burials have been excavated in Colombia. Their lids have somewhat comparable seated figures.

A double vessel with bridge and spout, about nine inches long, from the Colombia-Ecuador border, is interesting as a regional version of this well-known Peruvian shape [3.37]. The little figure is not dissimilar to the large Colombian urn just discussed.

Usually the Inca are credited with the introduction of the dignified form somewhat akin to the Greek wine jar known as aryballos. Two pottery containers from Colombia and Ecuador show that it was widely distributed through South America, though up to the present it has not been found north of the Panamanian Isthmus. A Colombian piece [3.38] comes from the Quimbaya region and is somewhat over two feet in height. Broad stripes tapering with the curve of the vessel bring out its sophisticated form. Each panel is decorated in a different way. A snake entwines the rim, curved into a fret design. Archaeological investigation in Ecuador was rare and far from coordinated, and the "grave diggers" and other plunderers in their search for gold alone were prone to cast aside, even destroy all other finds. A pottery aryballos, about twenty-eight inches in height, from Conchi Province is admirable for its grace and balance [3.39]. The negative painted pattern here is modest, but a change of motif on the neck lends a certain life to the piece.

The figure seated at the foot of a tall vase from Ecuador is quite different in type [3.41]. There are less than five digits on each hand and foot. This seems to have been deliberate—probably, it is symbolic—and in no way the result of lack of skill or carelessness, especially when the expertly turned shape of the vase itself and the incised pattern above the head are taken into account. The glyphlike design is not dissimilar to the Chavín-style gold ornament from the province of Lambayeque [see 5.1].

The province of Esmeraldas on the Pacific coast of Ecuador is noted for its pottery and goldwork, powerful in concept and execution. A pottery head [3.42] displays the local mode of headdress, a nose ornament that masks the mouth, and huge earrings of which there are numerous similar gold specimens still extant. The monster [3.43], with its open mouth and finlike extremities, suggests the sea. It forms the head of a clay trumpet, and its tone must sound something like the roar of a conch shell. Note the difference in the modeling of the eyes.

On another jar from Ecuador, the twin animals [3.44] seem to be either jaguar or puma cubs. Their strongly marked whiskers and prominent nostrils are definitely catlike. In this small piece, where the sculptural details have been worked out only as far as convention required, the general effect is playful.

The arid climate and the elaborate burial customs of coastal Peru have had a part in conserving hundreds of thousands of ceramic pieces that show changes in taste and development of style in many separate regions. There were exchanges of form and pattern, yet there are enough differences to distinguish the products of one culture from those of another, though the settlements may have lain less than a hundred miles apart, isolated by the desert.

Although in the pottery of Middle America considerable variety can be observed, its subject matter is mainly hieratic. In Peru, numberless scenes from daily life have been immortalized. As many books have been written on each separate region, here the attempt will be made to show, instead, the unusual and striking within the many styles.

Even early Chavín pottery has naturalistic representations of plants and animals. Revealing, often entertaining, are figural pieces from the Mochica and Chimú. The so-called portrait vases introduce a new element into the repertory of ancient pottery [3.45]. Although in other cultures one occasionally encounters representations that suggest portraiture, in many Peruvian pottery heads there is a sense of personality.

Small narrative scenes abound on Mochica ware. Events from daily life, at the seashore, on the water, on the hunt, in war, are portrayed, some in plastic representation, some silhouetted or drawn in outline on the rounded surface. Legends and ceremonies unfold. A dramatic scene outlined in brownish red on a Mochica stirrup jar [3.46] presents a seated hero throttling a sea monster that has a human head and arms and a scaly body. The vessel is as simple as possible in shape, but it strikes the attention because of the tenseness of the scene depicted on it. The hero wears long ear ornaments, a snake as a girdle, a jaguar-skin headdress with a feather bush, a poncho shirt with stepped yoke [see 4.18], and he holds a bladed weapon with a thong attached. Numerous other pieces from the same region show the same figure, indicating that it belongs to some fixed iconography.

The stirrup jar is characterized by two arching tubes that meet in a single spout, resembling a stirrup in outline. Death with his drum [3.48] offers another example of this form. Part of the body has been left more or less in the clay. The head is not fully skeletal; the eyes are open. This Death is alive and active, part of the Mochica pantheon, holding in wasted arms his fateful instrument.

Two young birds at the edge of a nest [3.47] come from a later period, from the Chimú culture when blackware, polished to a high gloss, was popular. Here true naturalism can be observed. The hungry beaks point straight up; the bowl of the jar forms the nest, while the spout indicates the branch on which it hangs.

Central and south coastal styles, also, show an amazing variety. The Recuay culture, which lies south of the Mochica-Chimú region, dates from around 500 B.C. It is characterized by three-color negative painting. The work ranges from smoothly turned jars with single bands of well-organized negative design to complex figural representations with elaborate surface patterns, rather restless in effect. Ancón, near Lima, a site that was among the earliest to be excavated, is early in date, also, being roughly parallel with that of Chavín. Tiahuanaco influences occur frequently in its ceramics, blended with local forms and motifs. Pottery from the Paracas Peninsula can be put in sequence by relating it to the textiles found in the same grave. It shows several periods of distinctive character, ranging from Chavín-influenced work to early Nazca ware made at the beginning of the Christian era.

One reason for the seeming abundance of Nazca pottery may be that in pre-Columbian times the style was adopted by neighbors as far north as Paracas. The early form is simple, painted in buff, cream, orange, and red brown. Fertility deities are shown with human, animal, and bird attributes, so that while one detail seems naturalistic, another is baffling to our modern eyes. In a round vessel with double spout and bridge, both plastic and painted means are utilized to represent a puma or jaguar [3.49]. The widely spaced spouts suggest ears. Modeling emphasizes the features, while paint defines whiskers, teeth, and spots. In contrast, all the decoration on an early Nazca globular jar of the same type is painted [3.50]. This is a shape that occurs also in silver. Here it is adorned by a demon with catlike whiskers. The outstretched tongue touches a trophy head, dangling upside down, as if drawing the life-force from it—a motif often repeated in Nazca pottery and weaving. The piece shows the high craftsmanship of these people in both design and coloring. It is, also, especially interesting because its original string and cotton stopper have been preserved intact.

Another Nazca pot represents a fisherman [3.51]. The head is three-dimensional. The body, draped with a net, and various marine motifs cover the rounded sides in fluent painting.

Elements of Coast Tiahuanaco appear in a juglike vessel [3.52]. The shapeless body and the spread hands (or gloves) attached to the sides without any arms suggest a mummy bundle. This is borne out in the face, bound round with a cloth, and its staring masklike eyes. A step design painted in a number of colors at the top of the headdress brings in favorite elements of the highland style. The markings under the eyes, interpreted as representing the tears of the rain-god, are also a typical Tiahuanaco feature. A bronze mummy mask with woven head band and a tapestry glove, both from Peruvian coastal graves, are illustrated in the respective chapters on textiles and metalwork [see 4.17 and 5.6].

The head of a toylike animal, said to come from Chancay on the central coast, is something like a llama's [3.53]. Otherwise, the thick neck, the short legs, and chunky body suggest the Peruvian tapir. This creature lives in high altitudes near streams, ponds, and lakes. It can be domesticated, and while young, it sometimes serves as a pet. If alive, its stripes would run horizontally, but here the painter may have improved on nature, thus emphasizing the animal's compact rotundity. The spots, on the other hand, belong to its appearance when young.

A large jar standing nearly four feet high presents a llama, strongly naturalistic in appearance [3.54]. Noteworthy is the color demarcation of its woolly coat. Its big dark eyes are glossy, as in life. On its back, where a pack would be laid, a spout rises, decorated with a Tiahuanaco fret design which recalls textiles of that culture. Again, stress must be placed on the technical mastery required to shape freehand, to color, and to fire such a large and complex ceramic piece.

The llama does not thrive at an altitude below five thousand feet. Likewise, the Quechua and Aymara Indians, natives of the Andean highlands, lost their energy and perished when forced by the Spaniards to hard labor in the lowlands. It is interesting to note that ceremonial burials of llamas have been found on the coast.

Inca pottery has a smoothness, a mellowness both in form and decoration with diminishing presence of the plastic figural. The performance might be compared to that of a conductor, who after years spent leading his orchestra, uses only gestures that are controlled and scarce. The period of complexity and exuberance has ended. Some of this may be due to the fact that many examples now classified as Inca pottery were tribute pieces—fashioned after a prescribed plan.

An aryballos with a rare decorative scheme [3.55] was found near Puno on Lake Titicaca. Characteristic of the type in this region are the low-placed handles and small plastic knob in the shape of an animal head at the top, which may have served to aid in tipping it. Rare is the double row of stag heads with their antlers strongly emphasized. This realistic representation of deer heads, together with the familiar geometric patterns, would suggest a date in the late Inca period.

The puma jar, fourteen inches high, from Tiahuanaco, Bolivia, was probably used as an incense burner [3.56]. The body of the animal is indicated by the broad painted band that curves down from the three-dimensional head and up again to the tail, which forms the spout or handle. In a manner characteristic of the style, the paws have been turned into the wings of not one, but two stylized condors. The rest of the decoration is made up of painted lines, squares, rectangles, with a step design along the base. Here again, one thinks of Tiahuanaco textiles, where motifs crowd one upon the other, in human, animal, or bird shapes, geometrically compressed.

Compared with some of the lively and immediate products of the coast, the designs have a hieratic character, closely related to the carving on the Gateway of the Sun. The repetition of a rather limited repertoire has led to conventionalization and sophisticated abstraction.

The burnished vessel shaped like a human head, five and a half inches high, strikes us first with its fierce masculinity [3.57]. It, also, was excavated near Tiahuanaco, Bolivia. The turbanlike headdress has lost much of its color; the eyes and mouth and the earplugs are emphasized by the twin arrows that descend from the forehead, perhaps representing lightning.

The word "primitive," when applied to art, has been so misused that it has lost its original sense. Here four pieces of pottery are illustrated from different regions of South America (Brazil, Chile, the Argentine, and Venezuela). They were fashioned by peoples on a lower cultural level at about the same time as the pottery we have been discussing, but they seem inferior in quality. If, however, we can disengage ourselves sufficiently from that sophisticated standard, we will find something interesting and praiseworthy in all four.

The simple form of the piece from Brazil is elevated by the exactitude of its painted pattern which gives it primeval power [3.58]. Contrasts of light and dark are used effectively.

The example from Chile has an unusual shape—some call it a bird; others, a shoe [3.59]. It suggests the *aquamaniles* ("water containers") of medieval Europe and probably served the same purpose. With its handle, it has a certain grace, despite the difficult shape, and the variation in the striated pattern lightens the whole effect.

The Argentine jar [3.60] is in shape reminiscent of the Inca aryballos. It is thought that children were buried in such decorated urns. The fanciful design may represent an owl—or, perhaps, a conventionalized human figure. Wings and/or clasped hands are suggested by the painted curves and low-slung handles. The contrast of light and dark in the negative design is used to excellent effect. The flange at the top is neatly turned, showing assured technique.

On the bowl from Venezuela [3.61], the two pairs of heads looking at each other across an open bowl are characteristic of the lowland tropics, as are also the four legs of the piece. The vicinity of Panama with its familiar Coclé motifs can be sensed in the wide painted scrolls. The little creatures are thought to represent squirrels or chipmunks. Their small, alert heads and their legs with rounded haunches have a certain naturalistic touch. Surely, such gaiety could not be unintentional.

[3.1] Anasazi pitcher. New Mexico.

[3.2] Mimbres bowl. Arizona.

[3.3] Teotihuacán vessel. Mexico.

[3.5] Colima drummer. Mexico.

[3.4] Jaina figurine. Mexico.

[3.6] Archaic mother figurin
Tlatilco.

3.7] Huastec figurine. Mexico.

[3.8] Pitcher. Cholula.

3.9] Mixtec jar. Mexico.

[3.10] Mixtec tripod bowl. Mexico.

[3.12] Colima dogs. Mexico.

[3.11] Nayarit painted figurine. Tepic, Mexico.

[3.13] Nayarit funeral procession. Mexico.

[3.16] Pottery mask. Mexico.

[3.15] Large pottery figure. Near Oaxaca.

[3.17] Zapotec jaguar-god. Mexico.

[3.18] Zapotec figurine. Mexico.

[3.19] Mixtec urn. Huajuapan.

[3.20] Zapotec fire-god. Mexico.

[3.21] Maya sculptured jar. Guatemala.

[3.22] Incense burner. Uaxactún.

[3.23] Sculptured vase. Ataco, El Salvador.

[3-24] Maya painted and incised jar. Copán, Honduras.

[3.27] Maya pottery calabash. Mayapán.

[3.28] Maya sculptured bowl. Yucatán.

[3.29] Pottery serpent head. Conacatepeque, El Salvador.

[3.30] Double vessel. Kaminaljuyú, Guatemala.

[3.31] Molded bottle. El Salvador.

[3.32] Tripod vessel. Costa Rica.

3.33] Painted bowl. Costa Rica.

3.34] Painted tripod dish. Nindiri, Nicaragua.

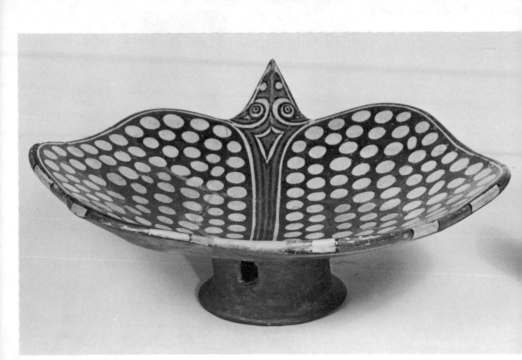

[3.35] Coclé platter. Panama.

[3.36] Veraguas dish. Panama.

[3.38] Quimbaya aryballos. Colombia.

[3.40] Chibcha figurine. Colombia.

.37] Double vessel. Colombia.

[3.39] Aryballos. Conchi Province, Ecuador.

[3.42] Pottery head. Esmeraldas, Ecuado

[3.41] Vase with human figure. Ecuador.

[3.44] Twin-animal jar. Ecuado

[3.43] Clay trumpet. Esmeraldas.

45] Mochica portrait vessel. Peru.

[3.46] Mochica painted stirrup jar. Peru.

[3.48] Mochica stirrup jar. Peru.

47] Chimú spouted vessel. Peru.

[3.49] Double-spout vessel. Nieveria, Peru

[3.50] Nazca double-spout vessel. Peru.

[3.52] Coast Tiahuanaco figure jar. Peru.

[3.51] Nazca jug. Peru.

[3.53] Chancay animal vessel. Peru.

[3.54] Pottery llama. Peru.

[3.55] Inca aryballos. Near Puno, Peru.

[3.56] Tiahuanaco animal vessel. Bolivia.

[3.57] Tiahuanaco portrait jar. Boliv

.58] Negative painted jar.
arajo District, Brazil.

[3.59] Diaguita pot with handle. Chile.

[3.61] Tetrapod bowl. Trujillo, Venezuela.

60] Painted jar. Tucumán,
gentina.

4/Weaving

One of the most spectacular of the arts of ancient America is weaving, which has still not received the appreciation it deserves. Certainly, more would have been made of this work had it been produced by a civilization in the Old World. Possibly, its tremendous output and manifold technical perfection have been overshadowed by the alien impression these pre-Columbian representations make.

The splendid apparel in which the Indian chieftains met the conquistadores has been described in various contemporary reports from the Mexican, Maya, and Inca areas. From the first two regions, however, there are practically no examples of weaving left, due to unfavorable climatic conditions. The high standard of work there can be only surmised from what remains painted on pottery and in murals, such as those at Bonampak, and is depicted in great variety of detail on stelae and other carvings. Moreover, what was woven by the natives in the colonial period and later indicates a talent that may have rivaled the Peruvian. Nearly forty years ago, on a street curb in Mexico City, this writer bought for one peso a bit of embroidery (now in the Textile Museum in Washington, D.C.) done in a running stitch in imitation of brocade, with bands of birds, flowers, and little human figures placed in telling sequence. In Guatemala, where the ancient girdle-back loom is still widely used, brilliant and characteristic designs are brocaded in with the fingers, at times using motifs and color sequences from pre-Columbian days. Some isolated sections of Mexico kept their folklore long intact; there within the last half century, brides starched and finger-pleated their wedding kerchiefs into intricate forms—symbolic birds, flowers, and figures. Feather-decorated huipils (women's upper garments) survive in Chiapas.

In our Southwest in pre-Columbian times, turkey feathers and strips of rabbit skin were fashioned into blankets. A few beautiful fragments of fine cotton cloth that have come to light bear witness to technical skill. One design in a damasklike technique shows interlocking frets, familiar from the pottery of the region; in another, the fret is used with openwork in a lacy border.

What really stirs the imagination and places reality before our eyes is the pre-Columbian material of Peru. Here the sandy soil, lack of rain, and this region's particular burial customs have resulted in the preservation of an amazing variety of fabrics. Inca graves were plundered for decades, and even by the nineteenth century, museums in the United States and Europe had received examples as gifts. When in 1932 this writer made his first survey in this country, he came upon pre-Columbian textiles in fine-arts museums framed under heavy glass, hung on the walls of dusky corridors and stairways, collecting the dust and humidity of the years. They were, nevertheless, the only pre-Columbian products that art museums then displayed.

Ocoña Valley, which lies at the delta of the Río Ocoña on the southern coast of Peru between Puerto Chala and Mollendo, is typical of the isolated sections where the varied pre-Columbian cultures throve [4.1]. It is very fertile, as is all of this land when water can be brought in, but even now it is sparsely populated because of its inaccessibility. In colonial times, vineyards and fig groves throve there, and "many buildings erected by the ancients" could be seen.* The natives were excellent fishermen, and a great variety of seafood was harvested beyond the pounding surf.

On the north coast of Peru, knowledge of weaving can be traced back to 1500 B.C., even before the development of ceramics there. When it first appears, the weaving is already quite advanced. Frequently new techniques appeared, already developed well beyond the experimental stage and sometimes to the point of complete mastery.

Among the most famous sites of ancient Peru is the vast cemetery on the Paracas Peninsula on the south coast, which was apparently used for centuries for the burial of personages of high rank, judging from the different types of tombs. The dead were usually buried in a seated position, placed in a basket, and surrounded by elaborate folded garments alternating with layers of rough, plain woven cloth and sacking. Pottery and personal possessions were included in the mummy bundle that might have as large a diameter as six feet and was finally enclosed in a protective covering of reed matting. Sometimes, an artificial head was attached, made of cloth and stuffed, and in the north at a later period, a mask of wood or metal might be added or features sewn on, cut from metal. At one counting, more than four hundred mummy bundles were unearthed on a single hill.

Some graves, which even today have been found untouched, lie in only a few feet of sandy soil or in one of the cavelike hollows of the soft coastal

*Antonio Vásquez de Espinosa, *Compendium and Description of the West Indies,* translated by C. U. Clark. Washington: Smithsonian Institution, 1942

rim. Anyone traveling along the Pacific shore in Peru on a road that was cleared of sand in the morning by American-made snowplows can observe that by afternoon it is practically obliterated again by the sand blown across it. It then becomes clear how, during the centuries, new dunes formed that, to our good fortune, hid the tombs.

As for the material in pre-Columbian textiles, cotton, which is native to most areas, was apparently the earliest fiber used. Some cotton cloth was of such fine texture and sheen that the conquistadores thought it silk. Animal and human hair, the fiber of various plants, and bird feathers were also utilized. The ancient Peruvian weaver had, besides, the fine wool of the llama, alpaca, guanaco, and vicuña, members of the camel family. We tend today to think of camels as belonging to Africa. Actually, they originated in North America back in the Eocene epoch and spread from there to other parts of the world. All four species inhabit the Andean region. The llama and alpaca have long been domesticated. The llama averages two hundred pounds in weight and was originally kept as a source of meat and a beast of burden—the only one in the American continent. It is able to carry a maximum load of a hundred pounds and to travel ten to twelve miles a day. The alpaca served as the Andean equivalent of the sheep and was raised for wool and meat. The guanaco and vicuña are still in their wild state [see 1.45]. The latter thrives at very high altitudes, above twelve thousand feet. Even in ancient times, it was protected, and its fleece, which has the sheen and suppleness of silk, is said to have been reserved for the use of the ruling class.

The numerous spindle whorls of pottery and stone found in all of these areas indicate that thread was spun by the same general methods everywhere, the strands twisted by hand and kept even by a revolving weight at the end of the thread.

Blue, derived from indigo, may have been the first color, dyed in the raw stock even before seeding. Mineral, vegetable, and animal dyes then came into use. A rich carmine was obtained from cochineal, a tiny insect that feeds on the prickly pear cactus. The dried and pulverized bodies were highly valued as trade goods throughout Middle America. Shellfish provided a number of other hues. Cotton grows in several natural tones, and even today eleven different shades of alpaca wool are available commercially.

In color, the tendency in pre-Columbian textiles is toward strong contrast, rather than delicate harmonies. A single piece can show as many as fifteen different hues. Red, yellow, and brown predominate, but every imaginable shade and combination can be found. Monotony in the pattern was subtly avoided by variation in sequences of color, often making the repeat difficult to trace.

Much of this highly sophisticated weaving was produced on the back-strap, or girdle-back, loom. This consisted of a loom bar, a stick holding the warp, that was hooked to a tree or a house wall or suspended between two posts. A belt encircled the waist of the weaver, so that the warp could be slackened or tightened with a movement of the body. The width of the material could not be much greater than the weaver's convenient reach, that is, about thirty inches. Similar hand looms are still used today, especially in the more remote parts of Middle and South America.

As certain Peruvian cultures produced cloth well over five feet in width, it must be presumed that this was set up on a larger frame or that backstrap looms were so arranged as to allow several persons to work together. The Peruvians used—and still use today—a horizontal loom that has the warp pegged out close to the ground [4.4]. It is a question whether the large-frame loom used by the Navajos in our Southwest in the weaving of blankets is not a heritage from pre-Columbian times. On it, the warp is set up on a horizontal pole supported by two vertical ones, and it is held taut by another pole at the bottom.

Most of the textiles were probably made for human apparel. Belts, straps, and carrying cloths were needed, and bags of various sizes and strength. Some buildings in the Mexican, Maya, and Andean areas seem to have had awnings and curtains—which may have consisted of straw mats in some cases; in others, of woven material. As has been noted, some textiles seem to have been specifically woven for burials.

Pre-Columbian garb was not tailored; that is, the pieces were not cut out separately and then sewn together. Every piece was woven to the required size and shape. Most Peruvian textiles have four selvages—an achievement almost beyond the conception of most modern weavers, as is the immensely complex technique of warp-interlocking. Costume varied somewhat according to period and area. Generally, the Peruvian woman wore a long belted tunic fashioned of a rectangular piece, a shawl, and a headband. The man's costume consisted of a long strip of plain cloth, which was apparently bound round the body and loins, with decorated fringed ends that draped in front; a tunic (called by the Spaniards a poncho, or shirt) that usually consisted of two strips sewn together, with a slit left open for the head; also, a broad sash, a cape or mantle, a headband or turbanlike headdress, and sandals. A few sets of garments with matching motifs have come to light. Shawls of huge dimensions have been found, hats and knitted caps.

A rare example is shown in the doll-like figure a foot tall from a twelfth-century coastal tomb [4.2]. Limited to whatever raw materials were close at hand, the craftsman fashioned the figure with its child or guardian spirit at its side from everyday materials. The body consists of dried vegetal strips available on the shore or in the dunes. The fingers and toes have been shaped separately to be as "realistic" as possible. The figure wears a fringed loincloth, a simple poncho shirt of rough cotton material, and a matching turban. The mask of wood with inlaid eyes has been perfectly preserved.

Excavations in Peru have revealed practically every conceivable textile technique, including every known form of tapestry, numerous types of brocade and weft-pattern techniques, as well as warp-patterning, and several sorts of gauze. Double cloth and even triple cloth were woven with the use of two and three separate warps of contrasting colors, the sets of wefts alternating so that the design appears as a complete fabric on both faces in reverse coloring. Several techniques were unknown to the rest of the world, notably three-dimensional cross-knitting, by which tiny elaborate figures were fashioned in the round.

Textiles were often embellished with embroidery of many kinds, by resist dyeing ("tie-and-dye"), and by the application of fringes and tassels, shells and spangles, cutout disks and squares of metal. The feathers of rare tropical birds were sometimes used. Frequently a number of these decorative techniques can be seen in a single piece.

The motifs vary from abstract geometric shapes—squares, oblongs, frets—to stylized representations of birds, fish, animals, and human beings. Flower and plant motifs are rare. In durability of material, fastness of color, strength and evenness of thread, modern textiles cannot compete. It is difficult to imagine any of the woven stuffs of today surviving in the earth more than a thousand years.

While all pre-Columbian weavers seem to have been equally expert in their craft, the textiles differ widely from one another in style, despite the short distances that lay between some of the cultural centers. Changes of fashion in technique, motif, and color can be seen. Like pottery, textiles are now classified according to the site where they were found or the cultural group that is indicated by their pattern and color. Indeed, the same motifs used in the textiles are recognizable on the pottery and in the metalwork from the same period and region.

A piece of eccentric tapestry comes from a late period of a coastal site, probably near Nazca [4.3]. Here, the use of nonhorizontal wefts has created in the pattern an unusual waviness and roughness of surface. Two stripes in a dark design alternate with one kept in lighter tones. The feline head at the top of each curve has been turned upside down at the bottom of the next adjacent one. The "claws" suggest the heads of birds. The same figure appears in the lighter strip with a different effect.

Chimú designs in pottery, stucco, and metalwork are echoed in a north coast sash or turban band, fifteen feet long by about six inches wide, a detail of which is illustrated [4.5]. Here slit tapestry and gauze work are enhanced by varicolored disks and tassels, woven separately, that lend three-dimensionality to the resplendent piece. As in much of this work, the warp is cotton; the weft, alpaca wool. As the alpaca does not thrive at sea level, the wool must have been imported regularly from the highlands even before the Incas took possession of this region.

Numerous stamps made of clay, possibly for the printing of textiles, have been found in the Mexican and Maya areas. Plain cotton cloth, however, was sometimes painted freehand. Such is the case in a mask for a mummy bundle, executed in dark tones and framed in red [4.6]. The nose with its suggestion of a skeleton figure serves as the axis of the composition, the upper section broadening to parallel the outline of the upcast eyes. Two stylized felines (jaguars, by their spots), also with upturned gaze, add to the richness of the design yet distract little from the solemn impression. The unfinished length of warp at the top served in the fashioning of a false head. Such painted masks seem to have been limited to the Ocucaje site on the south coast. This piece has been dated at several centuries before Christ.

Embroidered textiles are especially characteristic of the early Nazca and Paracas cultures. A large mantle from Paracas, over seven feet long and nearly four feet wide, has a dark blue ground of plain-weave cloth in alpaca wool with a cotton plain-weave border [4.7]. The embroidery, done in alpaca in rich and brilliant tones, shows a series of winged men holding trophy heads, remarkably diversified through the interchanging of the colors. More than fifteen different hues have been identified in the embroidery alone. The Paracas weaver dotted his textiles with mythical figures—sometimes winged; sometimes half-human, half-animal—motifs also familiar from the pottery. These figures reveal not only a developed imagination but, still more, the ability to express it graphically—all the more remarkable in that this piece, also, dates from before Christ.

On a mantle or shawl from the central coast at a late period, strips of plain weave in cotton alternate with cotton double cloth brocaded in alpaca wool [4.8]. The decorative motif is familiar—stylized little men with haloed headpieces, dressed in elaborate costumes and holding trophy heads. Smaller figures and tiny birds fill the empty spaces, and the curving band that frames each section suggests the serpent inherited from Chavín.

While Gobelin tapestries seldom have more than twenty warps to the inch, in one Peruvian piece some fifty-two have been counted. Conventionalized or even abstract designs are characteristic of Tiahuanaco work. In the poncho shirt of interlocking tapestry, a detail of which is illustrated [4.9], striped squares alternate with brightly colored, highly decorative stylizations in a rare checkerboard arrangement. A rampant jaguar can be identified, condors and other birds, an arm grasping a spear. Various winged men appear, familiar from the Gateway of the Sun at Tiahuanaco [see 1.46]. Incidentally, these figures, also, wear shirts in stylized patterns. Groups of step-frets, varicolored bands, and lightninglike zigzags bind together the composition.

Influences from the highlands penetrated not only the coast but also the southern slopes of the Andes and moved eastward into the plains. The valley of Belén, Catamarca, in Argentina, is quite far from Tiahuanaco, but the checkerboard pattern on a pottery vessel from that region indisputably draws its inspiration from highland textiles [4.10]. In the pottery, the pattern has a horizontal feeling; in the fabric, horizontal and vertical are subtly balanced.

Unfortunately, comparatively few textiles survive from the Andean highlands. It is increasingly believed, however, that a number of the pieces found on the coast, especially those from the period of Inca domination, came originally from the highland regions. In the fragment of a late south coast shirt, geometric forms including various interlocking designs have been fitted into a series of squares [4.11]. Other details suggest figural motifs, difficult to interpret without a complete iconographical key. This piece contains many Inca elements, in design as well as technique, notably the miniature checkered poncho shirts so exactly portrayed even to the **V**-shaped yoke.

Another shirt fragment from coastal Peru shows the dissolution of the Tiahuanaco style [4.12]. Staff-bearing men can be deciphered, as well as masks, birds, feline figures. Fragmented wings, hands, spears, and the teeth, eyes, spots of the jaguar, can be recognized, but they have become almost purely abstract decorative elements in the weaver's repertoire. The piece in the illustration has been folded to show the slit central square that formed a sort of yoke around the wearer's shoulders.

A bag of dovetailed tapestry, ten inches high, woven—as usual—of alpaca wool with a warp of cotton, belongs to the Nazca-Wari culture, showing early Tiahuanaco influence [4.13]. Five-inch tassels of coral-colored and white feathers are attached by embroidered shanks, adding a certain elegance. This is a fine example of shaped weaving, the fabric needing only to be folded and sewn up the sides.

A large openwork shirt, found in almost perfect condition, displays virtuoso craftsmanship [4.14]. Though said to have been excavated near Ancón, north of Lima, it shows characteristics of the Ica culture to the south. The weave is a rare variant of slit tapestry, with the design painted in dark blue, beige, red, and white. The processions of small animals at the bottom and on the fringed cuffs are tightly woven on the same warp.

A slit-tapestry panel comes from the central coast of Peru [4.15]. The main portion carries a step design as its most outstanding motif, with interlocking frets at the base of each. The border presents a row of figures holding staffs. Animation is produced by variation in the colors. Openwork above the fringe lightens the whole scheme—another instance of the pre-Columbian craftsman's assured taste.

The square cap with its tasseled pompons [4.16] was fashioned in cut alpaca pile on a knotted foundation, to form a silky plush ending in a soft, short fringe. The design of squares with stylized birds in different colors indicates a coastal culture with Tiahuanaco influence. Head coverings were also ornamented with multicolored feathers. This single piece goes far to suggest the picturesque appearance of some native dignitary.

A tapestry glove, from a tomb in the Ica Valley, is Coast Tiahuanaco in style [4.17]. The proliferation of feline animals on the fingers and above the wrist serves as framework for the human figure in the center. Trophy heads that resemble serpents surround him, radiating from his forehead, nose, feet, and from the shield held in his right hand, and suggesting to us great power, even magic, like electric shock lines. Decorated gloves of leather also have come to light. Though the glove is a piece of wearing apparel quite familiar to us, the complex symbolism used on it demonstrates the alien psychology of this civilization, which we shall never be able fully to fathom.

As we have already seen, in the art of the last period of Inca domination, a certain standardization can be observed, as if the various cultures that had been conquered contributed to a blend that was pleasing and quite sophisticated. The tapestry shirt of vicuña wool [4.18] is divided into four main fields and measures about a yard from shoulder to hem. Noteworthy is the **V**-shaped yoke, characteristic of the Inca, which is framed by a subtly designed border of small squares in four colors. It seems that toward the end of Inca rule, stylized plants and flowers—often with a sacred connotation—came into favor. Rows of such flowers decorate the contrasting rectangles that make up the body of this piece. Two bands of geometric design that might be called echoes from Tiahuanaco form a sort of girdle, and on the bottom, there is a border that harks back to late coastal styles. Although allegedly found at Pachacámac, the material and the decoration suggest that it may have been an offering from the highlands to this famous pilgrim shrine.

The pre-Columbian American also used innumerable varieties of nonwoven techniques, such as looping, knotting, braiding. The hammock is an invention of the tropical and subtropical regions, where garments were spare. Even today pride is evinced in the great variety of its execution and coloring.

.1] Water brings life to isolated valleys. . . . Ocoña Valley, Peru.

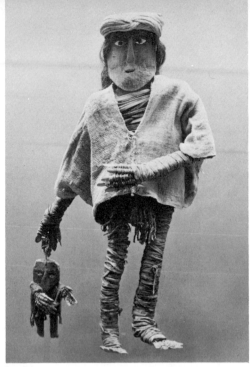

[4.2] Figurine from coastal grave. Peru.

[4.3] Eccentric tapestry. Coastal Peru.

[4.4] Highland woman weaving. Peru.

[4.5] Chimu slit tapestry and gauze. Peru.   [4.6] Painted mummy mask. Ocucaje.

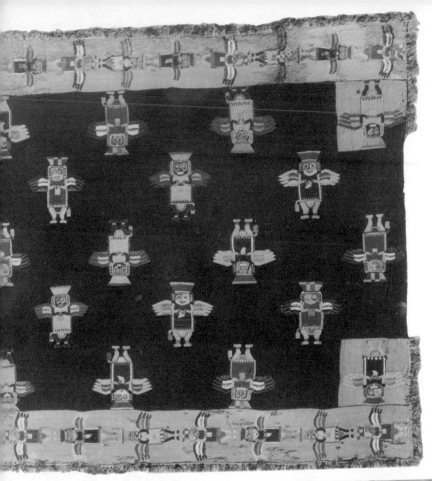

[4.7] Late Paracas embroidered mantle, detail. Peru.

[4.8] Central coast brocaded double cloth, detail. Peru.

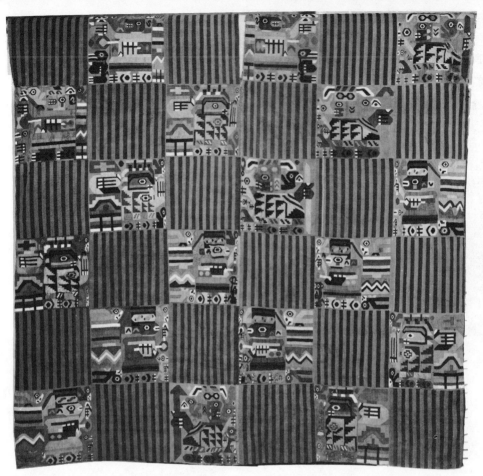

[4.9] Classic Tiahuanaco interlocked tapestry. Peru.

[4.10] Pottery mug. Argentina.

[4.11] Interlocked tapestry. South coast, Peru.

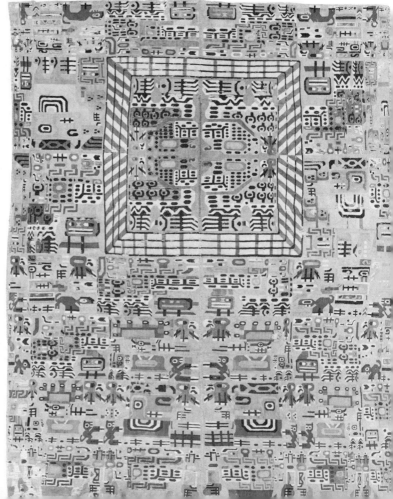

[4.12] Late Coast Tia-
huanaco poncho shirt.
Peru.

.13] Nazca-Wari tapestry bag. Peru.

.14] Coastal painted gauze shirt. Peru.

[4.15] Central Coast slit tapestry panel. Peru.

[4.16] Coast Tiahuanaco plush hat. Peru.

[4.17] Coast Tiahuanaco tapestry glove. Peru.

[4.18] Tapestry shirt. Pachacámac, Peru.

5 / Metalwork

In pre-Columbian America, as in many early cultures, gold was associated with the sun, silver with the moon. With the Maya and other Middle American cultures, jade—or more precisely several varieties of "green stone"—was more highly venerated. Trade was usually carried on by barter. The currencies of different peoples included cocoa beans, woven blankets, and T-shaped copper "axes," too thin for any utilitarian purpose.

The gold of pre-Columbian America was principally alluvial, obtained by panning in the riverbeds. Silver was extracted from surface mines. Copper, tin, platinum, and lead are found in alloy in pre-Columbian objects, and a number of delicate implements of bronze have come to light in Peruvian graves. Mercury appears in the form of cinnabar.

Hammering is perhaps the simplest method of working gold, as it can be done cold. Repoussé work, or die stamping, and incised decoration, or chasing, can also be done without heat. But the more sophisticated processes of casting, plating, gilding, inlaying, sheathing, some alloying and soldering, and incrustation with semiprecious stones were all practiced in ancient America. For these operations pre-Columbian goldsmiths had to be competent in the use of hammers, anvils, furnaces, blowpipes, heat-resistant crucibles, and various open and piece molds.

The lost-wax process, or cire perdue, was expertly employed. By this method, a desired object is first modeled in wax—sometimes over a core of clay—then enveloped with a clay mixture. When this is fired, the melting wax runs out of vents provided for the purpose, leaving a cavity within that exactly corresponds to the shape of the wax original. Molten metal poured into the mold takes on the desired shape. After it has solidified and cooled, the mold is broken away and the piece finished by hand. The nature of the procedure requires considerable plastic sophistication and invites the use of intricate detail.

The metalwork of each particular culture is so characteristic that, in the same way as pottery and textiles, objects can be classified on the basis of their artistic styles. Peruvian grave finds have revealed many sheet-gold objects with repoussé decoration using the same complex designs as the textiles. It is now believed that the first goldwork was produced in the northern regions of Peru. The Chavín-style gold ornament, six inches high [5.1], found on the north coast, shows what unusual decoration could be produced with a relatively simple technique. The main motif, a mask with open mouth and fangs, has remarkable lightness, freed from the frame that suggests the limbs of this mythical figure. Plain surfaces set off the series of serpent heads at the ends, which through their varied positions give the piece the effect of a medieval "mobile."

Another repoussé gold ornament, allegedly part of a headdress, combines realism with expressionism [5.2]. About eleven inches high, it comes from the Mochica culture. A conventionalized human face forms the center of the composition. The short legs suggest that it is the symbol of the moving sun. Two jaguar or puma bodies with curling tails appear in cut-out, adding to the "sparkle" of the aureole.

Also from the coast, found north of Trujillo, comes a ceremonial spear thrower, sheathed in gold, a detail of which is illustrated [5.3]. This work, also embossed, shows a giant condor devouring a dead man. The bird's comb is of coral, and its eyes are turquoise inlay. Its size compared to that of the prostrate figure indicates its symbolic portent. Imagining the chief to whose regalia such a piece originally belonged, one can readily understand the envy of the Spaniards.

A huge jaguar fang, more than five inches long, is utilized in the representation of a gold-sheathed jaguar with inlaid spots of turquoise [5.4], devouring an undefinable creature made of shell. The pointed end of the tooth forms the tail of the beast, stiff with savage tension.

Spanish chroniclers remarked on the Indian chieftains' elongated earlobes, stretched to accommodate the earspool, or earstud, that was part of the full-dress attire of an important personage. Most of these pieces were made in repoussé work and comparatively light in weight. Usually the figure of a warrior—perhaps a mythical hero—is depicted on the disk, sometimes with dangling earrings, nose plug, mouth mask. On the Chimú earspool [5.5] there are four figures, each holding out what appears to be a bird, perhaps caught in a net. One can discern a bordered tunic, a bag or short cape hung over the left shoulder, and at the side, a small attendant holding a monkey on a leash. The disks, five inches in diameter, are edged with a cast pearllike beading, like a fine rope. Note the chasing on the shafts.

A pair of heavy earspools made of pottery were found at Teotihuacán, Mexico—evidence of the wide dispersal of this type of jewelry. They, too, are beaded on the edge and have a helmeted head in the center.

From the highlands of Peru, as well as from the coast, one encounters beakers of gold or silver from various periods, both plain and with hammered designs, as much as thirteen inches in height [see 6.2]. Sometimes these have been fashioned into faces; sometimes they are inset with semi-precious stones. Small cast and sheet metal figures of humans and llamas were produced in the highlands. From northern Peru come magnificent gold ceremonial knives, as much as seventeen inches in length. Inset with turquoise, depicting a local god, they are composed of various parts, combining as many as six different techniques.

A mask of base silver from a mummy pack [5.6] is more decorative than the more frequently seen flat masks hammered of thin gold. The monkey heads that stare out from the eyes are startlingly effective. The beard of feathers is proof that an important personage was involved, for beards were worn only by high priests, chieftains, and rulers. A brocaded band frames the mask and probably once served to affix it to the mummy pack. Though this piece has Chimú traits, it is not entirely in their general convention.

The Inca silver dish [5.7], measuring five and one half inches across without the handle, is a rare piece, allegedly found near Cuzco. It was cast in such a way as to accommodate a mosaic of pink shell and turquoise, applied in different designs in exquisite proportion. One forgets with what simple tools such an object was fashioned.

By now the reader will have become accustomed to fantastic combinations of human and animal elements. The piece from Colombia [5.8] suggests a sea monster with a grotesque human head. Actually, a whistle cast in solid gold, it is only three fourths of an inch long, yet even the iris is marked in the eye.

Repoussé work was used also in Ecuador to fashion breastplates and masks, but these are so different stylistically that they cannot be mistaken for anything from neighboring lands. The bat-god appears frequently. A flowing decoration with punchwork is sometimes used to fill in the background, reminiscent of textile patterns.

The coastal section of La Tolita, Esmeraldas, is full of buried riches. Unfortunately, when a bulldozer was being used to clear the land, the uneducated workmen cared to salvage only objects made of gold and other precious metals. Whatever else was brought to light—stone, pottery, bone —was discarded, often having been smashed to see whether it contained anything they accounted of value. During World War II, a group of European concessionaires was discovered to be "mining" by turning high-powered jets of water on a hillside where archaeological objects were imbedded in undisturbed stratification. Most of the pottery was broken in the process, while the precious metal was melted down to conceal the illegal activity. At that time, this writer was on a mission to South America and spent several weeks in Quito, Ecuador. He was approached by a senator of the district to help him stop this barbarous exploitation. But though the operation was apparently widely known, no protest or appeal was heeded. Thus, the material on hand is reduced more or less to pieces that have come into collections through devious ways, without data as to their provenience.

Some of the most complicated techniques known to the pre-Columbian craftsman were practiced in Ecuador. The disk illustrated, over three and a half inches in diameter, from Pescadillo, Manabí, presents an astonishing virtuosity of execution [5.9]. Constructed in openwork, it presents a human figure with spread arms and legs, placed in a circular frame. The figure's head and legs and the beading are of platinum, while the plain ring of the frame and the lacelike scrolls are of gold. A double metal cord encircles the piece as well as the central medallion, holding visually together the composition. Several techniques are involved. So smooth are the transitions that one cannot feel with his finger where one metal joins the other.

Although many metal objects of colonial workmanship survive from the regions around the great mines of the High Andes, few pieces can tell us anything of the iconography of pre-Hispanic times there. The cast bronze plaque, four and a half inches high [5.10], is of a type said to be found only in and around the Calchaqui Valley and thus represents a rare specimen of pre-Columbian metallurgy. This valley lies close to the present-day borders of Bolivia, Argentina, and Chile. Closer to Chile than to Argentina in its decorative language, the piece shows relationship to Chilean pottery and reminds one, also, of the long pins that the Auracanian Indians, from that same region, still use to hold their mantles together, with a fish or small cross dangling from the silver ball at the top.

The plaque has a clearly defined and straightforward pattern. The combination of human and animal elements, so frequent in pre-Columbian work, is present here, also, in individual interpretation. A human head occupies the center, between two jaguars in silhouette, their spots punched deep enough to suggest inlay. The reverse side [5.11] shows the elaborated hair-do at the back of the head and two lizards on the broad panel. When compared with the sophisticated silver dish from Cuzco [5.7], the plaque demonstrates the divergent cultural and artistic levels of people who lived relatively near to each other. It is a border-line case, both culturally and topographically.

The Calchaqui Valley region, bordered by snow-covered peaks more than twenty-one thousand feet high, was even in post-Conquest days unsafe for Spaniards, and although it had very fertile land, a lovely climate, and abundant water, colonists did not venture there for some time.

Several Colombian cultures produced outstanding metalwork. Sometimes the work is named for the river valley where it was found—like Sinu or Tairona, for example; sometimes for a tribe, such as Chibcha and Quimbaya. Exquisite shapes in the round were cast, flasks sometimes resembling plants, human figures as much as eight inches high; and embossed gold ornaments produced for nose and ears in lacelike perforated patterns. Breastplates and knife-shaped pendants abound, often presenting anthropomorphic figures. Ceremonial staff heads and foot-long mantle pins carry carefully detailed birds, animals, and human figures in miniature. Many were executed by cire perdue, with intricate openwork contrasting with the solid surfaces.

An interesting composition, attributed to the Muisca culture, was fashioned in *tumbaga,* an alloy of gold and copper or of gold, silver, and copper [5.12]. Some six inches high, it was cast in several pieces, then soldered together. It shows a chieftain on a raft, surrounded by five attendants. The chief, taller than the others, with his staff in his hand, strikes the eye immediately. As so often in ancient American art, the heads are disproportionately large. The raft is amazingly simple, as we see if we look at it closely, but its production was rather an achievement. The piece follows a conventionalized tradition loosely connected with the Chibcha style. Though it shows technical limitations, it tells its story with impact.

A nose ornament large enough to mask the mouth is attributed to the Calima style. It is of hammered gold [5.13]; five inches wide, it weighs only twenty grams. The upper section, which was inserted in the septum, is simple, but the part below has a complex and well-coordinated design. Small disks vibrate above the semicircular band at the edge, with its embossed pattern, and two larger disks hang at the sides. Twenty-four lightly embossed cylinders add to the movement and glitter. The number twenty-four, as here, often occurs in such pieces. Similar elaborate nose ornaments can be seen, dangling free, on some of the larger breastplates and on plaques representing human figures [see 3.42].

On a large gold pectoral, a flattened-out bird shape serves as background for eight embossed figures [5.14]. Seven of them have beaded aureoles. The central personage is somewhat differently portrayed, wearing a bird's-beak headdress. Stylized bird heads and tails decorate the sides. A variant of this exists in the Museo de Oro in Bogotá; it has exactly the same shape but the figures are differently placed.

Staff heads cast in solid gold representing a human figure are characteristic of the Quimbaya. The little features are sharply modeled; headdress, ear ornaments, necklace, are depicted with precision. What makes this piece unique [5.15] is the bar of authority held across the chest. The striation on the face represents either tattoo or paint.

A blade-shaped pendant about eleven inches high comes from the region of Popayán, Colombia, where the Calima and the Nariño styles met. It is made of *tumbaga* covered with a thin plating of gold [5.16]. The central anthropomorphic figure and the four small mouselike creatures were cast—they are hollow behind—while the thin knife blade was probably hammered and the sections were then joined by soldering. The iconography is somewhat similar to the plaque illustrated above it [5.14]. The main figure wears a circular nose pendant. The body is picked out by delicate beading, and the knees are encircled with tight bands, which is also frequently the case in Colombian pottery. Though the meaning of the bird-monkeys and small mouselike figures is obscure, they add decorative diversity. The divided mass of feathers in the headdress counterbalances the upward sweep of the "knife blade," closing the composition.

A small helmeted warrior [5.17], only one and three quarters inches high, tops a gold mantle pin, cast by cire perdue, probably from the Calima culture. He carries a spear thrower in one hand, a ceremonial knife in the other, and the details of his costume are distinctly portrayed. As a final touch of virtuosity, his eyes can be seen shining inside his helmet. The tiny animal on his back may have totemic significance.

The realistic bird on the staff head from Colombia [5.20] is related in style to the figure on the previous page [5.15]. Indeed, it might have topped just such a staff of authority as that which the small human being is holding.

Some goldwork has been found in the tombs at San Agustín, in cire perdue, cast filigree work, and sheathing, dating between the sixth and the twelfth centuries.

It can be observed that the Isthmus of Panama acted as a funnel through which influences in art and technique were exchanged, perhaps not so much by way of land as on the water, skirting its shores. Gold helmets were made by both the Quimbaya in Colombia and the Coclé tribe of Panama. The tropical life of the Isthmus has been immortalized in golden sharks, alligators, frogs, and other reptiles. Breastplates, eight inches and more in diameter, carry demon figures that may have been gods, highly complex concepts clearly presented. Notable for their intricacy of detail and expert craftsmanship are animal and insect shapes that combine precious and semiprecious stones, such as uncut emeralds and rose quartz, with cast goldwork.

A thin gold sheet has been hammered over a form to very "modern" effect, showing two crocodiles, each carrying on its back a bird with spread wings [5.21]. Found in the Coclé region of Panama, the piece was evidently worn as a cuff. Although it appears in murals and on pottery, such an article is rarely seen in actuality.

So typical of the Chiriqui and Veraguas tribes of Panama are plaques of stylized eagles that they are popularly known as *veraguas.* Their heads and bodies appear in the round, often combining mythical elements, while the wings and tails are flattened out and unadorned, a pleasing display of pure gold. Also characteristic are cast figures of twin gods carrying weapons or blowing trumpets.

In Costa Rica, too, twin figures were worked into breastplates and heavy ornaments, in some cases with trophy heads hanging from their hands. Creatures of marine life are realistically depicted. Small bells and rattles in human and animal form were produced in copper, as well as in gold. The representations of a crawfish [5.18] and a shark [5.19] display their creator's amazing observation of the animal world coupled with a craftsmanship that can vie with anything produced in Europe during the Middle Ages. The solidity of the forms, even the rough finish, lend conviction and power to these small pieces.

Less metalwork has been found to date in Nicaragua, Honduras, and Guatemala. In style, however, it generally tends toward that of Costa Rica and Panama—even of Colombia—in both technique and subject. A very few pieces show the influence of the Mixtecs, who late in the pre-Columbian period proved themselves to be among the greatest in achievement.

A tomb containing four bodies was found during excavations now in progress at Iximché, Guatemala. The main occupant wore a headband of gold and a necklace of ten identical gold jaguar heads set off by small gold beads, forty in all [5.24]. The heads, with their glaring eyes and sharply defined fangs, were probably formed by pressing sheet gold over a stone negative. The style points to the south of Guatemala. In the Isthmian area, much of such conventionalized but expressive work can be found.

Iximché—a drive of about an hour and a half from the modern capital —lies at an altitude of seven thousand feet, surrounded by pine-forested hills. It is believed it became the capital of the Cakchiquel tribe of Maya around the second half of the fifteenth century. The ruined site seems to show some relationship with Zaculeu, but it has only been partly excavated. Murals have, also, been found in Iximché, in one case showing a personage performing a blood sacrifice by piercing his tongue. It is interesting that the style of painting indicates Mexican, rather than Maya, influence; it could be from a Mixtec codex. That would corroborate the lateness of date, when the region felt influences from both directions.

It is thought that metalwork was not generally practiced in Middle America before the tenth century; then it appears at a high level of technical skill. Some early examples of ancient Mexican silverwork have been uncovered in Guerrero, where in colonial times, a tremendous exploitation of silver took place—witness the church at Taxco. These ancient pieces are mainly hammered and repoussé work, with quite powerful designs. The Tarascan people, who also lived in western Mexico, were skillful in working copper in its natural state.

Gold, delivered in gourds or cane tubes, or cast into bars, formed part of the annual tribute paid by the southern provinces to the Aztec kings in the years before the Conquest. The names of the towns levied and the quantities demanded were recorded on tribute rolls, which later proved of great assistance to the progress of the conquistadores. Gold, silver, precious stones, and jewelry were sold in the great market at Tenochtitlán.

Oaxaca and its sprawling ambience saw perhaps the last and greatest flowering of pre-Columbian metalwork. The use of nose ornaments, lip plugs (labrets), and huge earrings may be rather repulsive to us, but the fantasy and the subtle craft involved cannot be gainsaid. A lip plug or labret [5.23] is Mixtec from the border between Veracruz and Oaxaca, and shows the head of a bird of prey in massive cast work. It is only about an inch long, but the open beak, the tongue, the tiny disks dangling down below, are executed with precision and finesse.

In the famous Tomb 7 at Monte Albán, discovered when the road leading to the ruins was widened, Mixtec jewelry in its most sophisticated form adorned the bodies of a number of dignitaries. Gold breastplates, nose ornaments, rings, necklaces, handles for fans, coronets decorated with gold feathers, testify to the Mixtec goldsmith's full command of his craft. It is remarkable that these people who surpassed all other cultures in the elegance of their work, seem to have taken it up so late.

A Mixtec pendant [5.22] is little more than three inches long and weighs around two and a half ounces. Here we have a glimpse of an enormously involved mythology. Produced by the cire perdue process, the piece represents the god Quetzalcóatl in his aspect of "the New Wind," signifying probably the change that heralds the coming of the rains after the dry season. His head, enclosed in the gaping jaws of a plumed serpent, emerges from the sun disk. The feathers and snout of this mythological creature form a sort of casque. The god wears a mask in the form of an eagle's beak and spiral earrings of conch shell, one of his symbols. Suspended from the beak is another sun disk with a feathery radiation, from which three loops carry the figure of another eagle with spread wings—

symbol of the rising sun—with a bell at each side. From his talons and tail dangle four more bells, which some interpret as the symbol of life.

The innumerable sections of which this complicated piece is made demonstrate not only how involved is Mixtec religious symbolism but also how the ancient goldsmith was able to render it three-dimensionally, in exquisite detail without clutter. Each section is subtly balanced against the others, and a high degree of fluidity is maintained between the various elements—fascinating to the eye, even without delving into the secrets of its meaning.

Prescott describes the conquests of Mexico and Peru in lively detail. A year after the fall of the Mexican empire (1521), a colony had settled in Panama, large enough to furnish Pizarro with ships for his exploits along the Pacific coast. His progress was steady though slow and far from easy. At Cajamarca, Peru, as ransom for the captive Inca ruler, he amassed gold estimated at fifteen million dollars—today perhaps worth some four times as much. There were goblets, ewers, platters, vases of various sorts, utensils for temples and palaces in many curious shapes. A golden ear of corn was sheathed in broad leaves of silver, from which hung tassels of silver thread; a fountain sent up a jet of gold, while golden birds and animals played at its base. For the Royal Fifth due the emperor, objects to the value of a hundred thousand ducats were set aside. Indian goldsmiths had to melt into ingots the rest of their own intricate creations. Nearly an equal amount was collected in Cuzco, where palaces carried friezes of gold embedded in the building stones, temple gardens sparkled with gold ornament. Embossed vases of gold, golden llamas, and statues of women—some in silver, some in gold—are recorded.

Cortés's Conquest of Mexico had been marred by greater setbacks. The greed of his troops on seeing the pomp of the Aztec capital, their cruel plundering of its treasures, turned the formerly mild emperor and his chieftains against them. Deciding on withdrawal, Cortés distributed the booty among his men. The capital lay in the middle of a lake, accessible only by means of three causeways. As the Spaniards retreated, the bridges broke under the unaccustomed weight of armored men and laden horses. Panic reigned as the Aztecs attacked. Those not laden with loot made it fastest and farthest. It is estimated that four to five hundred Spaniards perished that night. Rested, reinforced, and accompanied by the Tlaxcalcans, sworn enemies of the Aztecs, Cortés could return to triumph.

Cortés's first gift of New World treasures to Charles V was exhibited at the court in Valladolid, and again in Brussels. Albrecht Dürer saw them there in 1520 and wrote in his diary with enthusiasm about the size and craftsmanship of those golden things. In 1934 in Vienna, this writer found this entry in old volumes, still set in Gothic print, together with letters and rhymes of the artist. He translated and published it, for the first time in connection with ancient American art. Thus, this quote appeared first in English and several times afterward in American books and articles, before it was quoted in German. The perspicacity and broad interest of the artist of more than 440 years ago appear justified today.

Of the tons of gold and silver objects amassed in the first decades of the Conquest, not one piece survives. What the Museo de América, Madrid, exhibits came as gifts from Bolivia, Peru, and Colombia, on the occasion of the quattrocentennial of Columbus's first voyage. It appears that even the objects that the Vienna museum exhibits today were not among the first presents.* In the inventory made in 1596 at the medieval Habsburg castle, Ambras near Innsbruck, Tyrol, a golden casque with a large eagle's beak is already missing from the often-reproduced feather headdress. When the objects from the Habsburg curiosa cabinet were transferred to Vienna in 1878, of the more than one thousand small disks, sequins, scales, plaques, and minute decorations on the piece, not half a dozen were in place; a restoration done at that time replaced them with gilded bronze. Perhaps the only unplundered bit of original gold in the collection is the narrow ribbon outlining the fire-coyote on the Aztec shield [see 6.15].

Although many colonial silver objects, mainly household articles, are preserved in private and public collections in Europe, a colonial altar, entirely of silver, is probably unique. Spain's silver fleet preferred to land at the ideal harbor of Cádiz. Situated at the far end of the bay, the prosperous town of Puerto Santa María was an important Jesuit center, whence the missionaries sailed for the New World. Recently, a distinguished Mexican art historian was enjoying a free day in the environs of Cádiz. Wandering about Puerto Santa María, he entered the parochial church, once the Jesuit priory, and was attracted to the main altar.** Frontal, ciborium, and retable formed a cascade of silver, embossed with fronds, garlands, and medallions. As he focused his camera on the brilliant display, he noted an inscription, according to which the altar had been made by "Maestro Joseph de Medina" in the year 1685; it was the gift of Juan Camacho Gaina, captain general of San Luis Potosí and later viceroy of New Spain. Nobody knew about this gift from Mexico, no guidebook mentions it. A Mexican art historian, born in San Luis Potosí, discovers and writes about it. It is one of the flukes of history, which no author can invent.

---

* Karl A. Novotny, *Mexikanische Kostbarkeiten aus der Kunstkammern der Renaissance.* Wien: Museum für Völkerkunde, 1960.
** Francisco de la Maza. *Cartas Barrocas desde Castilla y Andalusía.* Mexico: Instituto de Investigaciones Estéticas, 1963.

[5.1] Chavín-style gold breast ornament. Chongoyape, Peru.

[5.2] Mochica gold headdress. Virú.

[5.3] Spear thrower with gold condor. Virú, Peru.

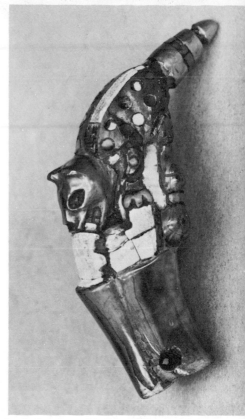

[5.4] Jaguar tooth with gold-covered animal. Coastal Peru.

[5.5] Chimú gold earspools. Peru.

[5.6] Mummy mask of base silver. Peru.

[5.7] Inca silver dish with inlay. Peru.

[5.9] Gold and platinum disk. Manabí, Ecuador.

5.8] Small gold whistle. Colom-
ia.

[5.10] Cast bronze plaque. Calchaqui Valley, Argentina.

[5.11] Reverse of cast bronze plaque.

[5.12] Figures on a raft. Muisca culture. Colombia.

[5.13] Gold nose ornament. Colombia.

[5.14] Chibcha (?) gold pectoral. Colombia.

[5.15] Cast gold figurine. Cauca Valley, Colombia.

[5.16] Gold alloy pendant. Southern Colombia.

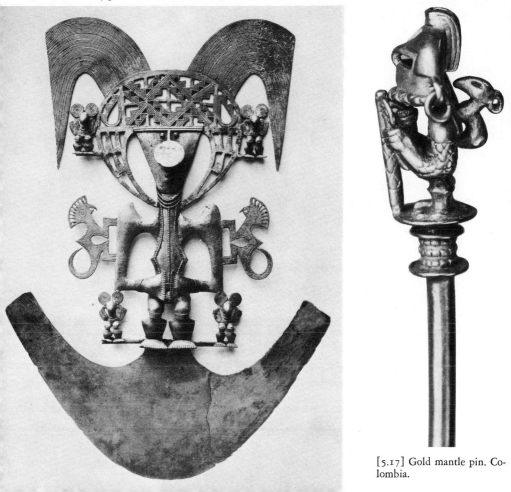

[5.17] Gold mantle pin. Colombia.

[5.18] Gold crawfish. Cartago, Costa Rica.

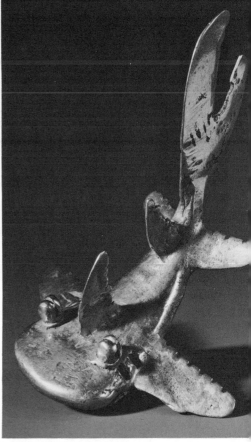

[5.19] Gold shark. Costa Rica.

[5.20] Gold staff head. Colombia.

[5.21] Coclé gold cuff. Panama.

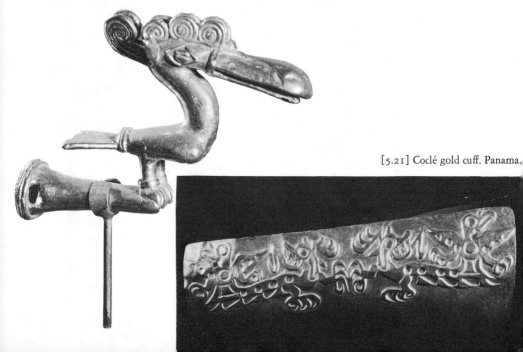

[5.22] Mixtec gold pendant. Tomb 7, Monte Albán, Mexico.

[5.23] Mixtec gold lip plug. Mexico.

[5.24] Gold necklace with jaguar heads. Iximché, Guatemala.

The Colonial Scene

A WORLD TRANSPLANTED

In the pre-Columbian era, we have been considering the cultures of separate peoples, with different languages and individual art styles. In the colonial period, we see the attempt of a European power to impose a single culture on these various folk, at a time when it was also populating the land with a number of its own citizens. Yet by the middle of the seventeenth century, the colonial population—whether Indian, mestizo (of mixed blood,) or born of Spanish lineage—had created their own artistic idioms, often quite different even from one another.

Until recently the art of the Spanish colonial empire in America (1530–1820) has generally been either ignored or treated as an adjunct to that of the Iberian Peninsula. As a rule, the more a building, statue, or painting resembles some European prototype, the greater the reverence accorded it. One of Hispanic colonial art's chief values, its peculiar originality—its "mestizo" (in Mexico, *poblano*) quality—is largely passed over as incidental. Nevertheless, it is the powerful non-European sources that give this art its special character.

The very countries that produced the greatest art in pre-Columbian times—Mexico, Guatemala, Ecuador, Peru, and Bolivia—have the most exciting colonial art. Highly convenient as the term "Latin America" is, it is open to criticism, for it is used to denote a territory where the majority of the population does not belong to the white race, and even after more than 440 years, does not speak much Spanish. All too little has been done to understand the languages—much less the psychology—of the Indian. Even for Quechua and Aymara, which are spoken by millions in the Andean highlands, the best grammars and dictionaries are those written by the seventeenth-century missionaries. A similar situation exists with the Otomi, Nahuatl, and Maya languages of Middle America.

Since the advent of Christianity, no single event in the history of mankind has produced such tremendous changes in the world as the Conquest of the Americas. To Spain and Portugal alone, a territory many times as large as Europe was opened up to material exploitation, and in the process, millions of natives became indoctrinated with the Roman Catholic culture of the Iberian Peninsula.

The Spaniards first settled the island of Hispaniola (Santo Domingo), then established a base in Cuba. From there, two expeditions set out to reconnoiter the mainland (1517–1518). The following year, Cortés landed his troops at a point on the Mexican coast which he named *Vera Cruz.* He consolidated his position as ruler over the Mexican empire in 1521 on the ruins of the Aztec capital, Tenochtitlán. In Peru, after the ancient Inca capital Cuzco, high in the Andes, had proven, for reasons of safety, untenable as a viceregal seat, Pizarro founded Lima near the Pacific Ocean in 1533 as his new capital. As early as 1524, Alvarado set up his first headquarters in Guatemala. In 1546, Montejo finally broke the resistance of the Maya in Yucatán; though poor in gold, this region was strategically important. The American Southwest, which yielded no precious metal in spite of abundant rumors, was opened up by Coronado in 1540 but remained an outpost. It is ironical that actually there was great mineral wealth there in the mountains, though it lay too deep to be reached by primitive methods. So powerful were the tribal kingdoms, however, that it took years to bring about their final subjugation, even though the conquistadores used horses, iron weapons, and gunpowder, all of which were unknown to the natives.

For the administration of this vast territory, the Spaniards established two viceroyalties—one north and one south of the Isthmus of Panama. This form of government had already proved itself useful to the crown of Castille in Aragon, Valencia, Sardinia, Sicily, and Naples; Venice had applied it in the Levant; and Portugal, in the Orient. The first viceroyalty in the New World known as *Nueva España,* or New Spain, was created in 1535 to rule what is today Mexico and Central America, with Mexico City as its capital. The second, the viceroyalty of Peru, was established in 1544, to govern all the Spanish possessions in South America. In 1717, this viceroyalty ceded territory to the new viceroyalty of New Granada, comprising Colombia, Venezuela, and later, Ecuador. In 1776, what is known today as Argentina, Bolivia, Paraguay, and Uruguay became the viceroyalty of Río de la Plata. Panama, closely tied to the transshipment of treasure from the Andean highlands to Spain, was for a time under the administration of Peru, then later transferred to New Granada.

The supreme civil authority in the Spanish colonies was the viceroy, under whom a gigantic bureaucracy flourished; all political and military matters came under his jurisdiction. Spiritual power was entrusted to the Roman Catholic church, represented by the secular clergy and conventual orders. Through these two channels—the civil and the religious—the Spanish way of life was introduced into the New World.

The viceroy ruled in the king's name, and his power was almost absolute. All officials were nominally answerable to him. He was responsible for the collection of the "Royal Fifth," the king's share of all the bullion mined, as well as for all other taxes. Since the Spanish crown also expected a share of all "Indian treasures," the viceroy was obliged to maintain a diligent search for hidden wealth in the wrecked temples and still undiscovered tombs of the pre-Columbian past. The Indians paid tribute to both the crown and the church—as they had to the hierarchy in pre-Columbian times—in grain, dyes, herbs, and other produce of the land, as well as in blankets and manufactured goods. Later they also paid in money.

The viceroy controlled the military and was responsible for the fortification of important ports. Early in the seventeenth century, the manufacture of armaments and gunpowder—the latter being additionally needed in great quantity for mining—became one of the few industries permitted in the colonies. And this, too, was under the supervision of the viceroy. Mints for hard currency, mainly silver coins, were established near the largest mines and placed under his jurisdiction.

The Spanish church was, in a sense, a national church, a hotbed of royal protégés and bureaucrats. The king of Spain was an apostolic monarch, that is, he nominated the bishops and other ecclesiastics upon papal suggestion. So absolute was his control in religious matters that not even a papal bull or brief could be circulated in the New World without the sanction of the Council of the Indies, that arm of the Spanish crown which ruled on American affairs from its elegant Renaissance palace in Seville. All ecclesiastic positions in the colonies depended on the king to whom all available data on an aspirant had to be submitted. Once a priest was in the colony, permission for him to return to Spain depended on the prelate, the diocese, and in the final instance on the crown itself.

Visitors to Spain's colonial empire wrote in astonishment of the vast holdings of the church. In 1620, the religious establishments in Lima with their related properties occupied more ground than all the rest of the city combined. After Alexander von Humboldt visited Mexico (1803–04) he reported that in some provinces as much as 80 percent of the arable land was in the hands of the church. Many of the prelates were earnest, sincere personalities; but the secular clergy was of very mixed quality and often corrupt; venality and embezzlement existed in the monastic orders.

With the passage of time, two classes of white religious personnel emerged: those who had been born in Spain and those of Spanish antecedents, who had been born in the colonies and usually educated there. The antagonism between these two groups had already made itself felt by the second half of the sixteenth century and continued well beyond the colonial epoch. Mention should also be made of the many priests and friars of mestizo background, who brought their own prejudices and superstitions into the complex religious climate.

Universities that prepared the student mainly for a theological career —and later, also, for the law—were founded in 1553 in Mexico and twenty-three years later in Lima. In 1576, a chair for Indian languages was established, as vital to the propagation of the faith.

For a time, the Indian was officially declared "not of sufficient intelligence and rational enough to be held responsible for his acts." Bishop Bartolomé de las Casas (1474–1566), an enlightened churchman, denounced this judgment as degrading, a great injustice to the native population. The ruling, however, had advantages, because at least temporarily, the Indian escaped the discipline of the Inquisition. This institution first functioned in Lima in 1569, in Mexico in 1571, and in Cartagena, the great port of Colombia, in 1610; and it continued to operate up to 1820, when the Hispanic colonies were struggling for their independence.

Whether active in the civil or ecclesiastical administration of the colonies, the Spaniards worked under heavy handicaps. They were affected by the trying conditions of the extremely high altitudes and the tropical climate and by a number of strange diseases. The unheard-of power and the fabulous wealth suddenly placed in their trust, the tremendous distances—not only from the motherland but also between one colonial region and the next—made rigid control impossible. Furthermore, despite the incredible riches that mining and agriculture yielded, colonial economic life was hampered by the many restrictions imposed by the crown. Certain crops were forbidden, in favor of Spanish growers; merchandise from other European countries was subject to high duty.

The mining of gold and silver, however, was free from all restrictions. The main reason for this encouragement was the Royal Fifth claimed by the crown. To collect the king's share, the silver fleet sailed out from Spain with goods for the colonial trade; it was escorted by armed galleons, for the treasure-laden flotilla was a prize much coveted by English, Dutch, French, and other freebooters and pirates. The Caribbean, with its many coves on its many islands, offered the predators excellent shelter close to the route of the silver fleet. The armed convoys could not always furnish full protection, and much of the precious cargo either landed at other ports than Spain's or sank to the bottom of the sea, where it still intrigues the imagination and is subject to modern diving activities.

Towns that could be approached from the sea were raided for their silver and gold, as well as for rare native products. Understandably, harbor fortifications were constantly being strengthened and enlarged, all laid out on a somewhat similar plan. One of the earliest and most monumental is that of Cuba's Morro Castle. The fortress of San Juan del Morro (also, a Morro Castle) in San Juan, Puerto Rico, shows the typical outline [see 7.1]—roughly star-shaped—that was judged the best defense for a small garrison. The buttressed seawalls still stand, the immensely thick walls at the heart of the defense system. There were drawbridges, assault towers, and lookouts, and beneath, underground passageways, ammunition depots, and dungeons. The island was unsuccessfully attacked by Sir Francis Drake, but some years later in 1598, the Earl of Cumberland landed, and the population of a little more than three hundred whites retired to Morro Castle. (At the time more than sixteen hundred Negro slaves lived in and around the town.) Dutch freebooters inflicted heavy losses in the early seventeenth century. The citadel now stands as a reminder of a very different past, about which many inhabitants of the modern city know only what they interpret from its massive, time-worn walls.

Veracruz, the main Gulf port of Mexico, handled all the wares transshipped through Acapulco from the Philippine Islands, as well as commerce to and from Europe. Portobelo on the Caribbean coast of Panama was important, because the precious metals mined in Bolivia and Peru passed through there. Cartagena in Colombia was the gateway to much of South America. All of these places were regularly scheduled ports of call for the Spanish fleet. On the Pacific coast, Callao, the harbor of Lima, was of paramount importance. Here the mule trains from the Andes, bearing bullion to be loaded into the ships bound for Panama, reached their destination. Acapulco, situated on Mexico's rocky Pacific coast, about 270 miles from the Mexican capital, offered the best port for the unloading of the Manila galleon bearing wares from the Orient by way of the Philippines. A sleepy village for the greater part of the year, it sprang into hectic life with the arrival of the fleet and of the merchants and mule trains gathered for that event.

At the time that artistic activity began to unfold in the Hispanic-American colonies, art in Europe showed a complex picture. National, even regional styles were already in evidence—the painting of Florence was considerably different from that of Venice, although the people spoke practically the same language and confessed the same faith. Byzantine art, together with Romanesque and Gothic, still lingered in many places. But the Renaissance, a powerful and universal movement, was implanting everywhere the spirit of the individual, stimulating the development of national schools.

At the end of the fifteenth century, no section of Europe had an artistic climate more diversified than Spain. The Iberian Peninsula lay off the main thoroughfare of artistic interchange. For some seven hundred years, until 1492, much of it had been occupied by the Moors. Moorish characteristics —called *Mudéjar,* the Spanish name for a converted Moor—persisted in many phases of Spanish art, notably in the treatment of brick, wood, and tile. Spain slowly found her way out of the long domination by Flemish and Italian models to artistic self-assurance. The term "Plateresque" has been given to the early flowering of the Renaissance there, where many motifs appeared as finely executed in stucco or stone as if worked by a silversmith. Though this style falls generally in the first half of the sixteenth century, its decorative ideals made themselves felt also in the Neoclassical period that followed the Baroque.

The Baroque was not merely an art style; it was a mode of living. It presented the last great spectacle of feudalism, and it also heralded the dawn of the epoch of the common man. Economically, Spain was approaching her zenith. Into the country were pouring the immeasurable riches from the New World, gold and silver mined in faraway America by Indian labor and agricultural wealth produced, also, by Negro slaves. After generations of domination by foreign artists and artisans, Spanish talent and ingenuity took hold and created its own form of Baroque. In architecture, the heroic, complex, and ostentatious were emphasized. In sculpture and in painting, one can observe a trend toward the mystic, the ascetic, and the sentimental, with a concomitant prudery.

The Baroque flourished at a time when commerce with the Near East thrived, and the style profited from the richness of form, color, and workmanship then current in Muslim lands. Its successor, the Rococo, reached full bloom in the eighteenth century when the Christian world was in communication with China.

Hispanic colonial art is far from being a mere transplantation of Spanish forms into the New World. It grew from the union of two civilizations that, in many ways, were the antithesis of one another. It incorporated, also, the Indian's preferences, his sense of form and color, and the power of his heritage, all of which modulated the imported style.

Throughout the centuries of Spanish rule, two major trends are noticeable. The first is a painstaking effort to imitate European models. Though satisfactory perhaps from the standpoint of iconography and craftsmanship, such work was often uninspired. The second trend emerged as native talent forged a new idiom of art, different not only from the European but, also, from region to region in the Americas..

Just as the artistic achievement of pre-Columbian civilization must forever remain a torso—grand but incomplete—so the splendor of the arts of the Hispanic-American colonies can never be fully recaptured. Ours is a hemisphere visited by volcanic eruptions, earthquakes, and tropical hurricanes. The colonial builders were never able to outwit such violent phenomena of nature. Furthermore, in the more than one and a half centuries of independence from Spain, insurrections, revolutions, and wars have occurred, and antireligious movements have destroyed many buildings and objects that would have added to our knowledge of the arts during those approximately three centuries of colonial regime. In proportion to the immense artistic output, the names of relatively few artists and craftsmen can be identified. Many of the most stunning achievements are anonymous.

6/Transition

The Spaniards in the New World had to bridge an immeasurable gap, to make Indian labor, skill, and talents useful to Spanish colonial policy and to convert the Indians to a new life and a new religion. This policy was, on the one hand, largely a matter of enslavement of the native population and ruthless exploitation of natural resources. Many Indians were taken into peonage by the Spanish landowners. Some Indian communities were approached through the native *alcaldes* ("mayors"), who selected the men and apportioned the work required by the masters. Others were herded into the mines, for the amount of metal mined was the major concern of the state. Indian labor turned the wheels of this vast new enterprise, constructed the roads, built the towns, the churches. The Spaniard lived on the principle that manual work was beneath his status as conqueror.

By the end of the sixteenth century, the Spanish feudal lords, usually knights in rank, numbered about four thousand. In the first decades after the Conquest, few women crossed the ocean, and even later when conditions were more favorable, the number of white families was infinitesimally small compared to the millions of Indians and mestizos.

As is usual under such circumstances, the treatment of the workers depended on the individual landowner and his staff. Aside from the murderous work in the mines, the service most dreaded by the Indians was that in the *obrajes,* establishments for the weaving of cotton and woolen goods. This industry, which was among the few fostered in the colonies, was run on the principle of a prison, the workmen being forced to live on the premises under intolerable and inhuman conditions. The catastrophic decline of the Indian population in the first three or four decades after the Conquest long lay buried in dead statistics and is only now coming to light in all its horrifying proportions. The abrupt drop in the labor force caused the Spanish government to import Negro slaves at an earlier date and in greater numbers than has until recently been realized. By the middle of the sixteenth century, slave ships were pouring Negroes into the New World by the tens of thousands.

On the other hand, there was concern for the Indians' souls. With the armies of the conquistadores came the friars from various orders: Franciscans, Dominicans, Augustinians, Mercedarians, and later, Jesuits and Carmelites, imbued with missionary zeal and bearing their crucifixes, rosaries, censers, painted banners, and books.

The Spanish conquistadores came to America from a world where Christianity was already fifteen hundred years old. The rites, the iconography, the philosophy of the Roman Catholic church had evolved out of the European mentality and were attuned to the European temperament. It was a religion stabilized not only in its ecclesiastical administration but also in its spiritual scope.

The complex imagery and the strange customs of the alien civilization of this New World perplexed, confused, frightened the Spaniards. They broke the idols and razed the temples. They forbade—indeed persecuted—former religious practices and social customs. Where there had been an important place of sacrifice or pilgrimage, often a Christian church went up.

For the Indian, the idea of a god who had to die on the cross to redeem his people was unfathomable. Their gods were all-powerful. Because the Indian was totally outside the intellectual and spiritual tradition of Christian Europe, he had to be re-educated, the Spanish believed. Dictionaries of the many Indian languages, from Mexico to Bolivia, were soon in the making. Sign language and the translation of simplified concepts into picture writing were used to bridge the gap. One Father Testera invented a combination of Christian and pagan symbols for his *Libro de Oración,* or catechism. There, in the Mexican manner, a foot denotes going or walking; the swastika, the sun. The figures of friars and IHS, the monogram of Christ, appear, together with Aztec glyphs for numbers. It was to the interest of the colony that the Indian and mestizo membership in the various lay societies—the *cofradias* and *sodalidades*—should take part in the religious and social life of the community. But behind the impressive façade, there were many pagan practices and subconscious reactions that added up to a very different religion from that of the Catholic European. While the Indians adopted the new religion, they brought into its art their own taste preferences and mental associations.

A seepage of artistic motifs—plant, animal, and human—from the former religion and life can be observed in what is today termed Christian art, not only in the many articles produced for social or civilian use, but in those made outspokenly for the ritual of the church. Although the model was European, the raw material was the same as in pre-Columbian times, and the technique sometimes similar. What came out as the final product was by no means wholly European; it spoke a new idiom, one perhaps more sharply identifiable today across the perspective of the centuries.

It is rare to find an outspoken pagan symbol in colonial work. Sometimes, however, one does appear in full significance, as in the case of Tlaloc, the rain-god, on the baptismal font, dated 1581, at Zinacantepec, Mexico. Another example survives in a sixteenth-century mural in the lower choir of a former Franciscan monastery at Cuauhtinchan, in the state of Puebla, Mexico. The subject is the Annunciation. An eagle and a jaguar flank the central theme in an unusual, if not unique, composition. The dark-spotted animal appears in a pose frequently seen in pre-Columbian representations; the eagle is related to Teotihuacán's sacred quetzal [see 1.7]. It is no accident that these animals appear in connection with the Annunciation. In pre-Columbian mythology, the jaguar and the eagle represent, respectively, darkness and light. This mingling of pre-Columbian symbols with Christian iconography indicates the difficulties the missionaries had to face. Apparently, sometimes pagan symbols were permitted, because they helped illuminate aspects of Christianity.

The ancient Americans had fermented drinks made from cactus, cocoa bean, maize, or potatoes. Social status and craftsmanship are evidenced in the containers. As we have seen, the pottery ceremonial beakers of the Mexican and Maya areas were artistically embellished with painted or plastic ornamentation. On a pleasant piece from Asunción Mita, Guatemala, fashioned by simple means [6.1], the horizontal band of the unornamented rim contrasts with the lively vertical fluting on the body.

In the Andean area, where precious metal was in such abundance, beakers were made of silver, or sometimes of gold, often expressly as funerary offerings. Such a vessel might be encrusted with turquoise or other semiprecious stones—even with shell; it might be embossed with the shapes of birds, fish, or symbolic motifs. An Inca gold cup from coastal Peru has a repoussé design of birds in flight [6.2]. Here the upper band carries the decoration, and the main body of the vessel is plain.

Wooden objects rarely survive the vicissitudes of centuries. Among the more interesting exceptions to the rule are the *keros,* as the wood drinking cups of the Andean highlands are called. Of rare solidity, all fashioned in more or less the same shape, they are decorated in various colors, sometimes with a lacquerlike inlay.

In the first kero illustrated [6.3], the upper section has a checkered pattern overlaid with a zigzag motif. The lower part again carries vertical fluting, interrupted by horizontal bands with conventionalized birds and flowers scattered in colored inlay. Opinions differ whether the kero as a form is pre-Columbian. From its decoration, this one could be late Inca.

The other more highly ornamented wooden cup stems from Hispanic times, as is evident from the figures of men in Spanish garb that enliven the broad frieze [6.4]. Fetching is the rider on a white charger. His costume with its flying cloak is well defined, the feathered bush of his shako depicted in the same way as his horse's tail. Here the limitations of technique when representing something new is apparent: the artist's vocabulary has not yet reached its full range.

The technical prowess of the ancient American weaver continued throughout the colonial period, but pattern and color preferences varied as time went by. Up to the time of the Conquest, the finest weaves had been reserved for the ruling classes. Now the dignitaries of the colonial and ecclesiastical administration took their place. Much work was also done for the churches and for the mansions of high dignitaries. Anyone who traversed the silver route a few decades ago—from the mines of Bolivia along Lake Titicaca and down to the Pacific coast—could have seen large colonial rugs spread before church altars and flowing down the sanctuary steps. Alas, this writer came upon a wonderfully woven, large-patterned, colorful rug folded and creased into a hassock not larger than a yard square. Despite its frayed edges and marks of wear and tear, remnants of impressive craftsmanship and subtle coloring were still visible.

A detail from a large pre-Columbian breechcloth shows small squares with figures evenly placed in horizontal sequence [6.5]. Even the narrow border has fish in an ordered procession.

Under Spanish influence, the old conventions slowly disappeared. A piece of Inca tapestry, woven for a noblewoman's mantle [6.6], features silver thread, an innovation from Europe. Although in the border the figural elements are still framed within squares, animals drawn from European heraldry are scattered in the open field. The horizontal trend of the design is no longer strong. With the many strange designs set before him, it must have been difficult for the native weaver to organize his impressions, and the result was often a delightful jumble of motifs. In this early seventeenth-century piece, even double-headed eagles appear. Their long tongues are extended, as in a speech scroll from ancient times.

In the pre-Columbian costume woven in the Andean area, the general effect was of horizontal stripes. The border was modest or nonexistent. Spanish influence brought in a different concept. The rugs of Persia and the Orient had long fascinated the wealthy European; they enrich many a European religious picture and portrait. A Persian rug symbolizes a flower garden with a fountain at the center and an enclosing wall. Thus, the large rug or hanging that was sent to the New World as a model had a central medallion, conceived as a separate entity, a surrounding open "garden," and often as many as three framing bands of border. The Andean weaver reproduced this scheme without its logic [6.9]. The tapestry illustrated has a heraldic device at the center. The harp-playing mermaids that strew the surface of the larger field, together with small animal and flower motifs, are in no way composed into a related pattern. In the narrow inner border amid masks, animal figures, and plant arabesques, little hatted men in European dress kneel to aim their long guns. In the wide border, women in straight nunlike gowns with varicolored shawls appear. Barefoot Indians hold fans above them, while other Indians—sandaled and more elaborately clothed—carry standards. In the center on each side, the façade of a church with twisted columns is outlined, decked with festive flags. [Compare 6.10.] The very fine quality of the weaving and the wealth of small motifs place the date of this tapestry at the end of the sixteenth or early in the seventeenth century. The development of this kind of hanging will be discussed later in the section on Other Crafts [see 11.11 and 11.12].

The Mochica craftsman had a remarkable talent with the paintbrush, defining his figures with a thin outline and keeping the composition light and intelligible. Many stirrup jars of this type are widely on exhibit, but flat vessels, such as illustrated here, with broad flaring rims are rare [6.7]. Here a battle is taking place—warriors in different attire, some in animal and bird masks, brandish typical knifelike weapons with thongs looped through the handles. At the top of the piece, two men are blowing on panpipes, and in between (smaller in size, suggesting distance) a third man beats a drum. The Mochica culture is thought to have come to an end about the eleventh century. Nevertheless, certain stylistic details of the Mochica recur in early colonial tapestries: the position of the legs and feet; the suggestion of distance by diminution in size; the outlining of nearly all the figures; and to a certain extent, the costumes.

A late Inca vase from the Cuzco Museum serves as a connecting link [6.8]. Its form derives from the aryballos. Inca maidens holding hands create a rhythmic wreath all around the piece. Parrots perch between them. The *ñukchu,* sacred flower of the Incas, placed above them, can be also seen on the inlaid Inca kero [6.3] and decorating many a colonial object. Small points that are easily overlooked show how difficult it was to change certain details in the manner of representation. The same stiffness of pose characterizes the Inca maidens and the post-Conquest ladies. The feet are all turned toward the left, though the figures stand *en face.*

In the Chimú earspool of fine workmanship in the center of the page [6.11], a plain circle frames the conventionalized central figure. He has two birds on his headdress and two serpent heads at the sides [compare 5.5]. Nine small human figures occupy the outer frieze, flanked by parrot-like birds. Eight of them carry bundles of rods like fasces, and one, squeezed in at the lower left, a dangling object like a shell. The arrangement of so many details within the double circle of the tondo is proof of advanced decorative skill.

All the animals on the gold armband illustrated below this [6.12] are represented in the same peculiarly gauche way. Certain small details are emphasized—the bulging eyes, the claws. Pumas, monkeys, birds, are interspersed as in pre-Columbian tapestry and recall the past. But the horse, with toes that belong to no hoofed animal, identifies this piece as post-Conquest. A rider holds the horse on a lead line, the whip in his left hand surmounted by a bird. Note that the horse's mane and tail are done in the same manner as those of the white charger on the kero [see 6.4].

The upper section of à trapezoidal silver plaque, some eleven by fourteen inches, represents a scene before a church, the towers and central dome extending to the frame [6.10]. Festive flags are hung out. An Indian woman stands in the arched portal. She wears the typical highland costume: a wide heavy skirt with fringed or lace edging, a short shawl, and what might be interpreted as a folded cloth on her head. A bird perches on her shoulder. She is feeding corn to two llamas with packs on their backs, while two men in bouffant garments and tall hats (one is barefoot) hold huge four-petaled flowers aloft, which are developed into a decorative pattern. The scene appears to be an early version of the Good Shepherdess in a rustic setting—a figure that was later worked out in more sophisticated form. The lower section with its diamond-shaped hammered pattern makes a lively contrast. The whole piece has that particular charm of the direct and unpretentious so often encountered in objects of the Transition period.

The silver basin [6.13], bearing on the reverse the date 1568, is an example of high craftsmanship from the first century or so after the Conquest. Four circular medallions interrupt the procession of human beings and animals impressively embossed on the broad rim. Designed in good Plateresque tradition, these show two men and two women variously costumed, who seem to have been copied from prints. What happens in the space between them, however, is more noteworthy. Groups of animals, both real and mythical, stand among elaborate vases. An ungainly bird with a human head and a bell around its neck has the body of the Argentine ostrich, the rhea.

One section is of singular interest [6.14]. At the right, we see a tethered llama with a pack strapped to its back, surmounted by a cock, while a crane flutters between its forelegs. A half-nude sprite emerges from the central vase, wearing a headband with a feather and wielding a bow and arrow. A tiny rabbit crouches at his feet. The scene on the left of the vase is more coherent. Another llama kneels there with its load. An Indian man, with a headband, seems to urge it forward, while a woman, also in Indian dress, bends to help it rise. Behind her lie articles for the journey—a gourd, a jug, and slung round with a thong for carrying, a typical Inca aryballos. In a third section, an Indian woman appears with a child at her knee, wearing the typical Inca skirt and overblouse and carrying a pack strapped around her shoulders. Houses, a small church, and sundry trees and grasses give the sense of a hilly landscape.

Only an Indian, a dweller in those regions, could have rendered with such accuracy the native costumes and poses depicted in the various scenes and scattered between the forms of birds and small animals in a style reminiscent of pre-Columbian work.

The amazing history of this basin has been traced.* Silver was not only transported along the prescribed royal route to the Pacific ports. Silver smuggling started as soon as the Potosí mines began to pour out their treasure. Between the 1580's and the 1630's, a great deal of the traffic—legal and illegal—took the more direct route to the Atlantic from Potosí down the eastern slope of the Andes, via Jujuy, Salta, and Tucumán.

At that time, the bishop of Tucumán was one Francisco Vitoria, a Portuguese. After Philip II of Spain became the king of Portugal (1580), many Portuguese adventurers came to the New World and found more lucrative positions in the Spanish-speaking viceroyalties than in the Portuguese colony of Brazil. Bishop Vitoria had established a mule stud on his large estates. Mules were used up at a devastating rate, not only in the deep mines—where, once taken down, they functioned continuously without ever seeing the light of day until they expired—but also in the trains that carried the ingots to ports on the Atlantic coast. His Portuguese origin gave the bishop easy access to the Brazilian colony, and the fact that mules were also needed there in the transport of sugar and corn made him a large entrepreneur, with sometimes thousands of animals waiting for the market. His overseers knew how to toughen them for hard work. From Jujuy on down, the landscape became a little more friendly, and below Salta, good grazing land could be found. Tucumán was especially valuable because although the winters might be severe, as the chronicle says "they saw the snow only on the peaks of the Andes."

Horses were also bred on the estate. The many riders who accompanied the bishop's caravans to and from the Rio de la Plata had to be persons of trust and their physical welfare was important, since the bishop wished to continue to use them for more than one transport. Records show that even the Indian muleteers liked to go with certain leaders, on account of the good treatment received.

This example of economic involvement by an ecclesiastic of the colonies is by no means unique. Lacking adequate income from the state, both in the American viceroyalties and in the Philippine Islands, the clergy were allowed to add to their incomes through noneclesiastical activities.

With the burgeoning economy, the importations of Negro slaves became general. The Africans were urgently needed, because no Indian had the physique to withstand the brutal demands of the Spaniards, and the slave trade became an especially lucrative business for Bishop Vitoria. Most

---

* Friedrich Muthmann, *Die Silberne Taufschale zy Siegen.* Heidelberg: Karl Winter, Universitätsverlag, 1956.

of the slaves came from the Portuguese colony of Angola on the west coast of Africa, which bordered the Atlantic Ocean and had been in Portuguese hands since the fifteenth century. The frequent animosities between the tribes gave the powerful ruler of Angola a good excuse to arrange for raiding parties to capture inland Negroes whom he then sold to traders at Luanda, his capital. There is data that some slave dealers had permits that allowed them to import as many as forty thousand slaves in the short span of a few years.

Elaborate gifts were an absolute necessity when an emissary or messenger was despatched to a friendly power, and the silver basin was probably presented as a gift to the African king by the bishop of Tucumán. Sometime later, in 1643, on the occasion of despatching a slave ship from Africa to Recife, Brazil, the African king, Manni Congo, is recorded as having presented the basin to the governor of the port, Johann Moritz, Count of Nassau. At that time the city was the capital of the highly lucrative Dutch colony on the east coast of South America, which only lasted from 1630 to 1654. In 1644, the count was recalled to Europe and, subsequently, was elevated to the rank of prince. As such, he became elector and participated at Frankfurt-am-Main in naming the new ruler of the Holy Roman Empire, Leopold I of Habsburg (1658). It is there that the silver basin probably received its base and the new prince's coat of arms, together with the dedicatory text that identifies it as belonging to the house of Nassau. Thence, it was presented by the prince to the church of St. Nicholas in Siegen, Westphalia.

This piece shows the real *mestizaje* or blend of Old and New World imagery. Many such objects have disappeared through the trapdoor of history, and many others have not been recognized as documents of the period in which the Americas contributed so much to the enrichment of Europe. It is one of the strange accidents of history that this Baroque silver vessel, which is the work of Indian craftsmen of the High Andes, should have passed from the hands of a Roman Catholic bishop to an African king, crossed the ocean three times, and finally come to rest in a German Protestant church where it still serves as baptismal font.

Birds are one of the attributes often used in allegorical depictions of the Americas. Papageno and Papagena, the birdman and his mate dressed in feathers in Mozart's *The Magic Flute* (1791), are relatives of Rousseau's "noble savage," migrants from More's Utopia. One of Jean-Philippe Rameau's ballets, *Les Indes galantes,* first performed in 1735, is laid in Peru. In a booklet published in Paris, the composer refers to Garcilasso de la Vega, the Peruvian mestizo who wrote the history of the conquest of his native land, and urges the producer of the ballet to use the "taste and scientific information" of that distant period so as not to lose the grace of the work. Alas, in a modern revival at the Grand Opera in Paris (1954), the designer overlooked the ethnological material available in the great museums there and produced imaginary costumes and scenery of an irritating falsity.

Feather mosaic, a fascinating pre-Columbian technique unknown to Europe, was expertly practiced in the Mexican, Maya, and Andean areas. Colorful plumage from native birds was affixed to the fabrics of shirts or mantles, arranged in flamboyant headdresses, applied to shields, standards, fans. In some cases, the feathers were glued to the base; the more usual method was to attach each to a thread and stitch this to the woven piece, row by row. When in place, the feathers were neatly clipped to sharpen the design. Feathers of domesticated macaws and parrots are quite commonly found in such work, offering a considerable color range. Others, still more dazzling, came from birds of the tropical rain forest—notably from the many varieties of hummingbird—or were imported from distant valleys. Some plumage, such as that of the quetzal of Central America, shimmering now green, now gold, was reserved for the ornamentation of the privileged class. Montezuma is said to have kept an aviary of exotic birds for his pleasure and use, and the Aztec tribute roll has a record of the bundles of feathers exacted from tribes of the lowlands.

An Aztec featherwork shield [6.15] is mounted on a jaguar pelt stretched on a wooden frame about two feet in diameter. The subject is a rampant coyote, one symbol of the fire-god of the Aztecs. Tufted fiery plumage forms a radiating fringe. The design is made up of turquoise-blue and purple feathers against a background of shimmering red. Mouth, claws, eyes, and ragged tail are outlined with thin gold strips to striking effect.

It is not clear how much the Indian understood of the pictures of holy personages he saw displayed on Spanish banners and in books. But what the native craftsman did with the models laid out for him to "copy" soon became evident.

In the illustration [6.16], we see a bishop's miter that was constructed in a manner similar to the pagan Aztec shield. This side is viewed from the back of the prelate, showing the *infulae*, or lappets—also in featherwork—that hang down across the shoulders. Depicted is the Tree of Jesse, branching up from the recumbent figure of the patriarch, who is flanked by two lions. On its branches, the twelve kings of the Old Testament emerge from lotuslike bases, surrounded by leaves, tendrils, and bunches of grapes. At the top, the Virgin and Child sit enthroned in a radiant aureole. A butterfly and a scattering of birds fill the spaces at the sides.

On the opposite side, which is the front of the miter, the Crucifix dominates [6.17]. Angels collect the holy blood in cups. Peter stands at the left, with two keys and an open book, and Paul at the right with a sword and a book. The Cross emerges as a tree from the tomb of Adam resting again on two lions. And the twelve Apostles, each with his own attributes and a book, emerge again from lotuslike platforms among the arabesques of the grape-laden branches. At the foot of the Cross, the Four Evangelists can be seen writing their Gospels with quill pens: Luke with his symbol, the steer; Mark with the lion; John with the eagle; and Matthew with a small angel kneeling before him dictating.

The jewel-like beauty and glowing tones of such a piece can scarcely be imagined. The sky in the background is an iridescent blue-purple with stars shading from pale to dark yellow. The closed eyes of the Christ are indicated by tiny crescents of gold feathers.

This miter is believed to have been made at the order of Bishop Vasco de Quiroga, who spent seven years in the state of Michoacán, Mexico, and is famed for his just and perspicacious leadership. He returned to Spain in 1547, and three years later, presented the featherwork miter to Pedro de la Graca, the bishop of Palencia in Spain, whose coat of arms is now quite crudely stitched on one side. The emblems on the lappets, also, refer to the family and order of the bishop who wore it.

Such feather-mosaic work was employed for various regalia connected with the Roman Catholic church. Holy pictures also were executed in different sizes. When I was making my first survey in the British Museum in 1935, an obscure person brought in a picture in feather mosaic, about eight by six inches, representing Christ at the Column. After I had exclaimed at the rarity of such work, the curator turned to me and asked whether I would be willing to buy it, because for such acquisitions the museum lacked funds. The miter reproduced here, I saw for the first time in Vienna in 1933. But the photograph I ordered in that inflation-torn capital was so poor that it could not be included in my earlier work, and another miter, now in Florence, was substituted. Besides the two mentioned, there are two others with more or less the same iconography now in Spain: one in the Escorial, the other in Toledo. The Viennese piece was originally deposited in Schloss Ambras, near Innsbruck, and is mentioned for the first time in an inventory taken in 1596 of the various curiosa that the Habsburgs had stored there. Some feather-decorated pieces occurred among the late Incas and perhaps in the early colonial period. *Huipils* with this kind of embellishment can still be found in the state of Chiapas, Mexico.

The methods used in these bishops' miters were those of ancient times: the feathers, not wider than one eighth of an inch, were glued on strips of *amate* fiber paper, so placed to overlap smoothly, then fastened to cloth. The glue was manufactured from the juice of an orchid plant. Though the Indian artist's comprehension of the various hierarchy of the Christian church can be doubted, nevertheless, following the models with an amazing skill and exactitude and adding some graceful decorative touches of his own, he has produced a beguiling document of the Transition period.

[6.1] Pottery beaker. Asunción Mita, Guatemala.

[6.2] Inca gold beaker. Peru.

[6.4] Inlaid wood kero. 16th century. Peru.

[6.3] Late Inca or early colonial wood kero. Peru.

[6.5] Central Coast tapestry and brocading, detail. Pre-Columbian. Peru.

[6.6] Colonial Inca tapestry. Peru.

[6.7] Mochica bowl. Peru.

[6.8] Inca vase. Peru.

[6.9] Colonial tapestry. Peru.

[6.10] Colonial silver plaque. Peru.

[6.11] Chimú gold earspool. Peru.

[6.12] Colonial gold armband. Peru.

[6.13] Colonial silver bowl. Peru.

[6.14] Detail of silver bowl.

[6.15] Aztec featherwork shield. Mexico.

[6.16] Bishop's miter in featherwork. Mexico.

[6.17] Front view of bishop's miter.

7/The Colony Builds

The first churches in the Hispanic colonies were simple barnlike structures; the first dwellings, merely shelters raised when some native building could not be adapted. Soon there was an effort to replace these with more pretentious edifices. By the early seventeenth century, the New World is said to have had seventy thousand churches and chapels—some twenty thousand in Mexico alone—and five hundred monasteries and convents.

The colonial builder was faced with a number of situations for which there was no precedent in the Old World. Plans for colonial buildings were not blueprints, neatly calculated to the sixteenth of an inch, but, rather, they were sketches. Sometimes they were sent from Spain. More often they were drawn up in the colony and—theoretically, at least—submitted to Spain for approval. However, of the more than four hundred plans for buildings in the Americas and the Philippines which have so far been published from the Archive of the Indies in Seville, less than 6 percent date from before 1610, and anyone who has studied the designs can see how many changes occurred in the process of execution.

The main labor force was drawn from the people of the countryside. They followed the instructions of the itinerant carpenters (*maestro canteros*), master masons, sculptors, painters, and *ensambladores* (best translated as the coordinator or foreman of the project, who might belong to any of the crafts). Books, drawings, etchings, woodcuts of European art and architecture, as well as treatises and handbooks on techniques, were the sources of information and inspiration. Printing—a new craft even in Europe—was introduced into the New World as early as 1539.

Building materials were available in abundance. In many districts, the natives were skilled in the manufacture of adobe bricks and blocks even before the Conquest. Some regions furnished a soft stone, easy to quarry and to carve, which hardened upon exposure to the air. Magnificent virgin forests provided extremely hard, durable lumber for beams, rafters, even columns. The Indians were accustomed to moving incredible weights over long distances without the aid of the wheel or beasts of burden. Highly skilled even with the primitive tools of ancient times, they soon became masters when hard metal tools were placed in their hands and the technical achievements of contemporary Europe were taught them.

There was an immediate need for offices for the administration of colonial affairs, where documents could be filed away and legal claims settled. The town hall at Ixtlán in southern Mexico is a relic of that bygone time [7.2]. A simple structure housing a row of rooms with windows at the back and a porch with plain columns across the front was enough to serve this community, though it soon became known for its silver and gold mines. Here is an early, rural version of the splendid colonnaded administration buildings that would later grace one side of the main plaza in numerous colonial cities—with the main church on one side, the governor's palace opposite, and a fountain in the center that provided clean water for the benefit of the community.

The lords of the civilian administration soon started, also, to construct houses for themselves. The walls might be of adobe or of stone and mortar painted over, the roofs of thatch or sod; but the coats of arms and decorations carved in stone give them distinction.

The heavy thatched roof of the Zavala mansion on the main square of Juli, Peru, on Lake Titicaca, harks back to pre-Columbian traditions [7.3]. It is practical and warm in a region that has little large timber and where the temperature plunges from the 60's and 70's to below freezing when the sun sinks.

Cortés established a seat for himself in the region of southern Mexico that the Indians called Huayacac, from which its present name of Oaxaca is derived. The first buildings were never substantial and, therefore, were soon either strengthened and changed or abandoned for another site. Meanwhile, legends developed, so that a number of buildings are today connected with great names from the first decade without any substantiation whatever in fact.

An old house popularly known as Cortés's is now ascribed to the family of one Laso de la Vega [7.4], according to records that cover the period from 1560 to 1578. Massive stone blocks form the walls. The windows are placed high for good ventilation. The modest Plateresque decoration of the doorframe and the balcony, with its broad heraldic panel containing two coats of arms, give the building character. Plain stone columns support a broad gallery around the second story of the inner court.

The evangelization of the Indians started even before the Conquest was consolidated. It was necessary to erect solid buildings that could house an increasing number of clergy and to create facilities for the mass conversion of the natives. The monastic churches of the mid-sixteenth century are lofty and stark. They frequently boast groined vaulting in the Gothic manner, and the decoration is often a rustic interpretation of the Spanish Plateresque. A predilection for the dome appears at an early date, especially in Mexico. The sturdy walls, massive towers, and even the atrium walls are often crenelated, suggesting the term "fortress church" to early investigators. In Europe, before Christianity was firmly established, and even later, when Tartars, Turks, and other foes overran certain regions, the solidly built, stone fortress churches, indeed, served for defense—Luther's "A Mighty Fortress Is Our God" did not have only spiritual connotations. Crenelation, however, long survived as a decorative element on the otherwise stark edifices.

The Dominican foundation at Tepoztlán, near Cuernavaca, Mexico, was established in 1559 and completed some thirty years later [7.5]. The fact that it is in a cul de sac, framed by mountains, and near a rather sleepy village whose population still speaks Nahuatl (Aztec) has saved it so far from much modernization. The complex stands on an unusually wide platform. Its walls are about twelve feet thick, and close-set pillarlike buttresses give the structure monumentality. On the façade, the unbroken pediment carries a carving of the Virgin and Child flanked by favorite saints of the Dominican order. The shallow-cut sculptural work gives the impression of a woodcut transposed into stone.

In spite of its severe lines and medieval appearance, the church of Aranzazú in Guadalajara, Mexico [7.6], is an eighteenth-century structure, part of a group of four churches, each of which occupied a corner on Franciscan property to form the so-called Garden of St. Francis. Built of rough stone and with little exterior decoration, in keeping with the Franciscan credo, it exemplifies the persistence of visual tradition. At an earlier period, such a fortresslike corner tower was needed as a buttress. Here, it is little more than a picturesque addition. A Basque family defrayed the cost of this building, commemorating in it a popular aspect of the Virgin in their native land. The interior is ablaze with an ornate main altar and homogeneously gilded retables at the sides.

An ingenious means of solving the immediate missionary problem—the instruction of the pagan masses by a handful of clergy—was the so-called open chapel. A church might have no more than its foundation laid, the friars sleeping in improvised huts, when the open chapel would already be in use. This was an apselike construction, open on one side to face the large square or atrium of the establishment—like the orchestra shell in a modern festival park. It was large enough to house an altar and the necessary paraphernalia to hold services before hundreds, even thousands, of Indians, whom frequently the military drove in to attend.

In a few Old World churches, a somewhat parallel architectural solution can be surmised. The Spanish chapel of Santa Maria Novella in Florence stands open on one side facing a spacious square, and although today shut off by grill-work, it has all the marks of an open chapel. Paolo Uccello (1397–1475) depicts a similar structure in the predella to his "Transportation of the Miraculous Host in the Corpus Christi Procession" at Urbino. A number of Italian churches have outside pulpits, projecting from the walls toward the piazza, where a priest or friar could reach a far larger audience than he could inside. An exquisite example survives in the Duomo at Prato in Toscana, Italy.

Another characteristic of these early monasteries were the *posas,* small pavilions situated at the four corners of the large enclosed atrium, which served as stopping places for out-of-door processions. The *posa* may have a distant relationship with the domed pavilions similarly placed in the courtyards of great Muslim mosques, where religious instruction was given and refreshment dispensed to weary pilgrims, and where usually a fountain of pure water still functions.

European practices suggest that the *posa* had a place there, also, for even today processions—praying for rain, giving thanks for the harvest, bearing an important corpse to a funeral ceremony—stop before improvised or permanent out-of-door shrines for prayers or a religious service.

Most of the surviving fortress churches of Latin America are found in Mexico—among them, Huejotzingo and Acolmán near Mexico City; Cuitzeo and Yuririapundaro in central Mexico; Yanhuitlán in the state of Oaxaca. The former Dominican establishment of San Pedro y San Pablo at Teposcolula, also in Oaxaca, presents a lesser-known though striking example of such a monastic complex.

The tourist who drives his car in an unceasing rush on the Oaxaca-Puebla-Mexico City road, to proudly make his five or six hundred miles a day, bypasses the town, though it would mean only a half hour's turnoff on a gravel road to reach a sight of rare quality. Passing through a shabby settlement and crossing an unkempt garden, the visitor comes upon a great sunken plaza, with a stone mission cross in the center, and on the left, the so-called open chapel [7.8]. Two flaring masonry arms thrust forward from the center of a rectangular colonnade. The multiple arrangement of arches—the tallest some forty feet in height—gives life to what otherwise might seem today a useless pile of stone. The paneling on the piers, the decorative moldings that garland the arches, the fluting of the columns, have a rare linear perfection, like architectural drawings translated into stone.

Whether the structure was designed to be as it stands or was planned as the beginning of a huge, never-finished church remains an unanswered question. It is said to have been begun early in the last quarter of the sixteenth century, at a time when the place was enjoying great prosperity. Teposcolula was among the first communities to produce silk. Salt was mined nearby, and it was here that the glowing red dye from the cochineal —so important even in pre-Columbian times—was prepared. But the Dominicans quarreled with the feudal landlords; sections of the town became waterlogged after the rains; and an epidemic of plague swept over the place. All three factors contributed to a sharp decline in population. The distinguished building was abandoned. The dome collapsed, taking with it parts of the roof, and whatever interior decoration there was has long since vanished. One of the few buildings having a true Renaissance flair has been left to the caprices of the weather. With its piers stepping forward into open space, the two winglike inner buttresses, the suave panel-like decoration, it has unequaled elegance.

As if to assert the range of artistic talent, to the unfinished symphony of distinguished quality, a folkloristic coda was appended. The rustic façade of the adjacent church shows classic leanings. The niches are high, but the statues within them are either oversized or have been brought from somewhere else. A figure in monastic garb [7.9] is apparently the seraphic St. Francis. On the stone at his feet, darker than the rest of the façade, is carved the bust of an angel in medieval warrior's dress, carrying a lance and surrounded by elements that have no relation whatever to the decorative scheme of the exterior [7.7]. A garland ending in volutes frames the top, its overlapping leaves strikingly like the overlapping plumes of the ancient Feathered Serpent. This theme is repeated in the bases of two other niches, each angel carrying a symbol of the Passion. One wonders if they could be the capitals of pillars that once decorated a far earlier building.

Inside, the cheap pews, the bare whitewashed walls, and the reconstructed main altar show the devastating effects of late-nineteenth- and early-twentieth-century taste. Luckily there apparently was not enough money to "modernize" a left side altar. A foliated niche, high up in the lavishly gilded ornate retable, frames a dramatic statuary group of the Descent from the Cross [7.10]. Christ's body hangs limp; the men leaning over the Cross make a desperate effort not to drop Him—the two Marys are too emotionally involved to be of much use. The scene, so often repeated in painting and sculpture, has more than realism here: one has the feeling of viewing a stage where the tragedy is being enacted. The directness of the presentation, the crowding of the group into such a small space, makes one speculate whether this sculpture may have originally belonged to some other building.

Though they are less known than those in Mexico, South America also had the same type of early missionary complex, of which the Basilica of

Copacabana, Bolivia, is an outstanding example [7.12]. Like many another Christian edifice in both the Old and the New World, it stands over a spot long held sacred by a previous religion—in this case, on a promontory over-looking the crescent-shaped bay of Lake Titicaca, a famous pilgrim sanctuary in pre-Columbian times. The present building was dedicated toward the end of the seventeenth century, incorporating an earlier structure. Some of the crenelated walls of the atrium are still standing. *Posas* can be seen in the four corners, roofed with tiles, along with the domes and tower of the main building. More and more *posas* are being identified in the Andean highlands as investigations proceed, and perhaps some will also be recognized in Central America, where large communities of Indians are still functioning.

A side altar in the Basilica of Copacabana [7.14] is one of the few remnants left from the earlier period. Documented as having been "made" by a friar, the prior of the place, and painted by an Indian in 1618, it was, apparently, the main altar before the enlargement of the building, and it remains a favorite with the Ayamara Indians who inhabit the region. The retable has the serenity of the Plateresque. Busts of the six sibyls who foresaw the coming of Christ adorn the sides—a study not only in color but also in costume and hair arrangement. Although, no doubt, retouched during its more than three hundred years of existence, much of its original appeal is still present.

The church of San Juan in Juli, Peru, clearly shows the changes an early colonial structure might go through in the course of time [7.11]. Erected by the Dominicans at the end of the sixteenth century, it was originally a simple barnlike building of adobe, rubble, and wood. About a century later, it came into the hands of the Jesuits; they added a Baroque side portal of stone—quite a contrast to the classically inspired main entrance—and built a new apse and side chapels of excellent masonry to achieve a cruciform plan. Inside, a series of paintings on canvas tell the story of St. John the Baptist. The elaborately carved and heavily gilded wooden frames form a veritable screen along the walls and give a warmth to the interior unsuspected from the austere outside. Windows are cut only in the thick left wall of the nave, which raises the question whether the wall seen in the illustration was once open like a colonnade, as is postulated in some early Mexican churches. Because no glass was available, alabaster scraped thin enough to be translucent or oiled hide stretched on a wooden frame was used for the windowpanes. In the church of San Juan, some of the alabaster is still in place.

A gay-flowered woven material once covered the ceiling. It now hangs in tatters, revealing the structure of the roof as it was made in a number of regions. The frame consisted of rough timbers, fastened with withes or ropes, and sealed, sometimes with close-woven mats of straw, sometimes with layers of reeds and twigs bound together. Here, it is capped with tile. Roofs of corrugated iron now cover many highland churches. As incongruous as this modern material is, it has proven practical in the face of the terrific electrical storms that frequently endanger these tallest buildings in a village.

In the rustic structure at Cahabon, Guatemala, one can see a Central American version of the early missionary establishment [7.13]. It is not for nothing that the district of Alta Vera Paz has the word for peace in its name. The Indians were reportedly mild and amenable. Thomas Gage— the Dominican, later turned Anglican—who visited the Americas between 1625 and 1637, mentions the pleasant living conditions of the padres who administered the order's vast hacienda in that tropical paradise, only 740 feet above sea level. He describes, also, the difficulties of access. Indeed, until quite recently, in order to reach the capital of Guatemala from Cahabon, it was better to go by water—down the rapids to Lake Izabal and thence into the bay which opens into the Atlantic—than to climb over mountain ranges and through ravines by the more direct route.

The extent of the property can be seen from the photo, taken before 1890. Within a spacious walled square, the great barn church reveals itself in full size. The façade is expanded into a towering wall with bells— the *espadaña*. The roof is tiled. One can see from the finials that decorate the crumbling enclosure that crenelation served here as ornament.

When Anne and Alfred Maudslay visited Cahabon, toward the end of the last century, the place had not a shadow of its former glory. The once main church of the Dominican Order now served only a small community. Its parish priest was a Dutchman who jovially remarked that all of the Indians in the community worked on his coffee *finca* and herded his numerous cattle. He said he charged two dollars for a marriage ceremony and one dollar for a baptism, and when a cow broke into the Indians' land, that meant trouble, unless it happened to be one of his, in which case it would be led out gently. Small wonder that such a paternalistic system has today broken down.

Another category of ecclesiastical colonial buildings comprises the churches of large cities, including the cathedrals where bishops and, later, archbishops vied with one another in erecting magnificent structures, straining their resources in labor and funds. The first cathedral in the New World was begun between 1520 and 1523 on the island that Columbus named Hispaniola—now Santo Domingo. Attributed to a Spanish architect, it has Gothic features but is outspokenly Plateresque in style.

The cathedral in Mexico City bears the mark of every phase in colonial history. Erected on the ruins of the main Aztec temple, it was begun in the somber style of the Spanish architect Herrera, but its interior represents the rich Baroque of later centuries. In the mid-eighteenth century, the Sagrario was built adjacent to it, the joint work of a Spanish-born architect, Lorenzo Rodríguez, and an Indian sculptor. Made of red and white stone, with richly carved façades on both sides, the Sagrario is considered to be the prototype of Mexican Churrigueresque architecture. The cathedral towers are still later in date; and the dome, designed by Manuel Tolsa, also Spanish-born, was completed in 1813. Tolsa is responsible, as well, for the equestrian bronze statue of Charles IV of Spain, "the Caballito," that stands at the beginning of the Paseo de la Reforma. Modeled and cast in Mexico, it is a notable piece of Mexican colonial craftsmanship.

Although the Madrid-born architect José Churriguera (1650–1723) never set foot in the New World, the style named for him—the Churrigueresque—became extremely popular in some regions of Hispanic America. Pomp was paramount in that age, and his designs created a furor in Spain. Combining elements of the Italian Renaissance and the Baroque, he produced a symphony for the eye, composed of wreaths, garlands, columns, scrolls, carved drapery, medallions, candelabra, flags, vases, balustrades, obelisks, religious and mythological statues. Imported into Mexico in the early eighteenth century and seized upon by the native imagination, the style reached a monumentality and picturesqueness that surpassed that of its creator. Characteristic is the *estípite,* the inverted obelisk, of Italian antecedence, which often replaces a column or pilaster.

The conquistadores had filled the canals that crisscrossed the ancient Aztec capital with rubble from the wrecked palaces and temples of Montezuma. The ground was often ill prepared, and even today many important buildings in Mexico City are sinking, some as much as a foot a year. Great cracks appeared on both the outside and inside walls of the magnificent cathedral. Caissons were sunk—as in modern bridge building—and concrete piers put in to support the old structure. While the work was in progress, one could see remnants of marine life under the rubble of Aztec building material, for the piers were placed on the floor of what had once been the Aztec Lake Texcoco.

In the spring of 1967, faulty electric wiring put up for a feast day caused a fire in the cathedral shortly before midnight. Not until the early morning hours could some official be found to open the doors. The cedar choir stalls were destroyed with their fine series of fifty-nine saints in relief, the work of Juan de Rojas at the end of the seventeenth century. Two splendid organs that towered like galleons of the faith above the choir were gutted. The organ pipes made of tumbaga, a metal alloy with a low melting point, hung limp after the fire like sooty stalactites. Another complete loss was the Altar of Pardon at the entrance of the building, which served as a decorative backing to the monumental choir. Since then, two opposite factions have been arguing whether the damaged parts of the cathedral should be restored or totally dismantled.

Cortés established his viceregal seat in the living heart of the former Aztec empire. The colonial administration, therefore, came into close contact with the multitude of pre-Columbian inhabitants. (Mexico is the only modern republic in which both the Indian and the mestizo population have a worthy position.) In Peru, Pizarro created a new city on the sands of the Pacific, and Hispanic colonial life there concentrated around that capital, named Lima from the small Rimac River nearby. The place was inhospitable in climate and plagued by frequent earthquakes.

The first cathedral there was completed in 1551 and very soon enlarged, so that by the end of the century a new structure had, in effect, risen. In the succeeding centuries, however, earthquakes wrought constant havoc in the city, and except for some retables and wood carvings, the entire cathedral is modern, though kept in colonial style.

The rich lands in the highlands were distributed among the families of the conquistadores, protégés of the Spanish king and friends of the viceroy, all of whom were drawn toward the capital in the lowlands. In 1650, Cuzco suffered a damaging earthquake, after which the city was practically rebuilt. The cathedral, which dates from that time, occupies a special place in the colonial architecture of Peru [7.15]. It is a noble and original building, that set the style for the whole highland region. Dominating the immense Plaza de Armas, which is fringed with colonnaded mansions from colonial times, it rises from a spacious platform adjoined, left and right, by smaller churches. Two elaborate belfries top its stalwart towers. Decoration is concentrated on the portals.

The Jesuit church, the Compañía, stands at the right, and next to it, the former seminary that today houses the University of Cuzco. All the buildings are homogeneous, built of the reddish-brown andesite of the region, and offer a characteristically unique aspect. Another devastating earthquake struck Cuzco in 1950, and reconstruction has produced a rather modern Spanish idealization of how a Hispanic-colonial city should look.

The peoples who built Tiahuanaco and Sachsahuamán had the talent to construct the superb masonry work, the lofty barrel vaults that mark much of the seventeenth- and eighteenth-century architecture of the Andean highlands. The gigantic church of Santiago, Pomata, built inside and out of rose-colored local stone, dates from approximately the first quarter of the eighteenth century. Its barrel-vaulted nave has a steely perfection of line, alleviated by elaborately carved cornices and the lacy ornamentation of the splayed windows that pierce the vault all down the left wall [7.16].

The dome is, also, a masterly construction, with rather sparse decoration.

Pomata seems to have been one of the relay stations to and from Bolivia even in pre-Columbian times. The colonial administration had no reason to disturb the communication network that now served their interest. Its magnificent and immense church can be seen as one approaches, looming across a shallow bay of Lake Titicaca, a contrast to the huts of the native population around it.

Relatively little change occurred in Tunja, Colombia, until the present century, and that city, once rich from nearby gold and silver mines, long retained many early local architectural features. A Mudéjar ceiling, constructed in wood, survives in the church of San Francisco there [7.17]. It is tray-shaped, and its beams carry an interlacing pattern reminiscent of Near Eastern tiles. The figures in the side panels of the main retable emerge from their gilded background in the half round—a type of statuary that later was no longer made. The framing is mild, with a series of cherub heads in the frieze and columns of a Renaissance type. The altar and pulpit seem contemporaneous in date. A golden ring on top of the baldachin encloses a carved crucifix, beyond which the face of a golden sun on the wall can be seen, surmounted by a dove—a striking and unusual presentation of the Throne of Mercy, an aspect of the Trinity that emphasizes the Redemption.

Another Franciscan church in the capital of a neighboring country—Quito, Ecuador—shows the evolution of an interior over more than two centuries [7.18]. Much of the wealth of this region was derived from traffic, both legal and illegal, in cocoa beans shipped out in great quantities through the port of Guayaquil. Quito itself, which lies at an altitude of nearly ten thousand feet—an arduous journey from the Pacific—was a center of missionary work from the earliest settlement. Its friars penetrated far beyond the eastern slopes of the Andes and into the north, as well as southward along communication routes established in pre-Columbian times. A number of excellent artists and craftsmen throve in this rich community. By the third quarter of the eighteenth century, the export of statues and other religious objects to distant colonial regions had reached considerable proportions.

The church of the Franciscan order, begun in 1564, is a veritable museum of Quito's colonial art. Mudéjar ceilings survive in the crossing and transepts, rimmed with panels of saints, again in the half round. The side aisles consist of a series of connected chapels, each crowned with a dome and lavishly furnished. The nave, damaged by earthquake in the mid-eighteenth century, is sheathed with gold motifs against rose-colored walls. The main retable, highly Baroque, fills the deep apse. At the center stands the figure of the Woman of the Apocalypse as described in Chapter 12 of Revelation. The statue is signed by Bernardo Legarda and dated 1734.

Legarda's masterpiece, another example of the same figure, is illustrated later. [See 8.11.] The elaborate pulpit, the combination of large paintings, statues, and gilded floral decoration, are in their richness almost overwhelming.

The Andean highlands produced a style often called "mestizo"—that flowering of Spanish architectural and decorative elements in the hands of native craftsmen. At Arequipa, an oasis of rich land and abundant water on the west shoulder of the Andes, one finds expressive polychrome stuccowork in this style. Characteristic work in stone can also be observed in the main façade of the Compañía, the Jesuit church there, which is covered with tapestrylike relief carving [7.19]. In a round medallion at the lower right, one reads 1698. Only the lower section of the columns is ornamented. The plain upper shafts divide the façade into various fields, each of which carries a somewhat different pattern. Note the treatment of the choir window. The main pediment is not only broken but separated at such a distance that one has to search for the two wings with their slight scrolls to recognize its original architectural elements. Unfortunately, a recent earthquake has so damaged this rarely telling structure that only the central portion of the façade remains.

The *corregidor* or mayor of a colonial city was a man of power, especially if the place was as rich as Potosí and covered as much territory. It is recorded that the office of alderman there sold for eighteen thousand silver pesos. There were thirty of these officials, and, indeed, in the early seventeenth century, it might have been well worth the price to have a hand in the affairs of such a city. At that time, the white population consisted mainly of mine and mill owners, to which, of course, must be added transient adventurers, merchants and tradesmen, officials on inspection tours.

The mayor's mansion at Potosí, dating from the mid-seventeenth century, displays the mestizo style with a greater depth of carving—all the more effective in a climate where sun and shadow produce an uncalculated aesthetic bonus. The house has three portals, each decorated somewhat differently. In this detail [7.20], the variety of motifs can be seen.

In the Compañía at Arequipa, the pediment is broken to near unrecognizability. Here the pilasters provide just another surface for decoration. The separate sections ornamented by spirals and wavy lines give especial life to the over-all pattern. The "leaf-sprites," little human figures emerging from foliage, are especially characteristic of this highland region. The central window with its heavy iron grille documents the security measures of a bygone century. When the Neoclassic reached these distant provinces, mestizo art came to an end, and with it a telling element of the colonial personality.

At Puno, on the north end of Lake Titicaca, with a large population of Quechua-speaking Indians, the mule trains with their burdens of silver converged, not only from Bolivia but also from Peruvian mines to the north. The cathedral at Puno dominates the landscape, standing amid a group of low-slung dwellings with their enclosed courts [7.21]. Its twin towers overlook Lake Titicaca. Heavy buttresses and built-on annexes bespeak the vicissitudes of time. The original vaulting, destroyed by earthquake or lightning, has been replaced by a wooden ceiling. The dome is typical, and so are the tall transepts that make the structure cross-shaped. In its present form, the building stems from the mid-eighteenth century.

The variety of architecture and art along the rim of this lake can be surmised by comparing Juli [7.3 and 7.11], Copacabana [7.12], Pomata [7.16], and Puno [7.21], in their diversity. Only by visualizing the region with its many Indian huts, its reed balsas on the water, and Indian population all about, can one realize the difficulty of attempting to transplant a European religion and method of living, and understand why the effort never fully succeeded.

The church at Asangaro is evidently an early structure. Built of adobe, it has an earthen floor, and being almost windowless, is very dark inside.

A visitor from the early seventeenth century described the town, which lies somewhat northwest of Puno and Juliaca, as rich and large. Great numbers of llama, sheep, and cattle were raised there, but since it becomes very cold each night, no crops could be grown except small highland potatoes; all other agricultural products had to be brought up from the lower, milder regions. The province had much gold, which was placer mined. Some four thousand souls were registered at that time, of which nearly a thousand paid tribute. The Indian population was forced into unaccustomed labor, and in the second half of the eighteenth century, a considerable reduction in the population occurred. Today the place exhibits only shadows of its former greatness.

The church's interior decoration, however, dating chiefly from the eighteenth century, testifies to the wealth that made it a veritable showplace [7.22]. Large canvases in heavy gold frames mask the walls, and where they could not be hung, mural painting covers the surface like tapestry. The large painting over the transept arch may represent the Adoration of the Shepherds, or more likely, since the Apocrypha was a favorite source of subject matter, the joyful reception of the Holy Family upon their arrival in Egypt. Note the sixteenth-century costume of the participants.

In coastal Peru, the styles are considerably different from those in the highlands. The region around Huanchaco, Department of Lambayeque, on the north coast is well watered, and from the beginning of the colony, labor conditions were better there than in many other places. Lucrative native crops, corn and cacao, and imported ones, such as sugar and rice, thrived. Chroniclers remarked on the masonry tombs from pre-Columbian times, rich with silver, gold, and other paraphernalia for the dead. Archaeologists have since made valuable finds of a distinctive character there. The church at Huanchaco [7.23] is dramatically situated overlooking the Pacific. It dates from the end of the seventeenth century but has since been renovated. Of particular interest is the vaulting of cane and plaster, an ingenious solution to the problem of weight in these regions plagued by earthquake. The sanctuary raised above the nave is a feature that can be seen throughout Latin America. The stone portal, also, with its twin columns, broken pediment, and central oval window is typical. The multiple cornices and pilasters of the sturdy tower lend suavity to an otherwise rather sober structure.

The frequency of earthquakes in this region makes it impossible to visualize the original colonial aspect of Lima. Of the once vast complex belonging to the monastery of Santo Domingo—to the administrators of the Inquisition—the Sala Capitular [7.24], or chapter house, retains its authenticity. The rustication, the deeply carved shells over the entrance and the niche, the massive volutes on the corbels, lend striking plasticity. The carved furnishings in the rich dark wood of the tropics add to the atmosphere of solemn authority. Scenes from the lives of St. Dominic and St. Thomas are depicted in the large canvases. Note the "loge" over the doorway, where dignitaries, unseen, could witness an assembly.

Some of the churches at Trujillo on the north coast of Peru have fared better than those in Lima, despite earthquakes and, in colonial days, repeated harassment by pirates. Built quite close to the site of the Chimú city Chan-Chan, the place was named by Francisco Pizarro after his native town in Spain. In the Franciscan church there, a gigantic retable devoted to the life of the Virgin reaches into the vaulted ceiling, with the jutting overhang characteristic of coastal Peru [7.25]. At the center, Mary floats heavenward surrounded by angels over the heads of the astonished Apostles. The carving is of a fine pale wood with some polychroming but no gilding. A companion altar in the opposite side chapel depicts the life of Christ. It, also, is in natural wood and is perhaps somewhat earlier, as the carving is less ebullient.

The conventual establishments for friars and (later) nuns reached a grand scale. Supported by contributions and bequests from the devout and by income from fertile lands, they provided an amazing display of ornaments, splendid robes, embroideries, and fine music at their public ceremonies. Like the Franciscan church in Quito, already mentioned [see 7.18], the Compañía there was long in building. It is made entirely of stone. Lunettes that pierce the barrel vaulting provide a clear and serene light. The walls are covered with an interlaced pattern in stucco on a red ground, and the altars display the somewhat pompous Baroque preferred by the Jesuits.

The façade of this church [7.26] was designed by two friars in the first half of the eighteenth century: first, a German, Leonard Deubler; then, an Italian, Venancio Gandolfi. The building's massive exterior and ornate interior, however, have a flavor not found in any European land.

Splendid organs, with their reedy-toned pipes enclosed in gilt and polychromed cases, were essential to the *comparserie* of the great monastic establishments. Nunneries, especially, were often famous for their music, and in some, singing and the playing of instruments were taught. At the beginning, organ works were imported from Europe, but even then the cases were generally locally made, as were later the entire instruments.

The organ in La Merced, the church of the Mercedarian order in Quito, occupies one arm of a **U**-shaped choir loft [7.27]. Resplendent in red and gold, with horizontal pipes held by angelic figures, it probably dates from the eighteenth century and is said still to function. The illustration gives an idea of the characteristic strapwork on the walls, rather similar to that in Quito's Compañía.

An especial solidity marks the buildings of Guatemala. Thick walls, massive buttresses, heavy squat towers, indicate precautions against recurrent earthquakes. There is a preference for brick domes. The lavish use of stucco ornamentation and color produces a particular combination of grandeur and naïveté that gives this "earthquake Baroque" its character.

Antigua, known in colonial times as Santiago de Guatemala, was the seat of a captaincy general with jurisdiction over the land from roughly the northern border of Chiapas to Panama. The city was laid out with broad avenues, spacious gardens, and notably elegant fountains flowing with clean water. Despite repeated earthquakes—in this case, of volcanic origin—the inhabitants of the capital rebuilt their city after each catastrophe until they could boast of having a cathedral, nine monasteries, five nunneries, more than a score of churches, a university, a seminary, schools, hospitals, impressive government buildings, and many mansions, all within little more than one square mile. In 1773, when the city was again ravaged by earthquake, the newly-arrived captain general decreed its abandonment and moved the capital to the site we now know as Guatemala City. The ruins, left unrepaired, constitute an open-air museum of an eighteenth-century colonial town. It has been declared a national monument and is undergoing carefully supervised restoration.

The builders of Central America used native limestone, mortar, and stucco, so ably handled by the Maya in pre-Columbian times. The church of Merced in Antigua, illustrated at the bottom of the page, is an outstanding example of this work [7.29]. Its walls are very thick, the windows small, the towers ponderous. But the lacy filigree of stuccowork over the entire façade lends an air of lightness, even gaiety, to the whole effect. The builders essayed a dome at the crossing and another over the sacristy, both of which survived the catastrophe of 1773. Sixteen large green glazed ceramic lions, locally made, guard the larger dome—a touch of the *chinoiserie* that had become popular through trade with the Philippines.

By the eighteenth century in most areas, the architect and sculptor had brought the design of the retable out into the open air, with its niches containing statues and flanked by columns, its broken pediments and garlandlike ornamentation. Here a statue of Our Lady of Mercy stands in the deeply recessed choir window, as in the central niche of a high altar. The pediment is playfully elaborated. Note the horizontally grooved pilasters on the upper members of the towers and the flattened urnlike forms just below them—features especially popular in provincial architecture of the region. The cloister entrance (left) is a model of balance and refined design. Some of the covered walks were roofed with corbeled vaults in the Maya manner.

The great pilgrim sanctuary of Esquipulas in southeast Guatemala [7.28] houses a much-revered crucifix, blackened with age and the smoke of incense and candles, to which a chapel was dedicated as early as 1595. Like many similar places of pilgrimage, it stands, apparently, on the site of a pagan shrine. Maya carvings have been found nearby, and an ancient road is said to connect it with Copán, Honduras, only a day's journey away on foot.

John L. Stephens in his *Incidents of Travel in Central America, Chiapas, and Yucatán,* published over a hundred years ago, brings the place alive in his description:

> We commenced ascending the great Sierra, which divides the streams of the Atlantic from those that empty into the Pacific Ocean. In two hours we reached the top. The scenery was wild and grand. The view from the top was most magnificent and descending, the clouds were lifted and running from the foot of the Sierra upon an almost boundless plain, afar off we saw, standing alone in the wilderness the great church of Esquipulas. . . .
>
> We entered by a lofty portal, rich in sculptured ornaments, the nave with two aisles, separated by rows of pilasters 9 feet square, and a lofty dome, guarded by angels with expanded wings. . . . The recesses were filled with statues, some of which were admirably well executed, the pulpit was covered with gold leaf, and the altar, protected by an iron railing, with a silver balustrade, ornamented with six silver pillars. In front of the altar, in a rich shrine, an image of the Savior on the Cross "Our Lord of Esquipulas", famed for its power of working miracles. . . .

The present building was completed in the mid-eighteenth century. Though in a book dedicated to the general reader, it would be inappropriate to enumerate craftsmen and artists whose fame seldom spreads beyond the scene of their activities, mention must, nevertheless, be made of the Porras family of Guatemala, some of whose members had a part in the erection of Esquipulas and were also concerned with the plans for the vast cathedral of León, Nicaragua.

Instead of the oft-repeated postcard view of the façade, the back and side of the building are seen, revealing unknown details to the armchair traveler. It is a rarity to find a structure with four towers. Heavy cornices emphasize the church's monumentality. Its several entrances are all equally elaborated. The dome is now covered with tiles, but in a photograph taken in 1887, it is ribbed.

Small, remote, folkish as it is, the Calvario at Cobán [7.30] in the province of Alta Vera Paz has something of the same solid warmth as the vast structure at Esquipulas. A Calvario, or Calvary chapel, usually stands somewhat out of town, if possible on a hill betokening the hill of Golgotha. Regular services are not held there, but statuary for the processions —especially for Good Friday and Easter—are often stored in the place. Its isolated and picturesque situation makes it a favorite spot for prayer and meditation.

Cobán, originally settled by the Dominicans, soon became an important center for agriculture and animal husbandry. Charles V recognized this when at an early date, he bestowed upon the town the title of "Imperial City" and a special coat of arms. At an elevation of more than four thousand feet, it was ideal from the point of view of climate. Soon plantations of coffee, tea, cacao, and vanilla were established by grants to favorite families.

A long winding ascent by stairs leads to the Calvario, which has an all-around vista of the region. Masonry finials cap the walls of the stairway along which the Stations of the Cross are marked. At the top stands the chapel, which allegedly dates from the middle of the sixteenth century but has been enlarged and spruced up to the present time. The façade is extended upward by a free-standing wall, called *espadaña.* Grooved pilasters, similar to those seen in the church of Merced at Antigua, frame the central niche. Related decoration is on the tower. It is a plain but powerful complex serving a Christianity still permeated with Maya religious customs. The dress of the Cobán women is noteworthy, among the many distinctive costumes of Guatemala villages. Usually the *huipil* or blouse of white material is brocaded in color, around the neck and shoulders at least. The dark skirt has light arrowhead or geometric patterns as decoration and two broad horizontal bands with separate designs.*

The population of the rural areas were left to their own devices to a high degree, and rural construction was conditioned by the economics of

* Pál Kelemen, "Folk Textiles of Latin America," *Textile Museum Journal,* Vol. 1, 1965.

the particular site, the raw material at hand, the craftsmanship available. Arcades and second-story galleries useful for shade and ventilation, especially in a hot climate, became general features.

The market place at La Leíva, Colombia, is paralleled in many other regions [7.31]. It is the gathering place for local Indians and is flanked by houses that serve administrative and business purposes. Here the early colonial style of a balcony all across the upper story is visible in several versions.

Among the cities of Argentina, Salta has preserved much of its colonial flavor. It lies near Jujuy—perhaps the most Indian town of the Spanish period—and thus received stylistic influences from both the High Andes and the Atlantic east coast. The Casa de Estancia—a ranch house—near this city preserves the bonhomie of colonial living [7.32]. A second-story gallery runs the length of the house, with the roof drawn over it, supported by tapering wooden posts that rise from the cobbled pavement and appear to be the trunks of tall straight trees. Each room opens on the gallery, and there is enough space in the courtyard for neighbors to drive in with their coaches for visits or overnight rest. Like many houses built in the tropics and subtropics, the rooms run straight through the building to a similar gallery on the other side, for the sake of better ventilation. And they are not covered by a ceiling but stand open above, while the roof shelters all like a huge extended umbrella.

The art and architecture of Hispanic America produced a unique amalgam of European models with what the Indian and mestizo craftsmen could digest and make their own. Until the early seventeenth century, hesitancy and vacillation are often apparent. Later, the imported seed grew into an autochthonous plant. Local materials were put to highly individual use by local talent. Regional differences became more and more evident as the eighteenth century neared its middle point. These differences can be observed more in the churches of the provinces than in the seats of bishops. The smaller communities relied strongly on native or regional craftsmen, and there the rustic, the folkloristic, the unsophisticated idiom of the art and architecture of America came to its most fascinating expression. Eighteenth-century Mexico is especially remarkable for the variety of its regional styles. Notable are the domes, the colorful use of tile, and a revival of the Mudéjar as part of that brilliant epoch.

El Pocito ("the little well") belongs to the pilgrim complex of Guadalupe in a suburb of the Mexican capital [7.33]. It covers a spring of healing water, which according to the legend, gushed forth at the feet of the Virgin Mary as she appeared to the Indian Juan Diego. It is noteworthy that both the association with healing water and the shape of the chapel built in connection with it go back in time and into the East. Buildings with octagonal, round, and mixtilinear ground plans can still be seen in Armenia, Sicily, the Scandinavian countries, and Central Europe, if fate has preserved them. When more spacious buildings were needed as Christian congregations increased, the old early structure was sometimes incorporated into the new one, sometimes kept in use as a separate baptistry (as at Florence and Pisa, Italy)—thus connecting the Eastern custom of protecting a sacred well and the Christian rite of baptism as practiced in the West.

The chapel of El Pocito was built in the last quarter of the eighteenth century, allegedly as an act of devotion by everyone connected with it—masons, painters, stonecutters. Francisco de Guerrero y Torres is recorded as the architect; he was born in Mexico and never left his native land. The large domed space with its two smaller domed adjuncts is constructed of a porous stone, easy to cut, and is roofed by tiles in an undulating pattern that seems to vibrate in the sunshine. The star-shaped flaring windows, the fanciful finials and lantern, all combine in a design not to be found elsewhere, either in the Old or the New World. It is an exquisite example of Mexican Rococo.

The city of Puebla, with its great artistic tradition of pottery making, became the outstanding producer of tile for the Mexican colony. Entire church façades were covered with designs in tile; tile made up the floors of dwellings, as well as churches, and sometimes decorated garden walls with narrative pictures. The color schemes and patterns often show the influence of commerce with Asia. For visitors to the region, the distant cupolas with their multicolored tiles glistening against the blue sky are a welcome vision.

The *parroquia,* or parish church, of Tlaxcala presents that regional style to advantage [7.34]. For their important role in the Conquest as allies of the Spaniards, the Tlaxcala Indians were granted a number of privileges that lasted beyond viceregal times. In the small dome of the baptistry (right) and the larger one over the crossing, we see the compact style of building typical of the late seventeenth century. But the notable façade, with its central statue, shows *estípites* and finials in the fashion of the eighteenth, as are the oval windows with their multiple moldings. On the twin towers, the staggered lines of diamond-shaped and oblong tiles in different tonalities weave the surface into one upward movement. The undulant cornices, the many angles and volutes, and the frosty vertical white lines on the towers make an engaging impression. It is believed that this building inspired the better-known Sanctuary of Ocotlán nearby, which was erected in the mid-eighteenth century.

The Yucatán Peninsula was until recently quite isolated from the main body of Mexico and developed its own psychology, with a population largely Maya and very different from that of the other Mexican states. Until recently, one could reach it only by boat, and until *turismo* discovered it, it seemed a separate country. Valuable woods were exported from Yucatán, exotic fruits and nuts and other tropical produce. The chief product was sisal fiber, or hemp, of excellent quality. Prosperity reigned until the Philippine Islands, after gaining their independence from Spain, started to compete and ruined the market for Yucatán.

Isolation, however, did not prevent the rich *hacendado* from keeping up with fashion, as can be seen in the Baroque gateway of a hacienda near Uman, about eleven miles from Mérida, the Yucatán capital [7.35]. Two fine masonry arches with graceful articulated lines stand one behind the other with a sort of ceremonial air as if to emphasize the importance of the passage.

As the seventeenth century came to an end, the growing wealth of the colonies created a class that in imitating fashionable Europe—albeit with a considerable time lag—sometimes even surpassed it in splendor. Not only ecclesiastical buildings in regional variety but palaces, schools, manor houses, haciendas, show even today the luxury of the colonial epoch. The windows, grilled with carved wood or ironwork, displayed impressive coats of arms. Brackets for lanterns and torches decorated the walls. In the patios, colorful with tilework, with flowers and tropical birds, the indispensable fountain of pure water flowed. The first patio was usually devoted to the reception of guests; the second served the family; and a third court accommodated the kitchen, servants' quarters, and laundry, often adjacent to the stables. The social rooms gave the place its real importance, with lanterns from Venice or Bohemia, carpets made locally or imported from the Orient, Baroque and Rococo furniture, carved, gilded, lavishly upholstered. Statues and paintings were omnipresent.

The various classes were supposed to wear distinctive dress. The affluent went around in silk, velvet, and brocade; their hats were trimmed with bands of pearls; their wealth was judged by the elegance of their equipage. Only certain classes were permitted to ride horseback. Women of rank seldom walked abroad but were carried in palanquins—rather a necessity when rain made the mud deep, mixed with offal from the open drains. They spent their days largely at home, where on large enclosed balconies, heavily grilled—a Mudéjar tradition especially favored in South America—they could observe the passing life unseen or hold conversation with gallants outside on the street. In some instances, a wealthy mineowner would have a theater attached to his sumptuous palace, which in its decoration and its performances would vie with similar establishments in Europe.

Luxury reached its height in the viceregal capitals and in the silver-mining towns. Fortune first favored the South American mines. The story of the city of Potosí, situated in the Bolivian Andes at an altitude of more than 13,600 feet and four hundred miles from the nearest seaport, is perhaps the most incredible in the Spanish colonial world. Founded in 1547, in less than two decades the place had earned the title of "very loyal imperial city" in recognition of the incredible sum of 350 million pesos paid to the crown. The population reached its peak of 150,000 in the early seventeenth century, with one Spanish household for every 10,000 souls. Thereafter, with the decline of production, it dwindled until by 1853 there were no more than 8,000. Many of the mines of Middle America were discovered soon after the Conquest, but intensive exploitation did not develop until some hundred and fifty years later.

How the silver mines could bring prosperity and distinction to a region is demonstrated in Tegucigalpa, now the capital of Honduras. Once a remote mining village named for the archangel Michael, the city is today connected with the world chiefly by air. Its cathedral was erected as a parish church in the mid-eighteenth century [7.37]. The community was wealthy enough to call on master craftsmen from Guatemala and Comayagua (at that time the capital of the province) to supervise the work. The material is brick, which was manufactured locally, plastered over and whitewashed. Statues of the seven archangels adorn the façade, flanked by the deeply grooved pilasters characteristic of Central American practice. Gateways on the sides, leading into a garden, lend balance to a scheme that is almost Neoclassic in its simplicity.

The interior preserves one of the most exquisite Rococo altars in the New World—a lacy shimmering fantasy of carved wood, featuring again the archangels guarding a figure of the Virgin. A fragile four-wheeled cart perches atop the matching pulpit—evidently the triumphal Chariot of Faith. When this writer saw it in 1947, the pale gold of the carving was in perfect condition, untouched by the heavy hand of the restorer. At an audience with the president of the republic that same year, this writer urged that the cathedral be declared a national monument, which then became a reality.

By the eighteenth century, the mines of northern Mexico were outproducing all others. Such silver cities as Querétaro, San Luis Potosí, Guanajuato, Durango, and Zacatecas are telling reminders of that splendid epoch. The parochial church of Lagos de Moreno in the state of Jalisco, though less well known, is an exquisite example of the work of that period [7.36]. Under the name of Santa María de los Lagos, it was founded in the sixteenth century as a place of pilgrimage, for this is a region of healing mineral waters. Lying in the rich silver-mining district of central Mexico, where the mule trains came and went with ore, the town was also a well-known stagecoach stop. With the decline of the mining industry, it wakes up now only on fiesta days.

The present church dates from the late eighteenth century, and although it has Churrigueresque elements, its effect is lacy Rococo. As fine stone carving as the style presents anywhere can be seen in the main portal, with its recessed central section. The niches are framed with curving lines; medallions abound; scrolls—once important—are here reduced in size. A statue of St. Joseph with the Christ Child stands above a large central window, and over them is God the Father with orb and scepter in His hands, no longer raised in the gesture of blessing. The two towers are tall and slim, rising in three tiers, each successively smaller, as if pulled out of a telescope.

Except for the ornate side portal, the rest of the building is amazingly plain. Curious stone tablets, believed to belong to an earlier church, are set over the entrance to the sacristy. Of a rebuslike inscription, "SS. Trinidad" can be deciphered, rather awkwardly carved.

Saltillo, just below the Rio Grande, was long a bridgehead of expansion toward the inimical north. Tlaxcalan Indians were resettled there to reinforce the sparse Spanish population, in an effort to keep the more savage natives under control. Although the Tlaxcalans had proved true allies of the Spaniards since the time of Cortés, their quarter was separated by a stream from that of the hidalgos.

The church of Santiago, the present cathedral, presents another local version of the Churrigueresque, a veritable embroidery in stone [7.38]. The shell, which had become increasingly popular as a decorative element, occupies a significant position above the main portal. The *estípites* carry elaborately framed medallions, as if to flaunt their carver's virtuosity. This structure features a high ornate dome, supported on arches and topped by an octagonal lantern.

Inside the building, figures of the Four Evangelists in bas-relief *argamassa* (a type of stuccowork) adorn the four pendentives. More striking is a series of eight panels around the base of the dome. A balustraded gallery is depicted in relief, with a number of figures looking down from it. According to the inscription, these represent the "choirs" of patriarchs, angels, confessors, virgins, and martyrs. The other three panels show scenes from Holy Week, culminating in the Last Supper, above the communion rail. Virtuosity in the handling of *argamassa* also appears in the multiple moldings, heavy garlands, and religious symbols that adorn the adjacent chapel.

As capital of this remote region, Zacatecas received the title "very noble and loyal city . . ." as early as 1588, implying an uninterrupted flow of silver into the royal coffers—and also into the pockets of the mineowners. In 1803 in Humboldt's statistic of mines, Zacatecas still stands in first place. Small wonder that Dominicans, Augustinians, Franciscans, and Jesuits maintained monumental establishments there, to back their missionary drives into the north. Many of these buildings were secularized after the revolution and turned into schools, movies, assembly halls, shops. This fate befell, also, the main church of the Augustinians. Luckily, the side portal was saved at the last moment through the generosity of some citizens

[7.39]. The photograph was taken during the work of restoration, now completed.

St. Augustine (354–403) was a North African. Although his mother was a Christian, he had remained a nonbeliever. According to his own description, he was at his mother's house in Africa, discussing philosophy and religion with a friend, when a sudden burst of emotion overwhelmed him. He rushed into the garden and flung himself down in desperation. Suddenly he heard next door a child singing, "Tolle, lege; tolle, lege" ("take, read"). Believing this a divine command, he returned to the house and took up a volume of St. Pauls' Epistles. It opened at a significant passage that led to his conversion. St. Augustine's *Confessions,* written in Latin, describe his tribulations at length. In this period, the Greek Bible was beginning to be translated into Latin, and thus through his numerous writings, St. Augustine has, perhaps, become the most influential of the four Doctors of the Church.

In the relief at Zacatecas, St. Augustine is shown lying in the garden, with the door of his mother's house beyond, surrounded by vegetation which is more Latin American than African. Dressed in sixteenth-century clothes, he looks like a Shakespearean figure. A large benevolent sun looks down, a frequent symbol of God the Father, or perhaps here of Christ as the Sun of Righteousness—a portent of the coming revelation. At the left, angels play on celestial instruments, and an angel at the right holds a phylacterium, a flowing ribbon, inscribed with the words *Tolle, lege,* or, with deeper significance, perceive the message.

The material of the carving is the same local stone, a warm rosy brown in color, that was used for the intricately carved façade of the cathedral at Zacatecas. The ornate decoration surrounding the scene—the curtained medallions with their monastic figures, the multiple cornices, the *estípites,* the asymmetrically placed scrolls, and enlarged foliage so typical of Latin American work—in no way detracts from the impact. It was obviously inspired by a print but translated into the sculptural with what flair and plastic feeling.

The Villa de San Sebastián is mentioned in a diary written between 1602 and 1603 of a Spanish expedition sent to explore the Pacific coast toward California. The ship's crew was decimated by sickness; food and water were giving out. They put in at the port of Mazatlán and were able to obtain help in San Sebastián, which is situated some thirty miles inland. A permanent Spanish settlement was established there in the last third of the sixteenth century as a stronghold to support further expansion into the north. It provided a convenient stopping place for those who crossed the pass from Durango to the Pacific shore. Today an excellent highway runs within a short distance. After the revolution, the anticlerical government renamed the place Concordia. Only the church still retains in its title the name of its patron saint as a memento of the proud title of Villa conferred by Philip II. Like so many others, the nearby mines are now abandoned or malfunctioning. The inhabitants earn their living mainly in agriculture or as hired hands. The climate is semitropical and languid.

In the second half of the eighteenth century, the mines in these regions —and there were several—seem to have been the property of Francisco Javier Vizcarra, later known as the Marqués de Pánuco. This name does not occur in the lists of the four military orders of Mexico, and it is probable that Vizcarra climbed onto the ladder of nobility after striking it rich. The European almanacs of aristocracy are filled with the names of the newly rich who were able to buy a title when the royal treasury was empty— and when was it ever full?

The church of San Sebastián y Santa Bárbara has many notable features [7.40]. Its stone is the golden beige of old ivory. The corrugated frame of the central window is carved with precision and delicacy. The basket-weave panels at the sides are like flattened pilasters. This decoration of the decoration is characteristic. Nevertheless, the curved medallions, cockades, small shells, columns with varied ornamentation, are so spaced as to give a certain balance. Two long engaged columns at the sides seem to hold together the entire design, extending from the ground to the very top where the ornate pediment begins. There, amid a jewel-like sprinkling of carved flower vases, cornucopias, angels playing instruments, the statue of the patron San Sebastián stands between two stocky scrolls, with a shell as baldachin above him. The Virgin of Guadalupe appears in the articulated frame of the pediment, and on the column at the right is the figure of Santa Bárbara, a later addition. She is invoked during thunderstorms and is the patroness of the artillery and those who work with gunpowder—significant for these mining regions.

The interior boasts a ribbed vault with wreathlike carvings. Finely chiseled frames enclose the windows on the single tower. To the left of the entrance, the simple weather-beaten wooden cross is a relic of missionary days.

The rustic manifestations generalized under the term mestizo in Peru are often called *poblano* in Mexico. Though this refers specifically to the regional style around Puebla, it is also used in a wider sense to denote buildings elsewhere, where local craftsmen introduced strongly folkloristic touches. A more comprehensive term is *popular.* The Puebla region is noted for the virtuosity in handling *argamassa,* as in the interiors of Santa María Tonancintla and San Francisco Acatepec, with its façade sparkling with many-colored tiles. Less known and less touched by restoration are the buildings of San Pedro Atlixco, about twenty miles southeast of Puebla, at the heart of a wheat- and cattle-raising region.

The use of the figural characterizes this popular idiom. On the façade of La Merced [7.41], leaf-sprites, *putti,* and mermaids attend the Virgin in her garlanded bower. The Mudéjar style is echoed in the multifoil arch of the main portal. In enjoying the ebullience of the work, one is apt to overlook the technical skill required to shape these playful forms, so that they have been able to withstand two hundred years of wear and weather.

The Latin word *missio* ("sending away") became associated with the sending away of religious personnel into heathen lands. Most of the old religious orders—Dominicans, Franciscans, Benedictines—were engaged in missionary work in Latin America. Later, the Jesuits came into the field, and not infrequently disputes broke out among the earlier established orders and the newcomers over their territory. Long after the military and civil administrations had carved out their framework, there was much need for missionary activity, whether surrounded by jungle or on the treeless Andean slope, on the high plateau of New Mexico or in the rich valleys of California.

Most of the Jesuit missions of South America were established in the mid-seventeenth century and functioned in Argentina, Chile, Bolivia, Uruguay, and Paraguay—thirty-two in the last province alone, along the Paraná River. The father provincial had his seat in Buenos Aires. As all were within one viceroyalty, only one man was nominated to rule over this vast ecclesiastical empire.

The Jesuit establishments were known as *reducciones,* where the natives of the rather sparsely inhabited regions were resettled to learn the Christian religion and a new way of life. These Indians were without previous experience, yet the buildings and crafts they produced reveal their talent. It is an everlasting loss to cultural history that so little is left. Here was the real laboratory where the native imagination assimilated and blended styles that came from abroad in books and prints and were brought to a three-dimensional reality under the so different sky of the Americas.

The side portal of the church at San Ignacio, Argentina, shows this talent [7.42]. The ruin is one of the most important in eastern South America. The buildings are of stone, quarried about three miles away, with roofs of layered cane. Constructed under the guidance of the friars, they nevertheless reveal the indigenous imagination: in the absence of uniformity in the columns, in the choice of motif, and in the proportions. The pediment is broken, with two wide scrolls; and two sirens appear in the heraldic emblem in the center. There is, also, space for two eaglets, the whole topped by IHS, the monogram of Jesus. The harmony of the design is linear, rather than sculptural.

The descriptions of eighteenth-century life here leave one amazed by what a handful of padres was able to accomplish. In 1767, when the

Jesuits were expelled, only twenty-three regular members of the order were administering that vast area, with its more than nineteen thousand Indian neophytes. These Indians had no knowledge of money. They received everything from the hands of the padres. They practiced weaving, carving, carpentry, smithery, soldering. They cultivated honey, worked in the fields, raising tobacco, cocoa, coffee. They kept doves, partridges, peacocks, pheasants, and bred horses, donkeys, mules, cattle, and sheep. The presence of strangers on the *reducciones* was strictly controlled. The padres sold the produce and animals in the high Andean regions, through other Jesuit channels.

With the expulsion of the Jesuits, there was not enough personnel in the other religious orders to take over their properties efficiently, and much of their holdings fell prey to the greed of landowners for more fertile land and more laborers. Today, vines and underbrush sprawl over the crumbling buildings.

In Bolivia, the mission territory comprised the present districts of Mojos and Chiquitos, which lie between Santa Cruz de la Sierra and the borders of Paraguay. Until recently, the region had no road and thus preserved its eighteenth-century aspect. While the Argentine missions were constructed of stone, the Bolivians worked in wood, carving effectively shapes and decorations that were essentially alien to them.

An engraving, made in 1870, pictures the mission of Exaltación de la Cruz, a port on the Madeira River, in the district of Mojos.* The church and its isolated bell tower occupy one side of the plaza, which is more than three hundred feet long, with the former Jesuit college at the left [7.43]. The gabled roof of the church rests on four carved wooden columns, forming a spacious forehall and protecting the painted façade from the weather. All the buildings are of adobe. The sidewalks of boards were raised for protection against water, mud, and dust.

The native animals of this region include the puma, peccaries, several types of monkey, toucans, hummingbirds, and other birds of brilliant plumage. Some of the indigenous plants are papaya, grapes, avocado, pineapple, cherimoya, maize. All of them appear as elements of ornament even in highland Peru and Bolivia—very far from their habitat—which suggests that some of the wood carvers from the tropical region were imported to work in stone.

The mission of Exaltación dates from 1704. Franz Keller, a visitor in the mid-nineteenth century, describes how on Corpus Christi Day the richest carpets, banners, and standards were hung out on display; flowers and green branches decorated the house fronts.

* Franz Keller, Engineer, *The Amazon and Madeira Rivers, Sketches and Descriptions from the Note-Book of an Explorer.* Philadelphia: Lippincott, 1875.

There were signs that there had once been a large library, but only a few written prayers remained. Scores of the *Missa Cantada,* and such musical instruments as violins, cellos, flutes, harps were at hand—also, a sort of trombone made of palm leaves, skillfully pasted together.

One of his illustrations pictures a musical Mass, sketched *in situ.* In the choir loft, two Indians in loose-fitting robes, blow huge panpipes made of hollow bamboolike wood, from six to eight feet long, while reading the music from sheets on a stand. Another sits by the organ, and two more—one wearing spectacles—play the violin. A group, leaning on the balustrade, sings from music held in their hands. (Handwritten music survives in various churches of this region, where not only compositions of well-known European composers were accurately copied out but original works were notated.)

A Mojos Indian is described as dancing at the church with a broad machete in his hand, while a chieftain carrying a heavy silver cross stood by. The dancer wore a white robe to the knees, belted with a lively striped material reminiscent of a snakeskin. He had rattles on his ankles and beads about his neck, and his headdress was of feathers branching into an aureole.

The traveler's chapter closes with a vignette: two violins with bows arranged against a few pages of music into a neat still life. In Spanish, this is called *naturaleza muerta.* A fitting tombstone to what was once living nature.

The work of the missionaries, whether in South or North America, was fraught with hardship and danger. Many were murdered as they pushed into unopened lands. The seven golden cities of Cíbola, sought by the Spaniards in the Southwest United States, proved a mirage. But a vast territory was opened up for evangelization and economic exploitation, though it was the second quarter of the seventeenth century before the Spaniards could secure a foothold there.

The Indian village of Ácoma, New Mexico, has one of the oldest churches preserved in the region [7.44], dating from about 1630. It lies on a mesa, the sheer walls of which rise three hundred and fifty feet above the surrounding plain. When this writer visited it more than three decades ago, one had to scramble up a rough path, hacked into the sandstone and ridged by animal and human tread. The building, an adobe construction with walls sixty feet high and ten feet thick, must have been erected with tremendous effort. All the material had to be carried up to the tableland— timber and stone, even the adobe, some from a distance of thirty miles. As the cemetery, also, had to be on consecrated ground, a section in front of the church was walled in and filled with soil brought up from the plain in baskets and sacks.

The Pueblo Indian revolt of 1680 killed the resident priest, and it was not until the very end of the seventeenth century that the building could be strengthened. The massive masonry, with its few small openings, makes it look from afar like a citadel from an alien civilization. Actually, it is in a way, harking back to the adobe community dwellings from pre-Columbian times that the Indians constructed for major defense. Recent "restoration" has made the building more conventional in appearance. Here its former aspect appears in all its ruggedness.

San José de Laguna, New Mexico, was built of the same material as Ácoma and with the same type of labor, but it differs in one respect. While Ácoma and some other Pueblo villages existed in pre-Columbian times, Spanish colonists founded this settlement and named it for a nearby lake (*laguna*) long since disappeared. Located on elevated ground, it serves today a widely scattered population. The church was begun at the end of the seventeenth century and consecrated in the eighteenth. Constructed of stone, it is in excellent condition and well kept by the numerous villagers who give it frequent coats of whitewash. A gateway of like material leads into the churchyard.

Inside, carved double *vigas* ("beams") of wood support the ceiling [7.45], as is common in that region. The retable reminds one of a gigantic icon. Its four twisted columns of wood taper to flamelike finials. A picture of St. Joseph with the Christ Child occupies the center, allegedly painted on elk skin. St. John of Nepomuk, the Bohemian saint popular in many regions of the Americas from the middle of the eighteenth century, flanks him on the left. Here he has an especial significance, for the cult of the Penitentes of New Mexico adopted him as a symbol of secrecy. Santa Bárbara, the early Christian martyr, is pictured on the other side. She holds a monstrance, and the tower where she was imprisoned is included in the scene. The top section of the retable is occupied by the Trinity, represented by three seated figures, all alike, with triangular halos. Although the Council of Trent in the sixteenth century forbade this representation as false, it persisted throughout the colonial empire up to the end of Spanish domination.

Side walls painted to imitate tapestry [see 11.11] enliven the aspect. To the right and left of the altar table, two small identical panels, like sand paintings, show the sacred mountains that define the Pueblo region, with a rainbow above, and on the ceiling, sun, moon, stars, and again the rainbow appear. Pagan and Christian symbols blend to present a microcosm of this world which created for its own use its own language of signs.

California, the last region evangelized, was administered by the Franciscan order from the very beginning. San Luis Rey, founded in 1798 and named after Louis IX of France (a member of the order), is the eighteenth in the California mission chain. Though its style is related to that of the other missions, it has special features: the very broad tower base, the elegant *espadaña,* and the now-restored living quarters of the padres shadowed by a colonnade [7.46]. Like many others, this mission gathered the converted Indians around the church. When it was opened, they carved for it a baptismal font from a single heavy stone that has the power and simplicity of those early Christian objects of the Near East, where Christianity was born.

Barracks were provided for the military, stationed there to protect the community from raids of wild tribes who coveted its sheep and cattle. Vegetables and fruits were grown on the mission. The Indians made tiles and bricks, tanned leather, manufactured candles and soap; and they wove cloth from the wool of their sheep. Excavations reveal an elaborate system by which water was brought to the compound and filtered through charcoal.

The present building was begun in 1811 and dedicated four years later. The mission, once the largest of the group, was abandoned in 1846, after the last padre died. In 1865, President Lincoln signed a document returning the missions to their founders, and some thirty-five to forty years later, the complex was rededicated. It has suffered greatly in the intervening years. Today, like many of its contemporaries, late nineteenth- and twentieth-century taste has "reconstructed" the buildings and "redecorated" the interior, with painted curtains, marbelized masonry, imitative paintings, and pseudo-classic architectural features, with a sentimentality that contrasts sharply with their former austerity.

In 1716, a Mexican armed expedition crossed the Rio Grande, with the purpose of gaining a stronger foothold in *Tejas* ("Texas"). An elderly missionary remained to teach Christianity to the nomadic Coahuiltecan Indians. He named his mission and the nearby river San Antonio de Valero. His buildings lacked solid construction, and in 1758, a more substantial complex was begun. Nearly forty years later, the church was still without vaulting when it ceased to function as a mission. However, the compound with its yards, its cell-like habitations surrounded by stone walls, could be conveniently used as barracks for a company of Mexican soldiery from the town of Álamo de Parras, Coahuila (Álamo signifying cottonwood). Thus, until 1836, it was an insignificant military post. Then, occupied by Americans in the Texas war for independence, it became a citadel of courage and personal heroism—the Álamo, a milestone in the history of the United States [7.47].

The achievements of the missionaries in Arizona, though divergent in many ways, are equally as interesting as those in the better-known missions of Texas, New Mexico, and California. There had been some exploration there in the mid-sixteenth century, but the road lagged on the western side of the Cordilleras, and the route was far more dangerous.

In the beginning all nomadic Indians were called Chichimecs by the

Spaniards. Later, they learned the differences. The Pima, Papago, and some Moqui Indians could be brought under Spanish administration, but Sonora and Arizona were the hunting ground of the belligerent Yaqui, Apache, and Comanche tribes, who fought among themselves and resented the intrusion of the missionaries and the Spanish settlers following them. This was the region, together with Baja California, assigned to the Jesuits to evangelize.

The Jesuits started their work in the seventeenth century with incredible courage, moving deeper and deeper into the untamed land; and long is the list of those who suffered death in trying to convert a people to whom the freedom of roaming the wide and magnificent land meant more than settling around a mission to become docile servants.

By that time, the Spanish crown was allowing Central European friars to come to the New World. Was there a shortage of Spanish and native padres? Or had the Europeans persuaded the authorities that they would approach the superhuman task with a new verve. Austrian, Bohemian, Polish, Croatian, Hungarian, Swiss, German names appear in the records of arrivals in the seventeenth and eighteenth centuries.

There was rich land in the river valleys, for raising wheat and grazing large herds of cattle. Mining, also, was becoming profitable. But before such expansion was possible, military posts had to be established and maintained. Often even before the secular administration came the Jesuit missionary. One of the pioneers who initiated real and lasting work was Father Eusebio Kino.

Kino reached Mexico in 1681. Some two years later, in the capacity of "royal cosmographer" and superior of missionaries, he set out to attempt once more the conversion of Baja California. Failing in this endeavor, he returned to the capital and 1687 ushered in his most effective period in northern Sonora and Arizona—called the Pimería Alta after the Pima Indians of the region. In that year he established his headquarters at Nuestra Señora de los Dolores—some hundred miles south of Tucson and today in the Mexican state of Sonora—and spent the last twenty-four years of his life exploring, colonizing, evangelizing, and writing.

There are, however, a number of misconceptions about this intrepid missionary, and since he is attracting more and more general interest, a digression concerning him seems not inappropriate. Eusebio Kino is known to have been born in the Tyrolean village of Segno, north of Trient, and to have been first educated in the Austrian town of Hall. Later he went for theological training and work to Landsberg, Öttingen, Munich, and Ingolstadt. When Herbert E. Bolton, the noted historian of the Southwest, went to Europe—about 1932—to look up local sources for his *Rim of Christendom*, the peace treaties of World War I had been in effect for fourteen years. Italy had been granted the territory of the South Tyrol, an integral part of Austria for seven centuries. The *irridenta,* which had long been working on such transfer of land, was jubilant. The administrative apparatus of Austrian rule was dismissed, and Italian officials, ignorant and often prejudiced, took over the reins of justice. The official language became Italian. No German newspapers were permitted. All names were changed.

One can imagine that Bolton, with no thorough knowledge of either Italian or German, could have mistaken the situation when he visited the place. No credit for anything of the Austrian past could be tolerated by Mussolini's henchmen. Kino was declared Italian in origin, and the often-repeated phrase that he was "Italian-born and German-educated" came into circulation.

There is not one Italian name beginning with *K* to be found in the Italian Catholic encyclopedia or in the American Catholic encyclopedia. All the letter *K* entries refer to North and Central European personages. The name might well have been Kühne or Kuhn. Spanish records abound in distorted "foreign" names, difficult to decipher.* On how such Italianization takes place, this writer can offer a personal experience. In World War I, he rode into a South Tyrol village named on his map Ghertele. An inn had been there with a fine garden which the Tyroleans called Gärtelein ("little garden"). The Italians, imitating the sound, spelled it in their own fashion.

Another argument for Kino's Germanic origin lies in the fact that he traveled hundreds of miles north for his education and theological training, journeying across the Brenner Pass, which is today the border. Verona, Padua, Bologna, Parma, all were notable Jesuit centers. He could have walked south to the nearest Italian Jesuit school available to him.

Kino came to Mexico with the prestige of a Central European education and of experience in teaching at a Jesuit institution there. He was warmly befriended by the distinguished Mexican scholar Carlos de Sigüenza y Góngora. Sigüenza had collected much data and had maps of the northern provinces, with the latest geographic findings, which he lent the Jesuit. Both men, however, became involved in a polemic over the significance of a comet which appeared in 1680–81. Kino's letters to his patroness in Madrid, the Duquesa de Abeiro y Arco, and the book on the subject that he published in Mexico City reveal his superstitious interpretation of the phenomenon as a harbinger of evil. The day before he departed for Sinaloa, Kino handed a copy of his book to Sigüenza, apparently in a somewhat patronizing manner. The Mexican savant, whose views on such natural

* Nicholas P. Cushner, S.J., *Philippine Jesuits in Exile.* Rome: Institutum Historicum S.I., 1964.

phenomena were remarkably modern, prepared an impressive rebuttal, which did not appear in print until 1690. Kino's rudeness in the incident was all the more marked by the fact that he dedicated his published work to the viceroy of Mexico whom Sigüenza served as an advisor in scientific matters.

It was nearly axiomatic that the European-born and educated scholar was superior to the American. Though the nimbus of the Central European Jesuit suffers in the historical perspective, he was, doubtless, a talented and intrepid man—a typical Tyrolese of the tough mountaineer type that produced Andreas Hofer, the peasant patriot.

The difficulties of the advance from the last secure posts into this vaguely charted land and the accomplishment of these intrepid men are evident even today, as this writer observed, journeying from mission to mission site of eastern Sonora in a Wagoneer Jeep over what could scarcely be called a road. In colonial times, the course of rivers and Indian trails were the routes of forward movement. Though the valleys were rich, even then the settlements were isolated and far apart. The solidity of the buildings erected in some places only a few decades after a mission's establishment must be seen to be believed.

The chain of missions stretching from the Mexican states of Sinaloa and Sonora into Arizona was nearly broken by the expulsion of the Jesuits. There were not enough Franciscans to take over this vast territory, which was left without ecclesiastical leadership. With the end of Spanish hegemony and the revolutions of the nineteenth century, the widespread region of Sinaloa and Sonora fell into a state of apathy. Without stimulus, these villages and towns—some of which once boasted families who ate with solid gold tableware—fell into decline, and today, without good roads, they have become real backwoods. Some churches disintegrated after secularization. Some lingered on, usually without a priest. Some were strengthened and restored, seldom faithful to their characteristic colonial style, and are now used as parochial churches. Others, like Cocospera in an idyllic situation near the United States border, are literally falling apart, prey to picnicking vandals.

Great dams are going up, to regulate irrigation and produce electric energy for those valleys once beyond the back of God. On the Yaqui River, numerous old settlements are now dead, abandoned, as the water begins to collect in those once fertile bottom lands. Gone is the massive stone structure of Tepupa, standing on a hilly shoulder like a citadel of faith, with its barrel vault of stone, some fifty feet long, still unshaken. Batuc's imposing church of red stone, each piece precisely dressed and polished, is being engulfed. Fortunately, the façade—a blend of Renaissance design with Baroque elements—has been transported to Hermosillo, the capital of Sonora, and re-erected on the main highway at the south end of the town.

The carved side portal of this church has been incorporated into the new plaza wall in front of the mission church at Caborca, also in Sonora.

A lovely chapel stood near the church at Batuc, constructed perhaps before the large building and dedicated to the Immaculate Conception. The roof was gone, but its graceful proportions and fine stone altar, late Renaissance in style, could still be enjoyed. In 1963, when this writer saw it, three crows sat on the crown on top of the belltower, as if heralding the coming dissolution of the building. A photograph taken in 1968 shows just the two highest tiers of the tower. The birds are gone, and water erodes the stones.

All the more miraculous is the survival of the mission San Xavier del Bac, near Tucson, in such good condition. Father Kino, it is known, once planned to move his headquarters to this northernmost outpost, which he founded in 1700. The name *del Bac* has been translated as "where water appears," for nearby, the Santa Cruz River, which runs underground for some distance, rises again to the surface. The mission stood close to a large settlement of Pima Indians at the site of one of their holy places. Under the supervision of Swiss, German, and Bohemian Jesuits, several successive churches were erected. After the expulsion of the Jesuits, the region was entrusted to Franciscans from Querétaro—a city that could boast not only of being one of the wealthiest in Mexico but of having some of the most exquisite colonial art in all the Americas. Friars from the new regime reached the Pimería Alta in 1768. Their church—the present one—stands not far from the site of the earlier structures [7.48]. It was completed in 1797 and must have been nearly twenty years in building. As one approaches the mission, the towers and the large spacious dome catch the eye from a distance. The white surfaces shine; the decorative balustrades, the towers, and the sculptured façade gain dramatic plasticity.

In this area of endless sand and sagebrush, what wood there was in the surrounding country had long since been used up. The building had to be made of available material. Brick could be burned there, as in so many parts of the Americas. Even the interior of San Xavier del Bac is entirely of brick—the retables, the niches, the columnettes, the statue bases, as well as the walls. Fragments of the wooden molds for fashioning such complicated shapes survive. In the main, the statues, some of which are half life size, are of burned clay. Stucco forms a great part of the ornament.

The nave and the side chapels are roofed with a series of domes, decorated with ingenious story-telling mural paintings. In one, angels are drawing aside the canopy of Heaven. Scenes are painted on the walls. The entire interior is wreathed with the Franciscan cord, in stucco, dangling from a heavy cornice. The hues are light and vivacious—a Rococo color scheme.

The dome of the right side chapel [7.49] has traces of a sculptured design. Noteworthy is the deep central niche with its fluted frame, which held a large rough-hewn wooden cross with the figure of Christ. The illustration, taken in 1963, shows only the left arm in place. The body of Christ, fastened at wrists and ankles with perishable sheepskin straps, must have fallen about a hundred years ago, as pictures from the last quarter of the past century show only what is in the photograph. During a recent restoration, the arm, also, was removed.

The silver-crowned figure of the Dolorosa on the altar below, together with that of the patron saint, Francis Xavier, in the main retable, was ordered from Mexico City in 1759 and first stood in the Jesuit church, since demolished. Both are built on a wooden frame like a dressmaker's form. They are beautifully handcrafted, joined with hand-forged spikes, and were intended to be dressed in fabrics.* Wooden angels, poised at the corners of the sanctuary, once carried tapers or lamps dangling on chains from their extended arms, as can still be seen in some South American churches and, indeed, in Spain. Today the complex is under the care of the United States National Park Service and is used by the Franciscan friars who serve the congregation.

It was three and a half decades ago that we first saw San Xavier del Bac. Tucson, not yet expropriated by the climate hunters, was a small town with one main street. The road leading to the mission crossed some gravel, some sand patches as are found in the Arizona desert, its ruts deepened by the hooves of horses and donkeys. At the mission, no guide service was offered, nor was there at the entrance a long sales desk with rosaries, holy pictures, postcards, photo negatives, booklets. One could go alone into the church, with no flare of flashbulbs, no milling tourists. Since then we have visited the place repeatedly. Very recently, we stayed after closing time to take photographs. We sat in the choir loft and pointed the camera for a long exposure toward the main retable with its *estípites,* its garlands and bevy of *putti,* and the great gilded shell that arches from the top to form the ceiling of the apse. Through a west window, the sun sent in its pale yellow rays. Tiny floating particles of desert quartz whirling like gold dust cast a shimmering light on the retable. We were conscious of the particular mood that radiates from La Verna, where St. Francis received the stigmata, and Assisi, where he built his little church. This, also, was a Franciscan interior—though thousands of miles away from the Apennines. The quiet was absolute. Now the pale gold turned into a rusty bronze, presaging the twilight. Color and light blended into a unique harmony, revealing some of the mystique of the place.

* Communication from Bernard L. Fontana and Richard E. Ahlborn, 1969.

[7.1] Fortress of San Felipe del Morro. San Juan, Puerto Rico.

[7.2] Colonial colonnade. Ixtlán, Mexico.

[7.3] Zavala mansion. Juli, Peru.

[7.4] Casa Laso de la Vega. Oaxaca, Mexico.

[7.5] Tepoztlán, Morelos, Mexico.

[7.6] Aranzazú. Guadalajara.

[7.7] Carved detail. Teposcolula.

7.8] Teposcolula, Mexico.

7.9] Detail of façade.

[7.10] Detail of side altar.

[7.11] San Juan. Juli, Peru.

[7.12] Copacabana, Bolivia, from an old print.

.13] Cahabon, Guatemala.

[7.14] Side altar. Copacabana, Bolivia.

[7.15] Plaza de Armas. Cuzco, Peru.

[7.16] Interior, Santiago. Pomata.

[7.17] Main altar, San Francisco. Tunja, Colombia.

[7.18] Interior, San Francisco. Quito, Ecuador.

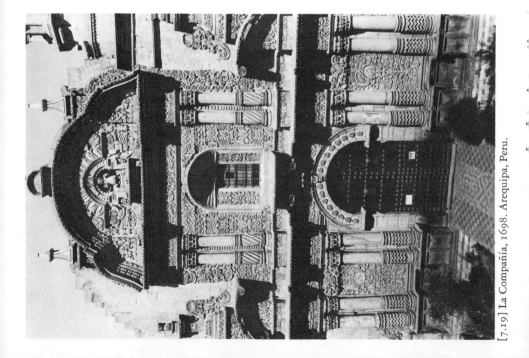

[7.19] La Compañía, 1698. Arequipa, Peru.

[7.21] Puno, Peru.

[7.22] Interior. Asangaro.

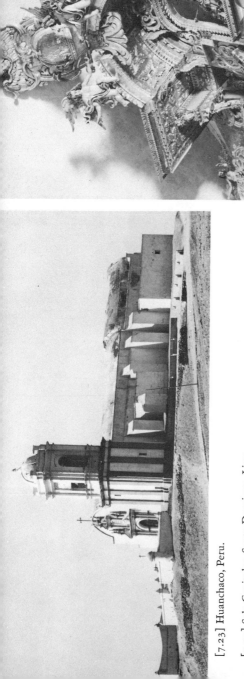

[7.23] Huanchaco, Peru.

[7.24] Sala Capitular, Santo Domingo. Lima.

[7.27] Organ, La Merced. Quito.

[7.26] La Compañía. Quito, Ecuador.

[7.28] Esquipulas, Guatemala.

[7.29] La Merced. Antigua, Guatemala.

[7.30] Calvario. Cobán, Guatemala.

[7.31] Main plaza. La Leíva, Colombia.

[7.32] Casa de Estancia. Near Salta, Argentina.

[7.33] El Pocito. Guadalupe, Mexico.

[7.34] Parish church, Tlaxcala.

[7.35] Hacienda gateway. Near Uman, Yucatán, Mexico.

[7.36] Lagos de Moreno, Mexico.

[7.37] San Miguel. Tegucigalpa, Honduras.

[7.38] Portal detail, cathedral. Saltillo, Mexico.

.39] Side portal, San Agustín. Zacatecas, Mexico.

[7.40] San Sebastián y Santa Bárbara. Concordia, Mexico.

.41] Detail of façade, La Merced. Atlixco, Mexico.

[7.42] San Ignacio Mission. Argentina.

[7.43] Mission church and main plaza (after Keller). Exaltación, Bolivia.

44] Ácoma, New Mexico.

45] Interior. San José de Laguna, New Mexico.

[7.46] San Luis Rey, before 1902. California.

[7.47] San Antonio de Valera. San Antonio, Texas.

[7.48] San Xavier del Bac. Near Tucson, Arizona.

[7.49] Side chapel.

8/Statuary

The construction of buildings in the colonial period was a venture in which many participated. It was like the performance of an orchestra, in which various instruments each had their part to play. In contrast, a statue or painting, when not too greatly damaged or overrestored, still preserves the mark of the individual artist.

Just as the art of pagan America has to be considered in terms of its calculated religious impact, so the art of the Hispanic period must be placed in the context of the Christian religion that ruled the imagination and the daily life of the colonial people.

The New World offered the inhabitants of the Spanish colonies precious materials from gold to mahogany, but ivory had to be imported from Asia by way of the Philippines. Ivory was always highly prized in Europe. Ivory bits have been excavated in the Near East, in Hungary, Austria, and even in north Italy. Ivory is hard to work, and a special technique was developed over the centuries in the Far East and in some parts of Africa. As the commerce from the Philippines increased—toward the second half of the sixteenth century—ivory crucifixes, statues of saints, and plaques fashioned by Oriental carvers appeared in the New World colonies. These show strongly Asian features; anatomy and coloring reveal an un-Caucasian approach. Later, raw ivory was brought in through Acapulco, and objects were carved directly in the colony. These were usually small in size—perhaps the central part of a portable altar or a reliquary, a tablet or a medallion.

An oval ivory medallion, eight inches high, five inches wide, and about one half inch thick [8.1], presents the Virgin *Tota Pulchra* ("all beautiful"). Its coloring adds to its attraction. Mary wears a red tunic and a blue flowing cloak edged in gold. She stands on the new moon, surrounded by the attributes of the Rosary, which moving counterclockwise from the upper right are:

The Sun	The Tower of David
Jacob's Ladder	The Sealed Fountain
The Olive Tree	The Palm Tree
The Gate of Heaven	The Closed Gate of the Temple
The Well of Living Waters	The Mirror of Justice
The Ark of the Covenant	(mirror without blemish)
The Enclosed Garden	Stella Maris (star of the sea)

The placement of the figure suggests that a separate crown, possibly of gold and pearls, was attached to an outer frame of some precious material. The hands are missing; they were probably carved separately and tenoned in.

The back of the piece, in particular, is executed with Baroque exuberance. Mary's hair hangs in long exquisitely defined curls [8.2]. The folds of the elaborately decorated robe, with remnants of gold tooling, are not standardized. She stands on three cherub heads, amid conventionalized clouds. Where possible, the figure has been freed from the frame, adding to the plastic effect. The carving shows considerable skill in the placement of the figure and of Mary's many attributes in clean and identifiable arrangement.

The text reads *Diego de Reinoso y Sandoval me fecit en la Siudad de Mexico 1637* ("Diego de Reinoso y Sandoval made me in the city of Mexico 1637"). Although archives in Latin America have suffered many vicissitudes over the centuries, it has been established that Diego de Reinoso y Sandoval was a native of Mexico. He was a Mercedarian, belonging to one of the most active orders of that time in the viceroyalty. A priest named de Reinoso published in Mexico in 1644 a vocabulary of an Indian language. The fact that it appeared within seven years of the ivory carving tends to strengthen the assumption that the author and artist are one and the same.

In pre-Columbian times, as we have seen, bone from the jaguar, boar, deer, and mountain goat served for small sculptured pieces. With ivory objects so in vogue, Hispanic-American ingenuity reached out for native raw materials. In Ecuador, a large nut was used; in some parts of South America, *piedra de Huamanga,* a sort of alabaster from the central highlands of Peru. One such carving represents the Virgin of Pomata, also with the attributes of the Rosary about her. Most surviving pieces are attributed to the eighteenth century. Special importance accrues to the Mexican medallion because of its early date and the fact that it has never before been published. The twenty-two ivory figurines of the Virgin, identified in a recent article as of Philippine origin, are carved in the round.*

Statuary not only decorated the many altars but played a leading part

* Margarita Estella Marcos, "Virgines de marfil hispanofilipinas," *Archivo Español de Arte,* No. 160, Madrid, 1967.

in the spectacular religious processions inherited from Spain. Saints were thus honored on their special days; their images visited each other in different churches; sometimes they went on pilgrimages. The pageantry reached its climax in Holy Week. Wood was the chief material used, ranging from feather-light balsa to solid oak and mahogany. Spanish cedar was often specified in contracts for retables, choir stalls, and fine furniture. Noteworthy is the fact that this material is neither Spanish nor cedar but a very strong native wood.

In the carving and coloring of statuary, sculptor and painter worked hand in hand. Roughly the same procedure and methods were used in the colonies as in Spain. The *imaginero* ("carver of images") executed the figure and covered the surface with a layer of gesso or of fine linen before he gave it to the painter. In the coloring, a waxy, tinted finish with a porcelain-like sheen, called *encarnación,* was used to represent the flesh. The result was lifelike and dramatic, especially in the flickering light of candles. The figured textiles of the garments were depicted with elaborate patterns in color, which were often applied over a gold or silver base in a technique called *estofado.* The religious statues of the Baroque period are frequently life-size or even larger, and have eyes of glass, human hair, and long, applied "real" eyelashes.

Three distinct types of figure can be seen: those carved entirely of wood, finished with *encarnación* and *estofado;* those dressed in garments made of cloth that has been stiffened, molded, and then painted; finally, those known as "candlestick" figures, which have head, hands, and sometimes feet of painted wood, but a body that consists only of an armature or is carved or stuffed like a mannequin; these wear real robes of velvet, brocade, and other materials, often embroidered with gold and pearls.

Two statues of the giant St. Christopher carrying the Christ Child across a raging stream might be said to epitomize the Baroque and the Rococo respectively. In the first [8.3], in the cathedral of Cuernavaca, Mexico, the saint's figure is over life-size, muscular and full of vigor. His garments are rich in gold and dark-colored *estofado,* and his staff is a real sapling. The Child, too, is sturdy, holding the orb in his lap. An expression of surprise and delight seems to be passing between them.

The Rococo figure [8.4], about three and a half feet tall, in the cathedral of Mexico, has a graceful pastoral quality. The coloring is delicate; the clothing falls smoothly; no gold is used. There is confidence in the long stride and assurance in the expression, but here there is no feeling of close relationship—both Child and saint look straight ahead.

Ayacucho (in colonial times, Guamanga or Huamanga) lies halfway between Cuzco and Lima, a main station on the King's Highway, from where an important road branched northward into Ecuador. In the first third of the seventeenth century, the city was described as having four hundred resident Spaniards and mestizos, plus a large contingent of Indians, Negroes, and mulattoes. It had a bishop, an office of the Inquisition, Dominican, Franciscan, Augustinian, Mercedarian, and Jesuit establishments. Even today, a number of colonial churches and chapels remain. The climate is excellent. Vineyards, fruit trees, wheat, corn, and other cereals were cultivated, and on the ranches, cattle, sheep, and hogs were raised. Precious metals were mined in the region.

The *corregidor,* or mayor of the city, who was named by order of the king, exercised jurisdiction over five leagues—about three hundred square miles—including all the Indian villages, ranches, and agricultural lands. In the first half of the seventeenth century the *corregidor* was Juan Gutierrez de Quintanilla, whose recumbent effigy [8.7] is unusual because it was carved in stone. The monument originally stood in the church of La Merced; today it is in the small local museum. What kind of a jurist he was is not known, but that he was a soldier is clear from the embossed helmet with visor, the armor beneath the vestments, the high boots. The long straight sword held over the chest with both hands is a symbol of the power he exercised in the name of the king over that vast, rich land. As he lies there petrified, he is still a commander. One is reminded of the ghostly scene in the cemetery in Mozart's *Don Giovanni,* where the equestrian effigy of the murdered Commendatore comes alive and accepts the reckless philanderer's invitation to a banquet.

Tomb sculpture was forbidden in the colonies by an early edict (1555), but effigies of benefactors were allowed to be placed in chapels they had donated. Francisco de Villacís, a royal commissioner of Quito, Ecuador, who defrayed the expenses of a chapel in the church of San Francisco there in 1661, is portrayed in the traditional pose of devotion, kneeling on a cushion, with his hands folded [8.6]. His cloak appears to be of starched and painted material draped over the carved figure. On the other hand, a Mexican effigy [8.5] is made entirely of wood, except for the Rococo touch of a silken scarf. Manuel Tomás de la Canal was a mayor and benefactor of San Miguel de Allende. Born in the capital in 1701, he was a member of the important exclusive military Order of Calatrava. In 1735, he had a votive chapel constructed in the Oratorio de San Felipe Neri in Allende, dedicated to the Virgin of Loreto and conforming to the measurements of the house where she is said to have lived and died.

The word Potosí has an auspicious, even magic, sound implying fabulous riches. When rich silver lodes were discovered in northeast Mexico at the end of the sixteenth century, the place was named San Luis Potosí. Within the next hundred years, it became one of the greatest mining centers. It was, also, situated on the road leading north toward Texas, a bridgehead of much missionary work. Nevertheless, it was not before the middle of the eighteenth century that it received a charter as "noble and loyal city," and thus, while other places can show earlier splendor, San Luis Potosí had its great surge of development at that time.

The sacristy of the Franciscan complex, newly decorated in the mid-eighteenth century, houses many paintings by well-known Mexican artists which are usually enumerated in the literature. But what is really unique is seldom mentioned. This is a large *argamassa* relief above a door, depicting St. Francis receiving the stigmata [8.8]. The saint leans against a rock, his open hands showing the marks of nails. His companion washes his wounded feet. A skull and scourge—symbols of his ascetic life—lie on the rocks beside him. At the upper right, amidst the clouds that separate it from the earth, the crucified Christ appears, upheld by seraphs' wings. The scene is framed by lush vegetation, richly tinted, and above it two, rather gay cherubs are holding a baldachinlike curtain with long tasseled cords swinging as if it had been drawn aside for the benefit of the beholder. Here the realistic blends touchingly with the legendary.

The tableau of the Nativity harks back to the grotto where Christ was born. It was depicted in medieval religious plays; sculptured groups appeared in churches in Italy and were erected in private homes. In Latin America, the group at the manger shows many European influences, but each area reveals individual taste preferences in style, arrangement, and presentation.

Querétaro in north Mexico developed a powerful school of sculpture. It had become the third most important city of the viceroyalty by the second half of the eighteenth century, through the vast commerce that moved to and from the silver cities. It was only natural that the arts and crafts should receive patronage. Querétaro sculpture can be distinguished by the use of hard wood, tall figures, and dramatic gestures. The *estofado* pattern is large with sprawling, continuous design and colorful floral display.

A kneeling figure of St. Joseph belongs to a *pesebre,* or Nativity group, from Querétaro [8.9]. It is in perfect original condition, having been handed down from the eighteenth century to the mother superior of the Santa Clara Convent and bequeathed by her to the father of the present owner for devoted medical service to her nuns. The figure of Joseph, having been treated for centuries as an aging bystander, came into new prominence in the Americas, and throughout the Hispanic colonies we encounter him as a vigorous younger man.

Here the pose is expressive without exaggeration. The carving is precise, the *estofado* masterly. The robe is a shimmering olive green, with red flowers outlined in gold and dark blue. The cloak is golden, lined in coral red and crossed by slender stripes of blue and gold. The *encarnación* has a fine waxy texture with glowing undertones.

Guatemala, also, was noted for its statuary; this writer has found records of holy figures being brought up on muleback as far as a Sonora mission in Mexico, close to the present United States border. The Guatemalan sculptural style was quite different from the Mexican, distinguished by its economy of line. The *estofado* is usually an over-all pattern, less rich in color and gold and using a smaller pattern. Moses [8.10] has the statuesque dignified pose expected of a leader. There is no gesticulation. Note the two flames on his head, emanation of his spiritual power. His costume is a blend of the biblical and contemporary as it existed toward the end of the seventeenth century.

Controlled gesture and gentle facial expression characterize the statuary of Quito, Ecuador. The Franciscan order there had from the beginning a great influence on the religious sculpture throughout the Hispanic colony. By the eighteenth century, the city was exporting paintings as well as carvings by the hundreds, some of which can be encountered even today in far corners of the former Spanish colonial empire. The first great period of sculpture in that region is connected with the name of Bernardo Legarda, a mestizo who was active in the first half of the eighteenth century; he is responsible for a version of the Woman of the Apocalypse found nowhere else in the world [8.11]. The Virgin Mary stands on the new moon, her feet resting on a serpent. She wears the three mystic robes and has a crown on her head. She is winged, as described in Chapter 12 of Revelation, and her gesture sets her apart from the many other aspects of the Virgin. Here she is depicted as a concept out of time, participating with the archangel Michael in the "war in Heaven." The javelin with its zigzag line in her upraised hand is not only highly decorative but deeply symbolic. It is a lightning shaft from the Godhead (notable, also, as the symbol of the might of Jupiter and Thor), and it is so placed that at certain hours the sun reflects blindingly on it. The Franciscans, always cognizant of mystic lore, saw in this representation the embodiment of that phase in the spiritual attainment of the human which Augustine describes as fear overcome and full confidence in the contemplation of Truth. Even those for whom the work has no religious message or iconographical interest can enjoy it for its human appeal and superb execution.

Ten or more examples of this figure survive, one on the main altar of Quito's Franciscan church [see 7.18]. The example reproduced here was found by this writer, closed away from the public in a domed chamber above the main altar in the church of San Francisco, Popayán, Colombia. How well the deep symbolic significance of the figure was understood is evident from the Noah's Ark painted on the dome of the niche in the background, calling to mind the flood that threatened the Apocalyptic Woman (Revelation 12:15).

A number of anonymous artists in Quito are recognizable through their different styles. In the figure of Mary Magdalene kneeling at the foot of the Cross, the bold and vigorous lines of the carving indicate another master of the eighteenth century [8.12]. The pose of the head, the gaze, the clasped hands, tell of grief and pain. The *estofado* shows a large, loose floral pattern on a silver ground, a rare untouched example.

Another artist in Quito of a somewhat later date was a full-blooded Indian named Manuel Chil, or Chili, better known as Caspicara from his pock-marked face. He, also, was closely connected with the Franciscan monastery. While Legarda specialized in large, sometimes life-size, statuary with sweeping colors and large patterns, Caspicara worked on a smaller scale. At that time, the Rococo, with its engravings and its vast repertory of porcelain figurines, was well known in the Spanish colonies. Caspicara produced graceful shepherds and dancers and touchingly sentimental saints in wood. Groups such as the Ascension of the Virgin and the Adoration of the Shepherds came from his hand, as well as exquisite doll-size figures for private *pesebres*. A miniature of his depicts Nuestra Señora de la Luz, Our Lady of Light [8.13], a missionary aspect that will be discussed at length later [see 10.18]. Here the skill should be remarked which could bring a concept that is essentially pictorial into the three-dimensional. The dainty flowered *estofado* characteristic of Caspicara's work bespeaks the Rococo.

Spanish religious sculpture tended to dramatize suffering, sentimental adulation, spiritual trance, and tortured bodies, even in the motherland. Horrifying details were sometimes put into a depiction of the head of John the Baptist. However, the seventeenth-century Mexican work illustrated [8.15] is not shockingly naturalistic. The saint's steadfastness is emphasized here, in the haggard face and firm mouth. The fixed gaze is not so much accusing as intent on what is beyond. The quality of workmanship is first rate. The head, once fashioned in a single piece together with the platter, was carved to the desired shape, then fine linen was glued on and worked into all the facial details, leaving the hair and beard free in the natural wood. When this became solid, a thin coating of stucco was applied, to receive the *encarnación*.

Especially in Mexico and its areas of influence, representations of the suffering Lord are numerous. The native, humiliated and degraded, knew what a broken body meant. Christ at the Column after the flagellation looks upward in agony [8.14]. His hands are tied together. Protruding veins cover his body like a network of strings from a crushed instrument. He is prisoner of the cruel mob.

In the far-flung territory of the Mexican viceroyalty, few regions were so isolated as New Mexico, like a single leaf on a barren branch, far away from its life-giving trunk. Only the Santa Fe Trail connected it. From the

255

seventeenth century on, Mexican and Spanish settlers plodded northward with their few belongings on oxcarts, through desert lands, the mesquite and rolling sagebrush blown by the wind. The nights were spent in a bivouac or open camp, unless some settlement or fortified hacienda offered shelter, fresh water, and human contact.

Mountain valleys had to be crossed even though Indian attack menaced. When they reached the land accorded to them, the settlers had to chop out a living from unyielding soil. And the danger was multiplied because now they were in a hostile region, without adequate military protection. They lived in solitary endeavor, in villages that grew up around mountain streams, in the shadow of peaks thirteen thousand feet high, one of which they named Sangre de Cristo. What they could bring with them of religious objects was scanty, and as the small adobe chapels grew into churches, the need for religious painting and sculpture grew also. But what craftsmen or artists were willing to come from more wealthy communities to a region behind the back of God himself, into the arms of Indian raiders? Local craftsmen developed a talent for furnishing paintings and statuary for the churches [see 7.45]. The wood carver who fashioned shovels and plows decorated the vigas and the supporting corbels and whittled cottonwood into statues of diverse sizes.

In the head of a standing Christ ("Ecce Homo") the carver has stepped beyond the bounds of realism [8.16]. The emphasis on suffering gives this figure something of the metaphysical, something of the fetish. One might say the piece has a touch of contemporary expressionism—but the anonymous carver of nearly two centuries ago believed the biblical story and made it tangible for his congregation. He put natural hair on the head, hanging down over the shoulders and around a face stained with sweat and blood. The beard and moustache are indicated in a dark area, and the sculptured lines that circle the great eyes emphasize their appeal. At first impression, one might think of an oversized puppet head, but there emanates a ray of agony that only religious intensity could evoke.

In New Mexico, where the carver worked in the framework of a strict local tradition and with limited technical apparatus, the elongated figure of St. Joseph, pared of all sculptural bravura [8.18], has the directness of Early Christian art. Such statues, called "bultos," were carved from the local cottonwood, colored with native pigments over stucco. In the same way, paintings, known as "santos," were fashioned on thin slabs of the same wood. The craft held into the twentieth century but now unfortunately is dying out.

Between 1548 and 1803, Guanajuato produced a quarter of all the silver that came from Mexico. Its mineowners lived in veritable palaces, erected lavishly adorned churches near their mines as if to appease the Divine Power for their excesses. The mineworkers devoted their free time to carrying out these noble works. From the churches which once dotted the broad and deep amphitheater that surrounds the city, amid the dead masses of slag, today Las Rayas, La Cata, La Valenciana are mementoes that astound the visitor with the richness both inside and out. Painters and sculptors of renown were called in, also, to produce portraits of the wealthy families and to supply decorations for the private chapels of palaces. Money was pouring in from the mines and did not count for much.

A life-size crucifix [8.17] was carved of wood by such a colonial sculptor and was sold, perhaps, when the Mexican mining operations became bankrupt. For, in colonial days, little of the tremendous production was plowed back into upkeep. The lodes became very deep, and when abandoned, they filled with water.

Crude crosses of heavy stone from the earliest period of the Conquest can still be found in some church courtyards of Mexico. These usually carry the symbols of the Passion, and sometimes Christ's face in the center where the arms meet. A unique example was discovered in 1967 at San Angel Zurumucapeo, Michoacán, where a life-size body of Christ was carved out of the same stone as the cross itself. This piece shows an unusual stylization, calling to mind the early crucifixes of Catalonia and the Near East. Other Mexican figures of the Crucified Christ, or of *Cristo Yacente*—laid out in the tomb—were fashioned in the same way as pre-Columbian idols, modeled from the pith of the maize made plastic with the juice of a native orchid.

The figure shown here stands at the end of a long line. Made by some unknown artist—like so much of the art of the Americas—it has a rare nobility that is difficult to match. The cramped right hand still holds the gesture of blessing. The crossbeam is painted with red roses, symbol of martyrdom and sacred love.

One must think of the mutations that this symbol went through even in Europe, from the twelfth- and thirteenth-century Romanesque figure, whose almond-shaped head stares with fixed open eyes on the visitor, to the expressionistic rendering in which a contorted body is displayed nearly falling off the cross. In the Mexican crucifix, the impact is not obscured by technical limitations or by modernistic pose. A most dramatic tension is transmitted. The famous "Crucifixion" of Velázquez shows four nails. Here, there are three, in older tradition, and their heads, too, have been turned into roses. The great Spanish painter's Christ, drenched with the sweat of agony, is a tortured human being that asks for pity. The Mexican Christ is an aristocrat—King of Kings.

257

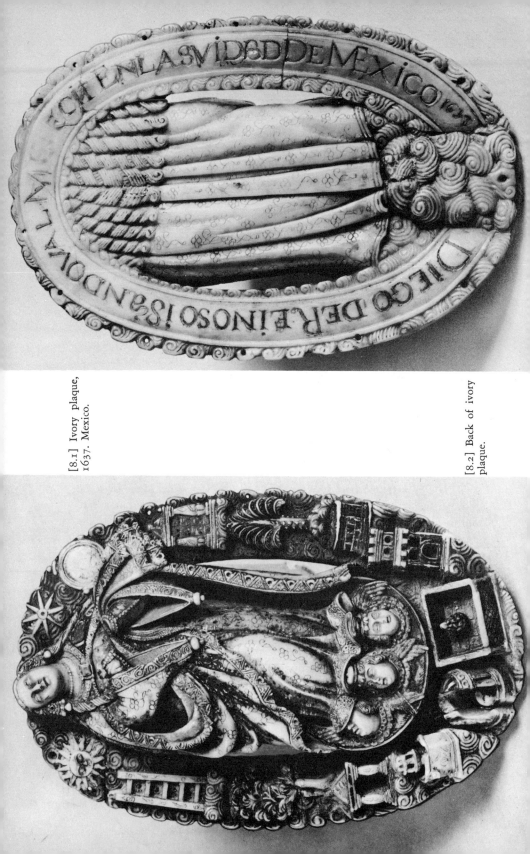

[8.1] Ivory plaque,
1637. Mexico.

[8.2] Back of ivory
plaque.

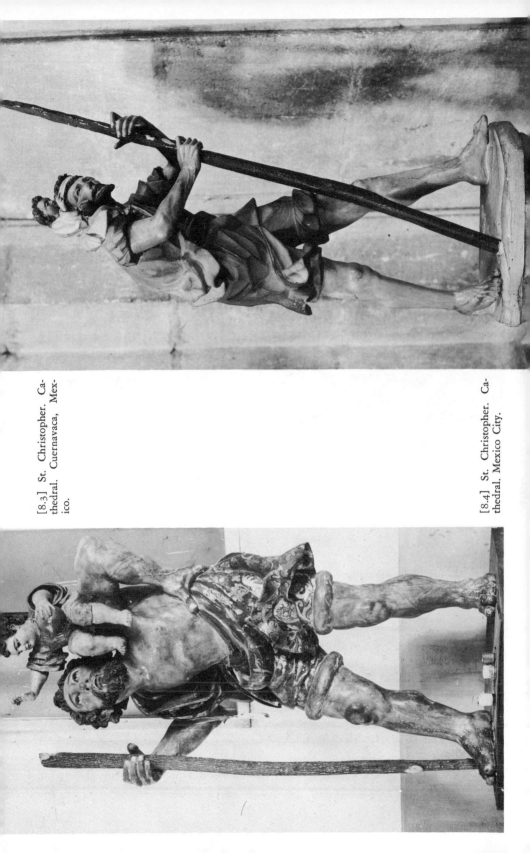

[8.3] St. Christopher. Cathedral. Cuernavaca, Mexico.

[8.4] St. Christopher. Cathedral. Mexico City.

[8.5] Manuel Tomás de la Canal, tomb effigy. San Miguel de Allende, Mexico.

[8.6] Francisco de Villacís, tomb effigy. Quito, Ecuador.

[8.7] Juan Gutierrez de Quintanilla, tomb effigy. Ayacucho, Peru.

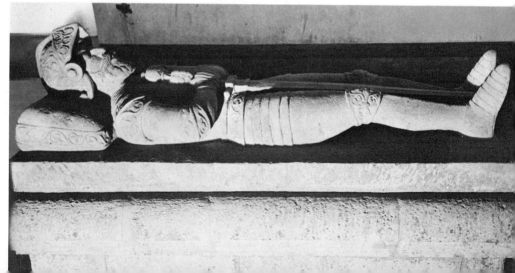

[8.8] Relief. Sacristy, San Francisco. San Luis Potosí, Mexico.

[8.10] Moses. Antigua, Guatemala.

[8.9] St. Joseph, Nativity figure. Querétaro.

[8.11] The Woman of the Apocalypse, by Bernardo Legarda. Popayán, Colombia.

[8.12] Magdalena. El Tejár. Quito, Ecuador.

[8.13] Nuestra Señora de la Luz, by Caspicara. Quito.

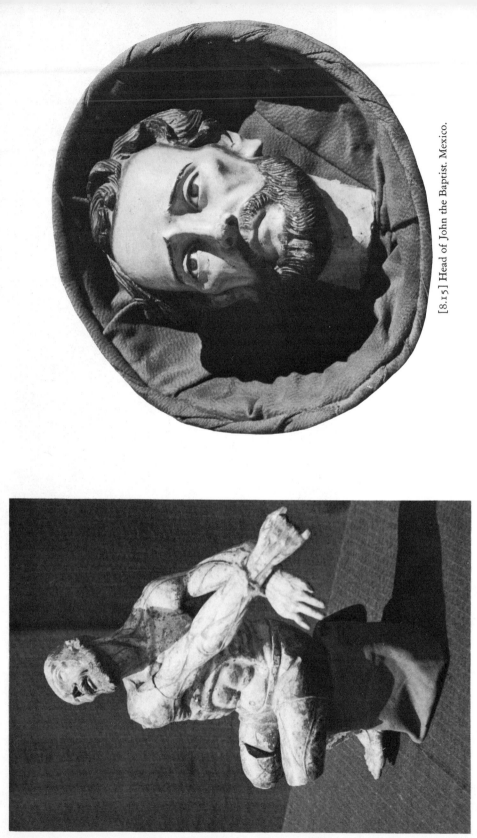

[8.15] Head of John the Baptist. Mexico.

[8.14] Christ at the Column. Mexico.

[8.18] San José. New Mexico.

[8.17] Crucifix. Guanajuato, Mexico.

[8.16] Ecce Homo. New Mexico.

9/Painting

It was a European custom to paint standards and the sails of ships with heraldic devices and holy subjects. Such paintings adorned the sails and flags of the fleet that carried the bride of Charles V from the Netherlands to Spain. The sails of Columbus's ships were decorated thus, and banners bearing pictures of Christ, the Virgin, and the saints landed in the New World with the conquistadores. Thus, painting in the European sense appeared on the American scene with the first Spanish invaders, to run a spectacular course. As we have seen, in certain pre-Columbian cultures, mural painting was used to depict historical events, calendrical and religious symbolism. All of it was done, however, in a flat technique. As is true of other non-European civilizations, there was no preoccupation with perspective. The highly developed technique of painting in oil was the fruit of sixteenth-century Europe, where the artist was often a prince of society. The subtleties in the manufacture of oil color, the blending of pigments, the secrets of grounding, and the application of varnishes were worked on and discussed in countless studios and described in books.

From both the inspirational and the technological point of view, the situation of the painter in the New World colonies was handicapped by a meager choice. His colors had to be imported at great cost or evolved from different raw materials. Oil color must be put on sound, tightly woven canvas to show true brilliance. Canvas, however, was a monopoly of the Spanish crown and had to be imported at a high tariff. On the other hand, cotton cloth abounded, manufactured from native raw material and woven on primitive looms. Here European techniques were not efficient. Cotton does not stretch evenly and soon sags. It absorbs much of the grounding, and especially when this is dark in tone, the highlights soon disappear— the first to suffer from age and careless treatment. For this reason, many colonial paintings lack sparkle.

The superhuman distances that separated one colonial capital from another also hampered the development of the colonial painter. He did not have the studios where great masters gathered to discuss art and philosophy before a group of disciples. His patrons were usually limited in their taste and requirements. He lived more or less in isolation, seeing only what his predecessors had done in a given area and the very few truly artistic objects imported from Europe. The main source of inspiration came from books and prints, which the Spanish crown imported as another of its monopolies.

One of the first printers whose books have been found in America was the Flemish Nuyts van Meere—from the first half of the sixteenth century—whose name was hispanized into Martin Nucio. Later, Cristophe Plantin (1514–1589) of Antwerp was named *prototypographus regius* ("chief printer") to Philip II of Spain. His books were attractive for their copious illustrations and because they carried a kind of royal seal of approval.

Twenty-eight paintings on the vaults of the lower choir of the parish church at Tecamachalco, Mexico, long puzzled art critics and scholars. They are scenes painted on stretched canvas—not the murals that were usual in the sixteenth century. It was observed that some had the shape and size of pre-Columbian shields. The rather gauche representations especially of animals, real and mythical, showed no European tradition. The painter was named Juan Gerson. Since reference books listed two Europeans of that name, it was supposed that the Mexican artist was a descendent. Some declared him of Flemish origin; some saw a Spanish, others an Italian background. One American professor declared him positively a North European, rejecting definitely any possibility of Indian blood. In the early 1960's, additional documentation proved that he was an Indian, a relative of the *cacique* Tomás Gerson; the family of the chieftain had received its name in baptism.

It was evident that the paintings were drawn from a book. A Bible was discovered that might have served as model, but as often happens, the opening section as well as the colophon was lacking. At this stage, this writer was given a copy of one page, picturing an Apocalyptic scene. We searched six libraries in Washington and New York, and in the seventh— the Episcopal General Theological Seminary, New York—we found a complete Bible to which the sheet from Mexico corresponded exactly. It was a pirated edition, printed in Lyons, France, in 1558, and as were so many, probably smuggled across the border into Spain, if not shipped down the river to Marseilles and from there to the Americas.

It is characteristic that scarcely any European artists with established names emigrated to the New World. The Flemish painter Simon Pereyns constitutes one early exception; he came to Mexico in 1568 and had a number of pupils. Several Italians were active in South America about the same time, the greatest among them being Bernardo Bitti (1548–c.1610);

a Jesuit lay brother, he reached Lima about 1575 and decorated many churches of his order. Paintings by Martin de Vos (1536–1593) are known to have been imported into Mexico. Francisco de Zurbarán (1598–1662) sent pictures to Lima and in 1649 exported a box of seventy-four canvases to Buenos Aires*—an amazing number for a city constantly snubbed in favor of the Peruvian capital. There is no like record concerning Bartolomé Estéban Murillo (1617–1682). However, as a youth he executed small panels and canvases of the Virgin for very little money that many a traveler to the Americas might have purchased for a talisman. Both these artists were active in Seville, a main harbor of transatlantic commerce; both expressed the religious fervor characteristic of their time. A number of anonymous colonial painters show their influence. However, the work of very few European masters can be identified in the colony. Aside from the ravages of time, restorers have often caused damage, painting the canvas over to a degree that obliterated its character.

Referring to sculpture, Juan Martínez Montañes (1563–1649) contracted for an altar in Lima,** and in the early eighteenth century, the Spaniard Jerónimo de Balbás personally supervised the building of the Altar de los Reyes in the cathedral of Mexico City, setting an elegant example for Mexican Churrigueresque.

In spite of the many handicaps, certain colonial painters rose to real eminence. In the sixteenth and seventeenth centuries, the Echave family furnished Mexico with three distinguished painters. Somewhat later, members of the Juárez and Rodríguez families attained widely deserved recognition in the same colony. In Colombia, Gaspar de Figueroa, in the midseventeenth century, and his pupil Gregorio Vásquez Ceballos became famous. In Ecuador, Miguel de Santiago and Nicolás Xavier de Gorívar were active in the last half of the seventeenth century, and Miguel Samaniego y Jaramillo should be mentioned some hundred years later. Engaging paintings survive in Peru from the brush of Diego Quispe Tito of Inca ancestry, and by Melchor Pérez Holguín in Bolivia. Other names appear in connection with illustrations of their work. The larger part of fine colonial painting, however, remains anonymous.

In the late seventeenth century, paintings began to replace sculpture on many retables. This, together with the erection of new side altars, brought a demand for literally thousands of pictures. By that time, also, the aristocracy, both civilian and ecclesiastical, began to have themselves immortalized in portraits, and other groups in society followed.

* Xavier Moyssén, "Zurbarán en la Nueva España," *Conciencia y Autenticidad Historicas.* Mexico, 1968.

** Beatrice Gilman Proske, *Juan Martínez Montañes, Sevillian Sculptor.* New York: Hispanic Society, 1967.

Melchor Pérez de Holguín, born around 1660, was a painter of distinction and considerable individuality, in Potosí, Bolivia. His last signed work is dated 1724. He was an albino, allegedly, whose weak eyes caused him to work only by candlelight. But in the Hispanic colonies, the word *albino* denoted someone with one eighth Negro blood—which seems the more likely interpretation.

Diego Morcillo Rubio de Auñon, the protagonist of Holguín's painting shown here [9.1], was Spanish born and a member of the Trinitarian order. He first became a bishop in La Paz, and later, archbishop of the diocese of Charcas. In 1716, he was also named interim viceroy of Peru, and in this capacity, he visited Potosí en route to the viceregal seat in Lima. Holguín depicts the event, which is described in detail by Bartolomé Arzáns in his history of Potosí.* In the painting the viceroy can be seen coming over the mountain in the distance. Having advanced into the city through a number of triumphal arches, he reappears in the foreground, riding a horse with a baldachin over his head, surrounded by ecclesiastic and civil luminaries, some of whom had journeyed to the city for this special occasion. Most of the other personages are on muleback, for the tight social scale of the colonial society prescribed who might ride a horse, who a mule, and who only with special permission could use any other conveyance than his own feet.

The parochial church in the background, labeled San Martín, is beflagged and hung with fine fabrics, as are all the other buildings visible. The arrival on the *Plaza Mayor* and the masquerade that took place the same evening in honor of the illustrious guests make up the two smaller sections of the painting.

There is a storybook atmosphere to the work, but it lacks the animation that so often characterizes such illustrations. It has a rather solemn touch, as the frail seventy-four-year-old man rides to what he must have known was a superhuman task.

Though not one of the many royal princes or heirs presumptive to the Spanish throne ever visited the colonies from which most of their revenues came, portraits of past and present Spanish rulers were reproduced in woodcuts and engravings, and distributed in the colonies. One should keep in mind the photograph of the incumbent President of the United States that hangs in all the post offices of this country. Here [9.2 and 9.3] the civil administration asserted itself with paintings of its supreme power, the Spanish king.

Ferdinand V (1452–1516), called "the Catholic," king of Castille

---

* Lewis U. Hanke, *Bartolomé Arzáns de Orsúa y Vela's History of Potosí.* Providence: Brown University, 1965.

and Aragon [9.3], is best known for driving the Moors from Spain. Ambitious to establish his power over a growing kingdom, he struggled to reduce the feudal rights of his landed aristocracy. Here he appears as stiff and unbending. His costume is that of the early sixteenth century with the round ruche and the tall light-colored boots that were the prerogative of only the highest in rank. His left hand rests on the hilt of his sword, his right on an inkwell in which a quill pen is stuck. All others in the scene, holding their books, are placed below him. One of the officials presents him with a heavy tome upon which the word *ordenamiento* can be deciphered. This word, repeated in larger letters above the king's head, is the clue to the scene. The painting represents Ferdinand's codification of law, assisted by the three worthies who are named in the long inscription in the upper left.

Philip II (1527–1598), son of Charles V, was very different from his father. While Charles, the multilinguist, was willing to listen even to Martin Luther, his son was obsessed with a mission to make the entire world Roman Catholic. Here we see him in late sixteenth-century dress, differentiated from that of Ferdinand by a daintier ruche, a shorter cape, and taller boots of dark material [9.2]. Like Ferdinand, he wears the insignia of the Golden Fleece around his neck. Once again, the ruler stands higher than his advisors; once again his left hand rests upon his sword; but in his right he holds a pair of gloves—perhaps to protect him from touching any of his underlings bare-handed. He also is accompanied by civilians with books, but the priest in the foreground, holding volumes of doctrinaire content, gives this picture its key. *"Nueba recapilación"* refers to the reaffirmation or repetition of the law as applied to the Indies, granting a great increase in ecclesiastical power. The erudite advisors are all named in the accompanying inscription, and the titles of their books are clearly written upon the volumes themselves.

Each of these canvases is over seven feet in height. Both were painted in Peru, even the one of Philip probably posthumously, with clumsy efforts at perspective—note the table and the pattern on the floor. Two rare surviving examples of the state portrait, they contrast sharply with the lovely characteristic style of painting and craftsmanship that evolved simultaneously.

The eighteenth century was the age of humanistic enlightenment and Encyclopedist writing. The great work of the Swedish botanist Linnaeus spurred other nationals to supplement his contributions. Among them, José Celestino Mutis (1732–1808), Spanish astronomer and botanist, asked help from the viceroy of Nueva Granada—as Colombia and its adjacent colonies were called—in gathering pictorial representations of the flora of the region. This resulted in Vicente Albán's making a number of paintings of the flora of his native Ecuador for Mutis. A member of a family of five painters, he produced religious pictures also, but it is these illustrations for which he is best known.

Altogether, seven paintings have survived. As a by-product of natural history, they also provide a detailed record of the festive costumes of various sections of the native population—Indian, mestizo, native Creole. The painting reproduced here [9.4] shows a town dweller in her best dress and jewelry. Her bare feet reveal her lowly station. Letters designate each plant represented, which then is described in the legend in the lower right corner of the work.

Storytelling pictures are frequently encountered from fabulous Peru, generally of biblical subjects. Favorite statues, especially at pilgrim centers, were often reproduced in paintings and carried far afield—much as a souvenir photograph is today. Such statue-paintings usually show the niche, the curtains, the baldachin, and accompanying decoration of the original, giving the impression of the three-dimensional. Especially in the High Andes, gold tooling in intricate patterns, such as those applied to leather, often decorates the costumes. Favorite Madonnas received gifts of gold or silver; jewel-studded crowns, brooches, necklaces, watches, and strings of pearls were sewn onto the canvas.

The Virgin Mary appears in a variety of aspects in the Americas, and there is virtually no end to the calendrical events honoring her in different costumes with different paraphernalia. Candlemas (February 2), the Feast of the Purification, is an important holiday, celebrating the presentation of Mother and Child in the temple, in a ceremony that involved the carrying of lighted candles. Torches and tapers always played an important part in ancient religion. So much more important became the role of the candles that the Spaniards introduced to the New World.

La Candelaria [9.5] is a statue-painting of rare impact. The Virgin stands on a silver crescent moon, looking straight out at one from the canvas. On her right arm, she carries the Christ Child; her left hand holds an elaborately decorated candle as tall as herself. She wears a flowered gown, picked out with gold, and a heavy gold-brocaded mantle. Lace of all sorts swathes the Baby and forms a jeweled band about her face. Even the dais on which she stands is edged with a delicate bit of lace. A multiple rope of pearls sweeps from her shoulder across the gown to a dainty purse fastened to her sleeve. Rich curtains frame the niche where she stands. Color and gold tooling encrust the figures like jewels on an icon. The decoration is not confusing but serves rather to emphasize the dignity and splendor of the protagonists.

Executed toward the end of the seventeenth or the beginning of the eighteenth century, the canvas probably comes from Bolivia or from nearby in the Peruvian highlands. Few paintings have survived from this period in which the coloring and the superb gold tooling, so characteristic of High Andean work, is so well executed and preserved.

Very different from the hieratic figure of La Candelaria is the gracious life-size representation of the Immaculate Conception in the cathedral in Cuzco [9.6]. Indeed, were it not for the crown that designates her as Queen of Heaven, this might be a young noblewoman in gala dress. No effort has been made to depict the three mystic garments. Bodice, skirt, and cloak are worked in amber on a gold ground. The crisp bows are deep blue, and silver stars of various shapes ornament the light veil over her hair like jewelry. The cherubs that push back the curtains are more *amoretti* than angels. It is a figure of girlish charm—a favorite of the Quechua Indians, who call her *mamacita* ("little mother").

The Near East, from Egypt to Greece, was the cradle of Christian art. It was there that the first pictorial representations from the Bible were made at a time when Europe was still in its so-called Dark Ages. For about a thousand years, the iconographical canons of the Greek Orthodox Church dominated the art of the Christian world, until the appearance of Duccio, Giotto, and their contemporaries in fourteenth-century Italy.

It was part of Byzantine tradition when a saint was represented as the central figure in a panel to place episodes of his life around him—a tradition that survived in the West. Colonial painters, also, made use of this device, as can be seen in a funerary procession of the Virgin Mary [9.7]. On the extreme upper right, a town appears. Two tall persons stand in the door of a church, whence a long procession of human figures marches toward the front. In a cave at the left, a man and a woman lift a lifeless figure, illuminated by rays from above. These are the opening and closing episodes, like the statement and coda in a musical piece, that serve to explain and underline the scene at the center of the canvas. There, her eyes closed in death, Mary lies on a gilded bed with curving footrest at one end and tall carved headrest at the other. She is covered with a lavish fabric. A golden light radiates from her head, and above her, seven cherub heads emerge from a semicircular cloud. John the Evangelist leads the procession of mourners. Prominent as pallbearers are Peter, in front, followed by Paul. All the main figures have haloes about their heads and wear garments tooled in gold in various patterns.

The landscape, with its sprinkling of flowers and many bright-colored birds, is typical of the Cuzco circle of painting in the seventeenth and early eighteenth centuries. There is a particular dignity in the movement of the procession—and it has an audience, at the lower left edge. In contrast to the figures in the visionary scene, these people are attired in colonial style. Their three-cornered hats and gold-bordered clothing serve to emphasize their status. They are the modern onlookers of this biblical story. Their alert air brings the scene closer to us. Here is not only a story depicted with naïve charm but effective drama.

At Chincheros, a large village of less than seven thousand people, about a hundred miles southeast of Ayacucho, a delightful episodic mural is preserved. It shows the flowing line of a religious procession, transcribed one might say into the local idiom, on the rough whitewashed outside walls of the church under overhanging eaves [9.8]. On the left, in the upper row, there is a portable organ. A small orchestra stands near—one man is playing the violin, another the harp, while a third seems to be directing a white-robed choir. Priests and notables in long cloaks, all kneeling, make up the lower row, headed by an ecclesiastic in ritual garments.

The procession has halted before a strongly emphasized painted frame within which the miraculous Virgin Mary holding Her Son sits enthroned. There are buildings at the right. Against the wall of one of them, which is marked with a cross, rests a ladder with a man beside it. Apparently, a fire burning a church roof has just been miraculously extinguished. Beyond the plaza on the hillside is a larger church with adjacent colonnade. On the left of the Virgin and Child, three soldiers with lances approach on horseback. In the nearer foreground, a young man with the help of an angel is handling an old-fashioned saw. This may be an allusion to St. Joseph the carpenter; the saw is a frequent attribute of his.

Here a bit of the life of the Andean Indian is recorded. There has been no attempt made to indicate perspective. The figures are made to flow or stand or move by the ingenious way they are placed and delineated. The style is reminiscent of that of the Inca writer Felipe Guamán Poma de Ayala, whose *Nueva Corónica y Buen Gobierno* ("new chronicle of good government"), written in the first decades of the seventeenth century, was illustrated with a quill pen, creating telling pictures with a simple line like comic strips today.

A building designated as San Martín is pictured in the background of the Viceroy Morcilla's entrance into Potosí [see 9.1]. This once important church, begun in the last years of the sixteenth century, has been much remodeled, but its original adobe walls and tiled roof are still intact. As if to compensate for what some might call just another primitive single-nave structure, large canvases in gilded Baroque frames cover the walls with lively color, bespeaking a luxury that rich Potosí by the middle of the seventeenth century could well afford [9.9]. At the left, Esther appears with King Ahasuerus, "which reigned from India even unto Ethiopia," and at the right, Constantine and his mother, St. Helena, the discoverer of the True Cross. It is interesting that in both cases the protagonists are women.

The style is European influenced by the historico-biblico tradition in which grand old palaces were decorated in the Old World. Apparently, the name "Francisco de Ol . . . Orozco," inscribed at the bottom, is that of the donor.

A row of archangels fills the space at the top of the wall. Their powerful wings are emphasized, and each carries some symbol of his identity. Pictures of archangels, sometimes carrying sixteenth- and seventeenth-century long muskets, seem to have been assigned a special place in Andean churches, instead of the Apostles, the Virtues and other allegorical figures, frequently seen in Europe and other parts of the Spanish empire.

When the superhuman task of missionary work demanded many laborers in distant and barbarous territories, "foreigners," that is, non-Spanish members of the Jesuit Order, were admitted to the New World. These non-Spanish priests brought with them a different training and, frequently, a different outlook on their duties—differences, such as an often-boasted superiority of education, and a secretiveness about their activities and their finances, that contributed to widespread animosity and ended finally in 1767 with the expulsion of the order.

They brought with them, also, the cult of different saints. One, who was never admitted into the list of Spanish saints, is John of Nepomuk. He was a priest, born in the Bohemian village of Nepomuk who became confessor to the queen. The king, Wenceslaus IV, jealous and suspecting intrigue against him, tried to extract the secrets of the confessional from John—and failing, had him thrown into the River Moldau from the bridge at Prague. For his inviolate vows, he became a patron saint of the Jesuits; he also watches over running water and bridges.

Although John of Nepomuk was not canonized until 1729, his figure appears soon afterward in the Americas. A painting from Ecuador tells his story [9.10]. The figure of the martyred saint occupies the center. His eyes are closed in death, and a halo of five stars surrounds his head. According to legend, he floated for a considerable time in the river with five brilliant stars hovering over him. The text reads *margaritum fulcens* ("the shining pearl"). The ermine collar is one of his attributes, symbolizing one who prefers death to impurity. Above him, there are three cherubs. One places the crown of martyrdom on his head. Another, with finger to lips, signifying silence, holds a rose and a padlock: *sub rosa, sub secreto.* The third important motto of the Jesuit order, *sub sigillo,* is inscribed on a sealed letter amid the gushing water of the Moldau, at the lower right.

John of Nepomuk's lifeless figure rests against a large shell, a reference to his watery death. A nymph decked with pearls, shells, and water plants lifts a fold of the drapery upon which the text is written *ab cundis ad coronam* ("from the wave to the crown"). In a scene below, reminiscent of the Byzantine tradition, John is shown being lifted out of the river.

One sees the arches of the bridge and the town of Prague beyond, with the biblical text, "He sent from above; he . . . drew me out of many waters. . . ."

The painting is signed *Bernardo Rodrigués fecit.* Dated works of this Ecuadorean artist range between 1783 and 1797. The fine execution of this canvas, the attention to details, the lovely expression of the nymph [9.11], raise it far above the usual didactic painting so frequent in that period. Even when we accept the fact that books and prints circulated in the colonies, it was Rodrigués who digested the whole complex legend of the saint and produced a picture of dramatic impact.

A painting of St. Joseph with the Christ Child [9.12] in the cathedral of Comayagua, Honduras, is little conventionalized. Gold tooling is limited to the scattered flowers on the garment. The Child is seated on the globe as if on a toy, and Joseph lightly holds the flowering staff, which the Apocrypha says burst into bloom as a sign that he had been chosen by God to wed the Virgin Mary. This painting is dated 1778 and signed by José Manuel Goméz, a native of Honduras, who later painted the dome and pendentives of San Miguel Tegucigalpa [see 7.37].

The hieratic spirit is weak also in an anonymous painting of the Immaculate Conception from Cuzco [9.13]. The tooling is sparse. The iconographical details are blurred. Mary clasps a book and looks, not heavenward, but out of the canvas; and the little angels would seem more concerned with forming a decorative garland around her than displaying the symbols of the Rosary. The dark object on the ground might be interpreted as a coffin, thus suggesting the Assumption, also.

In Mexican colonial painting, big bold compositions are characteristic. Among the many subjects from the Bible, few have the enduring charm of the Flight into Egypt. Here in Querétaro, Mexico, on a large canvas [9.14], seven by five and a half feet, a romantic landscape forms the background, with tropical vegetation, palms, and vines, and in the distance a wide sweep of valley and hill. A mule wearing the breastband of a draft animal is being led on a halter by two cherubs. Mary sits on a colonial-type saddle, with a water bottle at the pommel. She is depicted with delicate features, and her loving relationship with her Son is excellently portrayed in this family portrait. She feeds the Child discreetly, in contrast to what Titian or Rubens would have made of the scene. St. Joseph walks at her side, dressed in the costume of the seventeenth-century wayfarer, with the sturdy shoes and open-throated shirt that were the apparel of the poor, contemporary with the artist. Some of the light that illuminates the Mother and Child falls on him, also. His obvious concern for the members of his small family adds to the engaging quality of the portrayal, which is signed by Juan Rodríguez Juárez. There were four painters of ability in the Rodríguez family: Antonio, José, Juan (1675–1728), and Nicolás. Juan's father was Antonio, and his mother was the daughter of José Juárez, an earlier artist of fame, painter of the picture shown in 9.17.

Over the centuries, carpenters, painters, and sculptors of note were called in to construct many a triumphal arch and catafalque for solemn occasions, which were usually dismantled after they had served their purpose. Elizabeth I of England, on the way to her coronation, passed through arches decorated with portraits of her forebears with their heraldic insignia. Paintings for both catafalques and triumphal arches are mentioned in the inventory of El Greco's possessions, which his son wrote a few days after the Cretan painter's death. Military triumphs, the marriage of princes, or the birth of a royal heir were, also, appropriately celebrated in the colonies —even though they had taken place thousands of miles away and the news was reported months later. The death of a ruler was marked by special ceremonies centering around a catafalque set up in the main church of each town. Much illustrative and descriptive literature remains about the exequies of Philip II who died in 1598. A book, printed as a memento of the occasion, describes the funeral "pyre" of José de la Borda (1778), who financed the building of the justly admired church at Taxco, Mexico. An illustration shows a four-tiered catafalque, embellished with symbolic scenes and texts from Ovid and other classical authors. From a Franciscan chronicle in Guadalajara, we have details of a "tumulo," or catafalque, put up in memory of a beloved padre once active in that city, who died in Madrid in 1782. The population of the town was called upon to do him honor. The floor below the dome of the church was covered with rich carpets, upon which the cenotaph rose in four elevations. Half life-size figures of angels guarded the four corners, and twenty-four candelabra illuminated the structure, which was topped by a votive candle weighing six pounds. Such allegorical figures as the phoenix, the palm, the tortoise, decorated the sides, including a skeleton athwart an ascending eagle—a play on the deceased priest's name: Aguilár. The friars composed Latin and Spanish inscriptions. The catafalque appeared a blazing pyre amid the flames of torches and of the many candles "of purest white wax imported from the north."

All these catafalques are known to have existed through the written word only, or at most through representations in old engravings. In the Mexican town of Toluca, however, in a barren room of the art museum, this writer came upon an actual catafalque from the eighteenth century [9.15]. It is a four-sided, four-tiered structure.* On one side of the lower tier, there is the recumbent figure of a king in sixteenth-century garb. The corresponding panels show a pope, a cardinal, and a bishop. On the second

* Pál Kelemen, "A Mexican Colonial Catafalque," *The Art Quarterly,* Vol. XXVIII, No. 4, 1965; and *Americas,* Vol. 20, April 1968.

tier, we see Death and Amor in a symbolic scene. In the third, Death spins the wheel of life; here the skeleton is clothed, apparently out of consideration for the nun involved. On the top, in the smallest of the panels, a warrior in helmet and breastplate lifts a honeycomb from the mouth of a dead lion about which bees are still buzzing. Each picture is accompanied by a cartouche with a Spanish poem and a phylacterium with a Latin motto. In the last instance, the scene refers to Samson's taking honey from the dead lion of Timnath, described in the Old Testament. Thus, the topmost tier presents the résumé and lesson—Christ's victory over Death itself. In studying the various painted scenes, one is astonished at the amount of book-learning evinced by those friars who, as Carmelites, especially and continuously meditated upon death.

The panels on the catafalque could be folded away, so that they could be used whenever an important person died or when the anniversaries of his death were celebrated. After the secularization of the Mexican religious establishments, these paintings were placed in a storeroom in the church of Carmén, which then served the needs of the parish. Later, when the Mexican provinces began to reassemble their archaeological and historical material, the director of the Toluca Museum—just appointed—discovered the paintings and claimed them for his museum, since the parish church had no use for them; in the ensuing debate, the governor of the state ruled in his favor.

Both in the Old and the New World, there must be other similar paintings or statues, originally made for triumphal arches and catafalques. It would be a refreshing feat for some young art historian to search them out, rather than occupy himself with such a subject for his thesis as the furniture in Dürer's prints.

In the great cities of Hispanic America there was now a prosperous layer of society, conscious of its own taste and social ambitions, vying with one another in the display of elegance. It became the fashion to commission a religious painting for one's private chapel and/or have a family portrait done by a painter of name.

A child dressed in the costume of the mid-seventeenth century, with laces, rich braiding, and long-skirted coat, was portrayed by José Juárez (1635?–?1660) at the lower center of a large canvas representing the appearance of the Virgin to St. Francis [9.17]. Flowers strewn on the ground create a mild circle that separates the realistic little boy from the legendary gathering. He looks out of the picture, in contrast to the others who are involved in the religious drama. The shield that he holds with appropriate solemnity declares "the devotion of my father Alonso Gómes." The portrait, in all likelihood, is true to life. Much care has been given to the details of the costume. By that time in Europe, such groups were rare, but here portraits were quite often worked into biblical or legendary compositions. Such a painting served a double purpose—offering to the ecclesia a new pride, and also, perpetuating a scion of a family that has long since vanished and would have been forgotten, were he not thus immortalized.

By a lucky coincidence, two paintings of the same person can be placed beside each other, as both are in the same museum in the United States. In the first [9.16], María de la Luz Padilla y Cervantes of viceregal lineage appears as a child, and in the second, in a portrait by Miguel Cabrera [9.18], as a grown woman. Cabrera was born in Oaxaca—in 1695, according to one source; in 1719, according to another. He died in Mexico City in 1768. A painter with a smooth brush and ingratiating manner, he was a favorite of Mexican society. The approach to the subject is somewhat the same in both portraits, and certain common features—such as the pouting lips, the line of the nose—are recognizable. The use of jewelry, so important in the display of wealth, can already be observed in the child's picture, where a pearl necklace, showy earrings, embroidery and silks, and elegant ribbon bows embellish the child's costume.

The woman is painted in the skillful, smooth manner that made Cabrera so popular. Here he could display his talent in the delicacy of color and the sumptuous textures of the silk, the pearls over the wrists, in the heavy necklace, the earrings, and rings. Even the fan is lovingly detailed. Note the flowers on the veil-like headdress, painted like a bouquet, that connects the forehead with the silken cap farther back on her powdered hair.

Cabrera painted a great number of religious pictures—also, portraits of viceroys, bishops, and nuns. His best-known work is the posthumous portrait of Sor Juana Inés de la Cruz (1651–1695). A young Carmelite nun, she was the great poetess of her age, whose hymns evince a profound philosophy and whose sonnets reveal the subconscious of her dreams expressed in distinguished Spanish. Cabrera was once highly valued; then he was depreciated; now the judgment is at midpoint: he is seen as a representative good eighteenth-century Mexican painter.

When the colonies achieved independence, following the example of the United States, democratic institutions were essayed. Native strength and talent made themselves felt in the art schools. By the end of the nineteenth century, a storytelling art had developed, often naïve but usually charming; and for the first time, the Indian became a subject. In relatively unsophisticated prints, paintings on metal and wood, masks and wax figures, truly fascinating folklore evolved. From this, it was only a step for mural painters and contemporary artists to develop a style which although utilizing European tradition, is strongly the expression of the Western Hemisphere.

CANTERÍA.

LA PARROQUIA DE SAN MARTIN

AESTA BILLA IMPERIAL, DIA LOS M

[9.1] Entrance of Archbishop and Viceroy Morcillo into Potosí, by Melchor Pérez de Holguín.
Bolivia.

[9.2] Philip II. Cuzco, Peru.

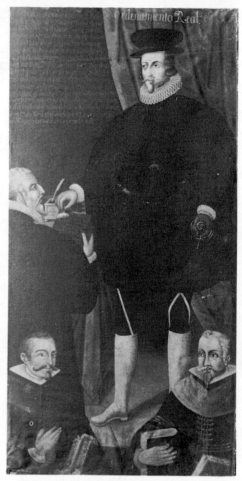

[9.3] Ferdinand V. Cuzco.

[9.4] Native woman with local products, by Vicente Albán. Quito, Ecuador.

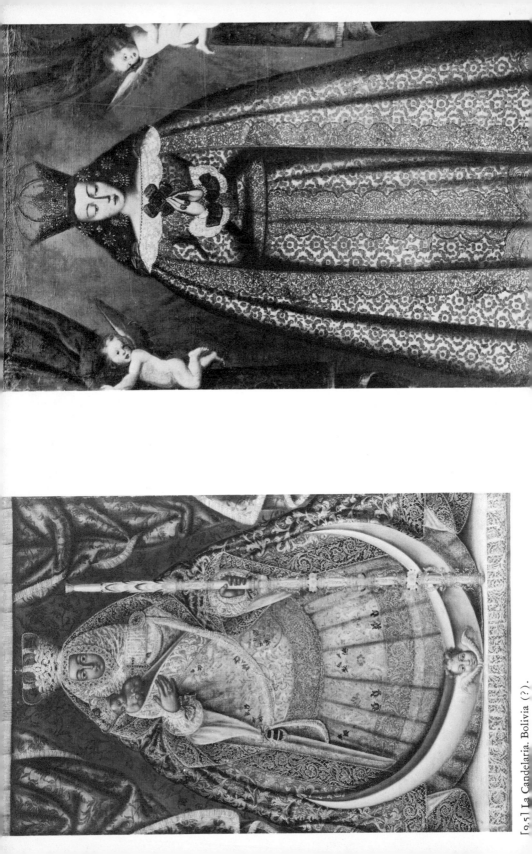

[105] La Candelaria. Bolivia (?).

[9.7] Funeral of the Virgin Mary. Cuzco, Peru.

[9.8] Mural. Chincheros, Peru.

[9.9] Paintings in chancel. San Martín. Potosí, Bolivia.

[9.10] St. John of Nepomuk, by Bernardo Rodrigués. Ecuador.

[9.11] Detail of painting.

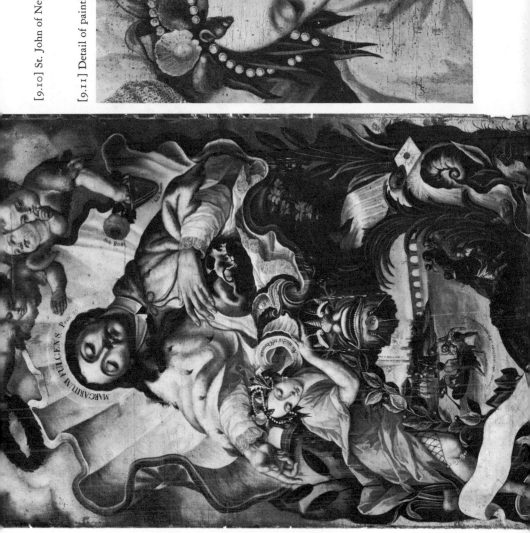

[9.12] St. Joseph and the Christ Child, by José Manuel Gómez. Comayagua, Honduras.

[9.13] Inmaculada. Cuzco, Peru.

[9.14] Flight into Egypt, by Juan Rodríguez Juárez. Mexico.

9.15] Catafalque. Toluca, Mexico.

[9.16] Doña María de la Luz Padilla y Cervantes. Mexico.

[9.17] Detail from The Apparition of the Virgin to St. Francis, by José Juárez. Mexico.

[9.18] Doña María de la Luz Padilla y Cervantes, by Miguel Cabrera. Mexico.

10 / Retables and Woodcarving

The cooperation between various colonial craftsmen came to its highest expression in the retable or reredos, that massive gilded wall rising behind the altar table, with saints and even entire scenes of the Bible placed on shelves and in niches. Sometimes a window was incorporated, which focused the light significantly through its gilded frame. Often a *camarín* ("little chamber") was constructed for the chief figure, sometimes comprising a small sacristy behind the main altar where the image was dressed and decorated. Occasionally, the *camarín* was built with windows on the outside, so that the image would be illuminated by natural light with very dramatic effect.

The wood carver's art forms in itself an expression of the period. The late Baroque employed as part of the composition inverted obelisks, or *estípites,* wreaths, elaborate consoles, columnettes, and other fancies. Lacy borders of gilded wood bound the piece to the wall of the apse. Paintings began to play a role in the composition, often giving the interior a drawing-room character. The gilded background shows a variety of surface decoration, ranging from broad basket-weave patterns to heavy swags. In the Rococo period, there was less gilding. Dainty multicolored bouquets were often scattered on a white ground.

Although, at first, this splendor might be dazzling, these retables show an amazingly harmonious spirit to those accustomed to the art. Great regional differences, however, can be observed. The style of the north Mexican eighteenth-century retable is fully distinguishable from anything carved in the Peruvian capital at the same period. The unexpected richness of gold leaf throughout Latin American colonial art far surpasses what contemporary European church art produced.

There were guilds for each of the crafts—for tailors, candlemakers, bakers, fishermen, tanners, cigarmakers, weavers, hatmakers, coach builders, barber-surgeons, innkeepers, dyers, confectioners, potters—as well as for the practitioners of the higher arts and crafts, such as masons, sculptors and joiners, cabinetmakers, painters, and gilders. In each guild, the senior masters held the authority. It was traditional for the son to take over from his father. The finished work was always inspected and judged by an official jury. Each guild had its distinctive dress and its patron saint, and celebrated his particular holy day.

Usually, the master of sculpture or of sculpture and joinery contracted for a retable, but other crafts had to be called in to complete it. This included the painter of the pictures, also the painter of the statues—the *estofador*—and the gilder, or *dorador,* of the carving. One master might submit the design, then turn it over to another to be carried out. There were also guarantors who had to promise to see the work through in case the original contractor failed or died. Generally, the details of the retable were specified, the kind of columns, what saints should be represented and where they should stand, even the sort of wood to be used. Sometimes a priest was named to furnish the proper iconographical norm for the various representations. The use of an older piece—a favorite Madonna or a series of saints—might be required or the altar of another church copied or the decor of an older one changed in accord with fashion.

The monasteries were rich and often called for masters from the large artistic centers to journey far afield. Sculptors seem to have been rather rare. The same names occur again and again in various contracts. The fact that they needed the assistance of local carvers, to get the work done on time, may account for the variety in the retables especially of the last half of the eighteenth century.

San Jerónimo near Huancayo, Peru, is mentioned as a prosperous Indian village in the early seventeenth century. Today in its parish church, part of a retable that might have once served as the main altar stands against a side wall with incongruous later additions. Its lower section, however, retains original parts [10.1 and 10.2]. Little individual style or regional preference is evident—only the attempt to follow a prescribed formula; the blossoming of originality comes later, leaving the groping beginnings far behind. The doors of the center section of this retable are painted with figures of the four Doctors of the Church, of whom San Jerónimo (St. Jerome) was one [10.1]. Note the even and unpretentious framing, the classically conceived but not fully executed twin columns, the crosses on the lower part of the two inner columns. To the right and left, two saints, possibly St. Jerome and St. Thomas Aquinas, are carved in the half round. Two cartouches [10.2] framed in scrolls and arabesques name the friar and the governor in charge at that time, with the date, 1609. The cartouches flanking the figures recall the Plateresque of sixteenth-century Spain, showing the time lag frequent in the colonies. But in a number of details, especially the general proportions and the relation of one motif to the other, the work is already removed from its model.

The road to Metztitlán, in the state of Hidalgo, Mexico, goes through the famous mining city of Pachuca and passes the Real del Monte, both of which poured out fabulous treasure for centuries. Beyond the miners' dwellings, it deteriorates, and after the bridge at Venado, it peters out. One graveled way leads steeply toward a high pass; another branches in a sharp descent to the left and runs along the green valley of a mountain stream. Curving hills keep the extent of the land obscured for a time, but the richness of the crops, burgeoning through expert irrigation, shows at once why the Augustinians selected it for one of their provinces. One passes several villages, and finally, after some forty minutes of slow progress on the bumpy dusty road, one sees the end of the valley closed off by rocky walls that are streaked with mineral colors. At the far end, on a promontory some four hundred feet above the river, the monastic complex rises above the surrounding settlement, calling to mind the castles that overlooked the vast holdings of the feudal and ecclesiastical aristocracy in Europe.

Some fifty feet of steep cobbled way lead from the main plaza of the town to the complex, which has an unusually extended oblong atrium, with some remnants of crenelated walls. Many of the accessory structures are in ruins; the stones have been carried away to repair the road. A battlemented roof and an espadaña filled with bells strengthen the first impression of medievalism. The complex is recorded among the first forty-five monasteries established in Mexico before 1540.

The façade of this church is mildly Plateresque. A large arched open chapel, adjoining the nave at the apse end, is now used for storage. The cloister, at the right of the church, is quite small with a pretty garden, though with little sunshine. Remnants of black-and-white murals adorn the walls, and below, a dado runs in fanciful arabesques. The designs are very bookish, probably taken from woodcuts, but enlarged and adapted with skill. There was much damage done to the complex in the revolution. The soldiers looted the archives; the only documents left refer to births, baptisms, marriages.

The church itself is a long barn, very high with a barrel vault. Under the choir gallery, the ceiling spreads like an umbrella and carries bright floral stuccowork, doubtless repainted on the original design.

The contract for the main altar—a rare find—is dated 1696. The friars were then affluent enough to bring into this remote valley a sculptor of renown [10.4]; Salvador de Ocampo is named as *ensamblador,* or general foreman. Son of the most famous sculptor of his time—Tomás Xuárez who is documented as an Indian, a resident of Mexico City—Ocampo is believed to have been born around 1665 and to have died about 1732. He held a master's degree "on what pertains to joinery, woodcarving, and architecture." Three other craftsmen are named in the contract: Nicolás Rodríguez Juárez as master painter, and a gilder and a maker of gold leaf as guarantors. Ocampo probably had several helpers—most probably of Indian or mestizo origin also. The late date of the retable proves that such work was done by native Indians and mestizos not only when Spanish craftsmen were scarce but throughout the colonial period.

Juárez's paintings on canvas show the wear and tear of the centuries and have greatly darkened, but the relief groups hold our interest in spite of the dust that has settled upon them. A magnificent carving of the Adoration of the Magi with rich *estofado* occupies the center; above this is a Crucifixion, partly in the round, partly in relief; and over all, the figure of God the Father encircled by angel heads. The statues at the sides are known to have been removed and may not all be the original ones. But the figures of the Four Evangelists in the predella at the base of the retable show the master's hand. Illustrated are Mark and John carved in three-quarters round [10.3]. The sculptor has admirably solved his task to encompass in the narrow space not only the two saints but their symbols, the lion and the eagle. The quality of workmanship is evidenced also in the excellent preservation of *estofado* and *encarnación*. The architectural framing of the retable is rich but organized and does not divert the emphasis from the central theme.

The Valley of Oaxaca is one of the most varied and picturesque regions in all Mexico, rich not only in agriculture and pasture land, but also in mines. Cortés received it, together with the title of Marqués del Valle, as a reward for his exploits. The Dominicans, who were among the most active in this remote domain, started their building activities here early. By the mid-sixteenth century, they had established themselves in a mining district known as Villa Alta San Ildefonso, which Humboldt lists among the eight richest gold- and silver-producing regions. The Mixtec gold jewelry of Monte Albán comes to mind.

To reach there from Oaxaca, one must travel for a while on the Inter-American Highway, then leave the broad pavement and begin to mount in a northerly direction. Dipping repeatedly from mountain saddle into deep valley and then climbing again, skirting the huge shoulders of steep hills, we caught an occasional glimpse of a ruined church or a distant crenelated monastery with no apparent path leading to it. After several hours, we came to a village where houses were being repaired and road markers whitewashed. This is San Pablo Gueletao, where the Indian national hero Benito Juárez was born. The place was being spruced up for the centennial celebration. From here on, the road deteriorates into a narrow graveled path, climbing and twisting. Toward noon, approaching the town of Ixtlán, we reached a church built of large massive stone blocks, with little outside decoration, perched on the precipice. A few more turns brought us to the main plaza.

Ixtlán is on the way to Villa Alta and close to the mines. It stands at a very high altitude, among peaks that reach over eleven thousand feet. Its town hall [see 7.2] shows at how early a date colonial life was established. There seem to have been at least three churches: the one just passed on the precipice; another on the main plaza—probably the earliest—which is now without a roof, its half dome still protecting a dilapidated altar. On the same level stands the third, an impressive building dedicated to the Apostle Thomas. A stone relief on the main portal of this church shows Christ standing erect with the flag of Resurrection in his hand as Doubting Thomas kneels before him. Some traces of dark color are still visible. The date 1757 is carved at the top.

By comparing the main retable at Metztitlán with this one at Ixtlán, Oaxaca [10.5], one can see the great change of style that took place within a span of a hundred years. In the earlier piece, the horizontals run through the entire design. They are evenly balanced with the verticals, giving a sense of serenity and poise. In the other, later piece, the horizontals are unconnected, and the verticals are emphasized. Upstriving is evident. In the earlier retable, the architectural elements dominate; in the later one, the sculptural subordinates all other details, including the paintings. The effect is aided by the fact that the sides are "hinged" forward, following the curve of the apse. The central section of this retable broadens like a stage setting. Columns have turned into *estípites*. Garlands, archangels, and scattered cherubs make a restless, scintillating ensemble.

The central group with the Doubting Thomas is recessed and lighted as if by a window, recalling the *camarín*. A curtained baldachin above the group adds to the feeling of depth. A splayed frame surrounds this section, carved and gilded in masterly fashion with shell-like volutes. The shell, which figures so prominently in the baptism of Christ and which became the symbol of Spain's patron saint, James the Great, gained an additional meaning throughout the Americas by the baptism of millions of Indians. The space where in the older altar stood a sculptural group, with Mary and John at the foot of the Crucifix, is at Ixtlán filled with a painting of the Assumption, as the cult of Christ began to be overshadowed by that of His mother. Unchanged is the figure of God the Father above, blessing this holy gathering.

The carving of the retable at Ixtlán was completed in 1760 and the gilding in 1770. The names of the sculptor and gilder are inscribed on the altar itself: José Villegas and José de Armengor Era. The latter is an Indian name.

As the day came to a close, and note-taking permitted us to sit a little longer in one of the pews admiring the splendid interior, a lady entered. She told us that she lived in Mexico City and each time she visited her relatives in Oaxaca, she took a day to come here, not minding the poor transportation, because she liked this church interior even more than Tepotzotlán, the guide-book showplace of Jesuit Churrigueresque. This retable has not yet been restored (1967); this interior still has a patina.

She left to catch the only bus back. We went out onto the vast church plaza, which once was possibly a Mixtec temple base. The sun was moving toward the range of the Sierra Madre del Sur. From the edge of the plateau we could see the valley below. The smoke from evening cooking covered the valley with a thin blue veil. The sun reflected red on the little pond of Gueletao, where Juárez as a small child is said to have spent a night of hazard and terror on a floating island, rather than desert the few sheep in his care. The spot of water fits well into this enthralling landscape. They call it *laguna encantada* ("enchanted pond"). This is the ambience where legends are born and one is inclined to believe them.

Whether it was an intricate retable, a beam in the ceiling, an organ case, native talent could always make it appealing. Andahuaylillas, some thirty miles from Cuzco, lies in a rich agricultural district of the Andean highlands. The parish church there, founded in late sixteenth century, is a barn-like structure built of adobe and roofed with cane and timber, as was usual at the time in that region. Mural paintings adorn the façade.

In 1631, the parish priest, one Juan Pérez de Bocanegra, had some of the interior redecorated. He is known to have published a dictionary of the Quechua language, and inscriptions in Quechua in various parts of the building may date from his time. Growing wealth tended to siphon off the wealthier landowners to the capital. Thus, this church remains a specimen of what was done in remote corners of the viceroyalty.

Painting covers the walls of the large choir like tapestry and embellishes the rough saplings that support the roof [10.6]. There are two organs. The cases, at least, are doubtless of local make, for they feature native instruments among more general types from the mid-seventeenth century. Illuminated books of anthems, celebrating the Incarnation, were discovered here.

On the main retable of the Jesuit mission church of San Miguel, Mojos, Bolivia, the archangel Michael stands at the center in fighting pose, where Mary is usually placed [10.7]. His wings are spread wide; his left foot swings to support the right which is thrust forward in attack. His flaming sword recalls that of the Apocalyptic Virgin at Popayán [see 8.11]. Everything shines with gold, even his shield, preserved by the excellence of the gilding for more than two hundred years. The surrounding architectural details of the retable, all of cedar, show considerable variety and durable construction. Note the silver altar frontal.

The town of Santa María de Comayagua, once called Nuevo Valladolid de Comayagua, the first capital of Honduras, was founded as early as 1537. It became firmly established as a city about fifty years later when a nearby silver mine began to thrive. The present cathedral dates from the early eighteenth century and boasts several fine domes, covered with shining tiles of local manufacture. The façade is decorated in stucco with regional motifs, palm fronds, and arabesques of grapevines.

Within, the vaulted ceiling still stands firm. To the right, at the end of a narrow side aisle, a retable rises against the same wall as the main altar [10.9]. Dedicated to the Virgin of the Rosary, it presents reliefs of the Six Joyful and Six Sorrowful Mysteries of Mary. The Glorious Mysteries— Pentecost, Coronation, and Assumption—are depicted at the top. The carving is clear and direct, the coloring enamel-like; the surrounding frame is rich but unobtrusive. Shallow relief work in an over-all design of gilded wood also covers the altar frontal to match the retable's base.

The contract for this retable, dated July 9, 1708, was discovered in Guatemala. It names Vicente de la Parra as the sculptor and sets the cost at 380 pesos. De la Parra was born in Guatemala about 1667. With this contract, his name disappears from the Guatemala archives, and it is thought that he may have remained in Honduras after finishing the altar.

Apparently, religious fervor and the pride of prosperity were not satisfied with the first retable, tall and effective as it was. Three large paintings surrounded by a lacy gilded screen fill the space above it. Although somewhat later in style, the group is harmoniously designed to supplement the lower section.

The once great wealth of this community is even more manifest in the adjacent Sagrario chapel to the left of the nave. On the pendentives, four archangels in stucco support the unusually high dome, where the sun is depicted at the zenith with large flowers striving upward toward it. On the tabernacle of the altar [10.8], the Four Evangelists appear in high relief. Its central columns, with four varieties of motif, contrast with the taller twisting ones at the sides. The door to the small cupboard is tortoiseshell inlaid with silver. A fine contemporary statue of Mary praying occupies the central niche. There is nothing flamboyant about this church, although some motifs show awareness of current fashion. Elegance is preserved in this sleepy town, the name of which even some specialists may disregard.

Some of the difference between colonial art and its European models is due to the great variety of new materials in the New World. The virgin forests of the Americas supplied durable wood of excellent quality in hitherto unknown quantity. The Spaniards contributed highly efficient metal tools. The Indians, who had an inborn plastic talent, came with the passage of time to command the métier. Whether a retable, an altar frontal, a ceiling, a chandelier, or furniture, there were few problems these craftsmen did not overcome. Sometimes it would seem that they enjoyed compounding the details and raising the complications of their work to the highest degree.

In the early churches, Mudéjar ceilings of carved and gilded wood alternate with Renaissance patterns. Later, the Baroque used gold over large shapes in a truly lavish manner. The Rococo reduced the dimensions of the motifs and began to apply white lacquer and mille-fleur colored designs, even painted scenes enclosed in medallions.

The small nunnery of Santa Clara, Ayacucho, Peru, was founded in 1568 by Antonio de Orue—later *corregidor*—and his wife. Their five daughters became nuns there; in 1637 the pulpit was donated by an abbess who still bore their names. The ceiling over the sanctuary in the convent church [10.11] is one of the earliest still existing in this region, dating not much later than the church's foundation. It shows the typical Mudéjar construction, adapted from Spanish tradition, in which double beams are overlaid with an intricate geometric pattern of different colored woods. The octagonal concavities thus formed are embellished with vari-colored inlay and ornate bosses. It is fortunate that the hanging candelabrum in the center has been preserved also. It, too, is constructed of wood, tastefully though elaborately decorated, with holders for nearly fifty candles. Alas, in many places, such a work of art is now replaced by a single naked electric bulb hanging on a long wire.

In the church at Potosí, dedicated to the Miraculous Virgin of Copacabana, an octagonal tray-shaped ceiling in the Renaissance style is preserved over the north transept [10.10]. It is fashioned in a checkerboard design with carved rosettes, each with a boss protruding from the center. A detail [10.12] shows the exquisite workmanship and its durable quality. Similar ceilings over the crossing and the chancel were also intact in 1945 when the photograph was taken.

Enticing nosegays of red and blue flowers are painted in squared-off panels under the choir loft of Orcatuna's unpretentious rural church [10.13]. Note the careless repairs—a bit of carved wood and a piece of painted mural showing a human arm. The village, situated some twenty miles northwest of Huancayo, is described as having been in the early seventeenth century predominantly Indian, situated in a very fertile valley that produced perhaps the best ham and bacon of the whole region, "with prices very low." Standing on the King's Highway, it was known for its Indian silversmiths, who used not hammers and bellows in their work, but blowpipes and their ancient tools; and many ancient monuments were situated on the neighboring hillsides.

It is interesting to note that a similar type of decoration was widely used in rustic European churches during the seventeenth and eighteenth centuries when Protestants took over former churches of Rome.

Because of its great agricultural potential, the province around Uruapan, Mexico, was another early field of intensive missionary work. Some of the settlements are still difficult to reach and preserve rare exam-

ples of colonial art in their churches. In the village of Naranja—the name
evidently refers to the cultivation of oranges there in colonial times—
a remarkable wooden ceiling over the church's sanctuary embodies many
traditions [10.14]. It is tray-shaped. Its crossbeams are painted with colored
flowers, but a simplified Mudéjar interlacing is carried on the ladderlike
supports that divide the various sections. Notable is its parade of holy
figures, drawn in outline. From an archangel playing a lute to a saintly
bishop, from such symbols of the Virgin as the sun, crescent moon, stars,
and crown to the Dominican seal in black and white, it presents an amazing
array of biblical and ecclesiastical figures, unconnected in sequence, an
interpretation as far from the tenets of the Council of Trent as the village
is from that Tyrolean town. As has been seen in examples from such
separated regions as Andahuaylillas, the Andean highlands, and Mexico,
this technique was practiced in rural churches from the end of the sixteenth
century, though in widely diverse idioms. It is possible that here, in the
course of repairing, saints who became popular in later centuries were
added.

Pulpits, also, received much attention. Usually carved of wood, with
panels or open-work balustrades, gilded and colored, they seem great
jeweled chalices, with the *portavoz,* or sounding board, suspended from
above or worked into a decorative canopy. Sometimes, the pulpits hang on
the wall like a balcony; sometimes, the stair is turned into an ornamental
feature.

The village of Piribebuy stands on the Paraná River in Paraguay.
Neglected today, its church retains its hexagonal colonial pulpit nearly unchanged [10.15]. The graceful cartouches are Rococo in spirit, as is the
series of tassels fringing the lower edge. It has been said that the trees of
the region were so gigantic that each could serve alone as a single column.
Here the strongly folkish angel—also sometimes called "Samson"—that
upholds the pulpit might have been carved from such a trunk.* The figure
might have been inspired by a caryatid, such as supports a Baroque balcony,
but the pose, the size, and the proportions are native American. It has the
drollness of a cigar-store Indian.

Even the confessionals, the furniture in the waiting rooms, tables,
benches, and chairs were often works of art. The interior of the church at
Asangaro in the Peruvian highlands [see 7.22] seems to have remained
more or less intact. Only with the coming of trains and trucks were the old
objects discarded. Here intricate carving, heavily gilded, covers a colonial
confessional [10.16]. The Tree of Life in the form of a large vase of flowers
can be seen on the side. An ornate roof with a lantern on top covers the

* Josefina Plá, "Apuntes historico-descriptivos sobre algunos templos para-
guayos," *Anales del Instituto de Arte Americano e Investigaciones Estéticas,* No. 21,
Buenos Aires, 1968.

whole, as if it were a separate building within the building. The flanking volutes and garlands, minutely carved and gilded, apparently served as candelabra, and bring a certain lightness to the piece.

Like much of colonial Cuzco, the monastery complex of the Mercedarian order, including the much-admired cloister, was rebuilt after the earthquake of 1650. The miniature scene of the Three Wise Men, illustrated here [10.17], has the seventeenth-century spirit, a testimony to the sculptor's devotion as well as his skill, far removed from mass production. Mary and the Child display the regal dignity to be expected of them, but also a human touch, as she allows the Infant Christ to lay His hand on the head of the kneeling king. The fine coloring, the differentiations of costume in all their biblical splendor, make a beguiling piece of genre art.

Though in the majority of instances in Hispanic America retables were made of wood, it is interesting to note that at the beginning as well as at the end of the colonial epoch, other materials were used. Masonry altars and stone shrines in the piers of the choir loft are found in Juli and Pomata [see 7.16]. An entire retable, made of a local form of alabaster called *tecali,* and dating from the last third of the eighteenth century, stands in San José Chiapa, a village seventy miles northeast of Puebla.

As one nears the northern border of Mexico, where productive mines functioned, the scarcity of wood in church interiors becomes marked. At San Luis Potosí, the interior screen to the shrine of Carmén is of carved stone as intricate as if it were a retable. Between Torreón and Durango, in the large village of Cuencamé, the pulpit as well as the altar is of masonry. The same is true in the parochial church at Batuc, Sonora, now engulfed, and at Bacadehuachi, situated farther north in the same state. During the restoration of some Pueblo village churches in New Mexico, retables of brick, adobe, and burned clay were discovered under the wooden panels. The interior of San Xavier del Bac is an outstanding example of virtuosity in molded brick [see 7.49].

It is difficult for the present-day reader to realize that until iron came into use to bear heavy weight, the only available material for such purposes was wood. Magnificent trees stood in the forests of Hispanic America. In the early decades, they were usually quite near the settlements where they could be used. Wood, however, was not only at hand for the convenience of the population. The main consumer was the miner, who to augment the fifth of the mined metal claimed by the king, had permission to cut logs and collect wood wherever needed. The tunnels in the mines were supported by wooden beams. All lifting apparatus was made of wood, and perhaps the greatest quantities were burned for the charcoal needed in smelting. Wood even made up the machinery of the mints [see 11.15].

By the middle of the eighteenth century, the American forests were greatly depleted. There was no reforestation; erosion set in. Since mining operations took priority over all other activities in the colony, the Spanish king Charles III (1716–1788) issued a decree forbidding the use of wood in retables.*

It was somewhat of a shock to us, who had been moved by Willa Cather's *Death Comes for the Archbishop*, when we first saw in 1936 the cathedral in Santa Fe, New Mexico, for which Jean Batiste Lamy strove all his life. It is a pseudo- and neo-Gothic structure, plebian in every aspect and out of place in this landscape. The interior is no better.

A curtain was lifted at the right of the main altar, and we stepped in to find that the wall behind was not more than five feet away. There was only space and light enough to see a tall carved stone piece mortared into the wall. By bending and peering, we realized that here, behind the late-nineteenth-century carpentry, a stone retable was—vertically but veritably —buried [10.18]. Its history has an especial appeal. New Mexico was a territory allotted to the Franciscan missionaries. By the eighteenth century Santa Fe had a growing Spanish and mestizo population, with a parish church and several chapels for the use of the Indians, Negroes, and other nonwhite population. In mid-century, a large chapel was erected for the military personnel, dedicated to Nuestra Señora de la Luz (Our Lady of Light)—an aspect of the Virgin brought over by a missionary from Sicily only a few decades earlier and widely adopted especially in Mexico and the north.** The military chapel having fallen into disuse, its stone retable, dated 1761, was transferred to the new cathedral, where Bishop Lamy hid it in 1859, and it remained almost forgotten until 1939. Then, the Anglo-American community, which has done so much to preserve the Pueblo architectural style of Santa Fe, arranged a deservedly dignified place for it in the apse of the church of El Cristo Rey (Christ the King).

God the Father appears at the top of the retable, with hand raised in a gesture of blessing. Beneath is a Spanish version of Mary, "Our Lady of Valvanera," and below this, a large relief of St. James the Great— Santiago on horseback—with Joseph and the Child at the left and John of Nepomuk at the other side. In the lower row, Ignatius Loyola, founder of the Jesuit Order, stands at the left, and Francis Solano, known as the Apostle of South America, at the right. It is interesting to note that the two saints in the right-hand section were canonized only a few years before the altar was carved. Traces of color can be seen, especially on the caryatids and the arabesques surrounding the panels.

An opening in the middle of the lower section may have been a niche

* Francisco de la Maza: personal communication.
** Pál Kelemen, "The Significance of the Stone Retable of Cristo Rey," *El Palacio,* Vol. 61, August, 1954.

for a statue or a tabernacle. Now it is occupied by a carved panel of Our Lady of Light, not quite tall enough to fill the space. It seems that this panel was on the outside of the original garrison church. Although the Virgin Mary thus appears on the retable for the second time, it is a better solution than if this important stone tablet had been placed anywhere else in the new building.

The depiction has missionary connotations. On her left arm, Mary carries the Child; with her right, she lifts a soul in the form of a terrified human being out of the gaping jaws of Hell. In each hand, the Child holds a flaming heart, symbol of Christian devotion; others lie in the basket proffered by an angel. The relief is a faithful rendition of the original canvas venerated in the cathedral of León, Mexico; Caspicara's fine miniature carving of the same figure from Quito has been discussed earlier [see 8.13].

The retable presents a highly unusual piece of eighteenth-century stone carving. It was believed earlier that the carving was brought from Zacatecas, where such work reached a high level [see 7.39]. But although in technique it may be distantly related to the splendid exteriors of that silver city, there is a rustic air about it. The quarry from which the stone was taken was discovered just a few miles from Santa Fe. When the garrison chapel was excavated, chips of this same stone were unearthed, proving that the work was done *in situ.*

Since there is a ruling that consecrated objects in a church shall not be disposed of in an undignified manner, Bishop Lamy, undoubtedly, walled in and covered over the colonial retable, to have it out of his way and at the same time to act according to regulations. Further, knowing that in the community to which he had become the first bishop, the stone altar had served the faith for a long time, it might have been a sort of talisman to him to have it in his new building, although completely obscured. It is perhaps understandable that the bishop, born of peasant parents in the small French village of Lempdes, could not appreciate the architecture that the Pueblo Indian produced, which blended so perfectly into the landscape. But that he did not feel the spiritual effort in this work, the striving to express a religious concept, shows not only how insensitive he was toward the traditions of the land in which he became the highest ecclesiastical authority and from which he earned his living, but how little he had changed in his attitudes from his inarticulate adolescent years. His ideal of culture and art was the one he bore with him from his provincial beginning.

Bishop Lamy was certainly neither the first nor the last European to lack completely any understanding and appreciation of the art of the Americas. His figure is touchingly idealized in Willa Cather's book, and only those who now see the church of Cristo Rey can perceive how distant the actual facts are from the book's fiction.

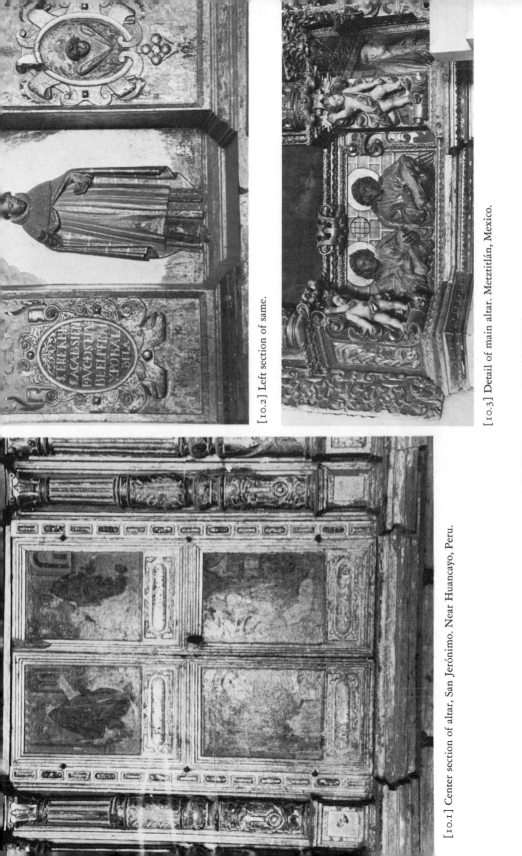

[10.2] Left section of same.

[10.3] Detail of main altar. Metztitlán, Mexico.

[10.1] Center section of altar, San Jerónimo. Near Huancayo, Peru.

[10.4] Main altar. Metztitlán, Mexico.

20.5] Main altar. Ixtlán, Mexico.

[10.6] Organ loft. Andahuaylillas, Peru.

[10.7] Detail of main altar. San Miguel, Bolivia.

[10.8] Detail of altar, Sagrario Chapel, cathedral.
Comayagua, Honduras.

[10.9] Side altar, cathedral. Comayagua.

[10.10] Chancel ceiling, Copacabana. Potosí, Bolivia.

[10.11] Chancel ceiling, Santa Clara. Ayacucho, Peru.

[10.12] Detail of chancel ceiling, Copacabana. Potosí, Bolivia.

[10.13] Painted ceiling under choir loft. Orcatuna, Peru.

[10.14] Chancel ceiling. Naranja, Mexico.

[10.16] Confessional. Asangaro, Peru.

[10.15] Pulpit. Piribebuy, Paraguay.

[10.17] Detail of side altar, La Merced. Cuzco.

10.18] Main altar, Cristo Rey. Santa Fe, New Mexico.

11 / Other Crafts

In the applied arts, the different fantasy world of the native American affirmed itself with more and more assurance, blending imported patterns with a play of mestizo fancy. The distinctive quality of the Hispanic-American style can be recognized in silverwork, pottery, and furniture, in rugs and wall hangings. Some of the examples illustrated may give an idea as well of the capacity for luxury in the New World colonies.

A gilded plaque of solid silver, from the cathedral of Sucre, Bolivia, dating from the sixteenth century [11.2] presents two scenes in repoussé, each some three and a half by eleven inches. In the upper one, the Last Supper, notable are the rhythm of the apostles' gestures and such details as the elegantly laid table and the numerous dishes portrayed. Everyone is barefoot, after the Washing of the Feet, which became a mark of humility and austerity. In the lower section, the Taking of Christ, there is a very different movement. The turmoil, Peter's hacking sword at the left, the blaring horn on the right, produces a strong contrast to the quiet mood above. While the apostles wear biblical garb, the soldiery is equipped with the weapons and armor of the late Middle Ages. Compare the workmanship, strongly Renaissance in feeling, with the silver vessel in the chapter "Transition" [see 6.13 and 6.14].

The triptych or small traveling altar from the end of the eighteenth century is constructed of silver and wood with figures in gesso [11.1]. Some ten by eighteen inches, it gives the impression of being much larger. Chased on the back of the frame with its striking crown in silver repoussé is an **S**-shaped serpent pierced by a sword, the Dominican seal, and the monograms of Jesus and Mary. The figures are arranged as if they were on a large retable. Mary stands in the middle with the Christ Child, surrounded by men and women saints in the garb of their orders, the martyrs holding their own symbols. Evidently the commission was to include all the owner's favorite saints. Iconographically the piece is rather pleonastic— the Christ Child is seen on the arm of Mary and then again (in the lower left) standing beside St. Joseph. Though somewhat worn, it nevertheless makes one regret that more of such revealing pieces have not survived.

A viceregal coach from Lima [11.3] is only one step from the sedan or palanquin. The tall enclosed box accommodates only two, but instead of having poles for carriers, it is placed over wheels, swinging free on heavy leather straps. The driver's seat is part of the chassis, and in the back there is a platform for two footmen to stand on. The heavy underbody seems out of proportion to the graceful Rococo box, which was once gilded and bright with paint. But the large iron-shod wheels and the general massivity give us an idea of road conditions in mid-eighteenth-century America. Harness and reins were often decorated in silver, as shown in the illustration [see 11.6].

When a woodworker had the skill to produce such a coach, the making of furniture was no problem. An airy cupboard [11.5] from La Paz, Bolivia, with its finely carved columnettes and deep-cut plant motifs shows variety and a good sense of proportion. The angel head in the center relates it to a religious setting, probably the sacristy of some church.

A cedar cupboard in the Sucre cathedral [11.4] is of a different type. It rests on two crouching lions and is richly inlaid with different colored woods and mother-of-pearl. In its diversity of motif, the decoration shows an organized world of contrast and connection. The religious is more emphasized here, in the crucifix on top and in the round plaque on the pediment with the IHS of Jesus.

The abundance of silver in both viceroyalties, Mexico and Peru, seems at times incredible. In one instance, a mine owner is said to have had the way from his palace to the church laid with silver ingots on the occasion of his daughter's wedding. In another, he planned to have all the balconies of his new palace made of silver and covered with gold leaf; he was stopped only by royal order, for the king himself had no such pomp. Where such luxuries were possible, one can understand that the leather leading rein from Peru should terminate in silver beaded bars, decorated with cast and hammered silver figures [11.6]. On it, a rider with a hound pursues a deer and a mountain sheep. The stick end, at the left, is a horse's head, looking like a knight in the game of chess. In the right half, horns and a drum are being played, and a tiny Indian trudges along with a loaded llama behind him.

Likewise of South American provenience is a mug [11.7] of heavy silver with a massive handle, ending—top and bottom—in a bird's head. A flower motif, done in fine tracery, circles the middle of the cup. The lobed silver vase beside it has a more complex shape [11.8]. From both handles, a monkey looks over the brim, giving the piece a humorous touch.

A great number of regulations were issued to control silversmithing in the colonies, and hallmarks and official inspection seals were mandatory. Today, however, many pieces of colonial silver in collections and museums bear neither hallmark nor tax-inspection seals. Control, apparently, was more rigorous in Mexico and Guatemala, because of more numerous personnel; in the Andean regions, the laws were only loosely observed, possibly because for a long period silver was so plentiful that it was physically impossible to keep track of its production. In the Jesuit missions of South America, Indian silversmiths fashioned not only objects for the church but also for the household, even silver harness and spurs—often for the trade.

The incredible variety in technique, color, and pattern of ancient American textiles has been seen in the chapter on weaving. Sarapes, blankets, poncholike woven mantles, still produced in various regions, give an idea of what must have been woven two hundred years ago.* But the indiscriminate destruction of fabrics and the natural deterioration of fragile material make the full elegance of colonial weaving difficult to reconstruct. This writer has come across Indian-woven blankets used to patch the seats on a truck; others used as doormats and hassocks.

It was an early medieval custom to veil all the altars before Easter; on the morning of the Resurrection, they then again appeared in golden glory. In Europe, this still is done for Holy Week; in Latin America, often on Passion Sunday—two weeks before Easter.

The huge Lenten veil reproduced here was once the pride of the church of Santa Teresa in Ayacucho, Peru, a building dedicated in 1703. The greater part consists of squares of lacelike net upon which symbolic motifs are embroidered or woven in [11.9]. The walls and part of the retable are visible through the net in the illustration. In the center, in a section [11.10] of more solid plain weave, embroidered scenes of the Passion appear, making a colored relief over the simpler fabric and so placed as to form a cross. One can make out the Washing of the Apostles' Feet, with the date 1727. Above it is the Last Supper. The largest section depicts the Crucifixion, and over this is the Entombment, surmounted by the Risen Christ. The deep jewel tones contrast with the airy ground, which is lavender.

This extremely rare textile has a counterpart in Gurk, a remote Carinthian town of Austria. The first church there was built in the millennium, and until the eighteenth century, it was a bishop's seat; thus, it was continuously enriched, though today the community is small and poor. One hundred square meters make up the piece, with a hundred scenes painted in tempera, the left half representing the Old Testament, and the right half, the New. The colors are dim, since it was in 1458 that people from all over Austria first came to gaze at it in wonder. Thirty-six sections were recently repaired, and the altar curtain of Gurk is today a part of Austria's national

* Pál Kelemen, "The Weaver's High Art," *Americas,* Vol. 18, December, 1966.

treasure. Has anyone in the Peruvian government or the ecclesiastical hierarchy, who continuously publicize their rich cultural heritage, taken pains to preserve their unique piece? It is not even situated in some tiny, inaccessible place, but in a very large and prosperous city. Already this wonderful memento of colonial weaving may have been cast aside for a shiny, harsh-colored expanse of rayon.

The pictorial representation of biblical and allegorical scenes in tapestry started in the Netherlands, where the technique of the Gobelins was invented. Since the Netherlands and Spain were politically connected for a time, such work soon came to the New World, and the weaving talent of the pre-Columbian Indians was transorchestrated for the use of the Spanish overlord. Raw materials were at hand; to wool from the llama family was added that from sheep; silk and the use of metal thread were introduced. The possibilities multiplied. In the large and often unheatable halls in which the descendents of the conquistadores established themselves, there was need for woven materials to cover the floors and walls, even the doors. They helped keep out the cold, and at the same time made living more cheerful.

A Peruvian colonial tapestry [11.11], most probably a wall hanging, has a complex coat of arms at the center, considered by one expert to be that of a captain general, by another of a viceroy of Peru. Whoever it was that ordered this piece, his name has been forgotten. What remains is a woven document in which a Spanish heraldic emblem is framed in a field that echoes pre-Columbian work.* The warp is cotton; the weft is wool. Small birds and miscellaneous flowers are sprinkled among the larger, more organized motifs; variations in the color scheme are observable. Shades of blue and red, white, brown, and gold make up the colors. If the coat of arms is that of a captain general, the piece would date from the end of the sixteenth century; if that of a viceroy, in the first half of the seventeenth. An exalted motto in Latin—"To God alone honor and glory"—is woven over the heraldic shield—a motto seldom lived up to, in a land where arrogance was paramount and exploitation of the peon was often extreme.

From the modest reception room of a papal nuncio in Central America to the sumptuous reception hall of European royalty, the throne is usually placed on a dais elevated by two or three steps. Behind the chair, a fine fabric customarily hangs, with a coat of arms in the center surrounded by allegorical and decorative motifs. It is possible that the tapestry illustrated served a similar purpose.

The Peruvian tapestry measures something less than eight feet square. A Mexican embroidered rug, of which only a detail can be reproduced, measures around twenty-four by thirteen feet. The variety revealed [11.12],

* Pál Kelemen, *Peruvian Spanish-Colonial Textiles* [an exhibition], Washington, D.C.: The Textile Museum, 1961; reprinted 1968.

however, gives an idea of the richness of motifs that makes this gigantic piece unique. The imagination is led to see hills and mountains depicted in the Chinese manner amid the euphoria of motifs that the skill of the craftsman unfolds. The ground consists of five widths of plain weave in wool sewn together. The embroidery is largely in long-legged cross-stitch, combined with stem and satin stitches. In the center field, six large baskets of flowers are featured, portrayed on a cream-colored ground. Trees, flowers, birds, small animals, of different shapes and in many colors, make up a fantasy world. Four siren heads adorn the corners. The border is largely red and blue with an arabesque of flowers and fruit amid which small animals are scattered in typical colonial fashion. The piece is signed "Ponce," and in a central medallion, dated "the year of 1783." European and Oriental echoes mingle here with additions from the local artisan. But with its distinctive idiom, the piece could only be of the Americas.

After an earthquake about 1920, the Carmelite nuns in Guatemala City sold fragments of a very large rug from their reception hall to defray the cost of repairs to their buildings. On analysis, the rug was found to contain alpaca wool, indicating Peruvian provenience. It is known that in the late seventeenth century the motherhouse in Lima sent a friar and nuns to Guatemala to establish a foundation there. Evidently they brought gifts and kept in touch with their sisters far away.

The conquistadores remarked on the good quality of native pottery, but brought in new shape and color preferences, and introduced the potter's wheel and glazing, basically changing native techniques. Mexican ceramic ware, especially that from Puebla, dating from the mid-seventeenth to the mid-eighteenth century, is the best known. However, what remains today of the colorful tiles of Guatemala, the figurines of Ecuador, the lavabos from Peru—to mention only a few—shows that superior ceramic work was produced over a wide stretch of Hispanic America.

In the first hundred years or so, the Moresque tradition was prevalent, as was the Mudéjar in architecture. By the beginning of the seventeenth century, a later Spanish style was being followed. With the commencement of trade with the Philippines, the influence of the Far East became a strong factor. Vessels were shaped in imitation of the Chinese, such as the form of jar known in Spanish as *tibor*. The end of the seventeenth and the beginning of the eighteenth century saw the climax of luxury in all the viceroyalties and a demand for the best and most ostentatious ware. As in Europe, some families could indulge in the luxury of tableware made in China with their own coats of arms; but the great mass of colonial pottery, as can be seen from collections, was produced in the Americas.

A majolica bowl, about the 1680's in date, shows clearly Spanish influence with Moorish echoes [11.13]. The buildings portrayed could be mosques, but might also be twin-towered churches so popular in the environs of Puebla. The prancing animal, the bird in the sky, and the vegetation are colonial in spirit. But the water basin with its reflection goes back to the Near East, where the combination of water and gardens started its fashion. This tradition of story-telling designs on majolica dishes survived into the twentieth century, when this writer was able to buy a pleasing flat platter with a somewhat similar picture.

The *tibor* [11.14] might date a little later, although its admirable shape and coloring place it in a high category of excellence. The medallions show Chinese influence, but the vigorous placement of the flowers is a mark of the local craftsman. The loosely arranged garlands at top and bottom, with their trefoils reaching into a yellow field, make the piece appealingly friendly.

At its height, Potosí, the fabulous, sustained large establishments of the religious orders. There were 1,050 Dominicans in Potosí, 1,800 Franciscans, and as many Mercedarians, 1,300 Augustinians, 1,100 Jesuits. In the city's heyday, its merchants traded in textiles and laces from Flanders, satins from Florence, fine blown glass from Venice, paper from Genoa, wools from England. On that forbidding plain, nearly fourteen thousand feet above sea level, there was traffic in the perfumes of Arabia, spices from Malay, fine porcelain from China, and diamonds from Ceylon. Potosí was the precious heart of the Spanish colonial empire, and its silver was the blood which invigorated that vast world. At first only silver ingots were cast at the Casa Real de Moneda, or Royal Mint; silver and gold pieces of given weights were pressed into irregular disks that were made into coins in Spain. In the mid-eighteenth century, machinery was installed to mint the coinage.

The illustration shows three ancient machines at Potosí, made entirely of wood, for rolling out silver ingots [11.15]. Each has four frames grouped around a large horizontal wooden cogwheel, which was worked from the floor below, by eight mules toiling round and round to provide the power.

All the best talent was called upon in the enlargement of the Casa Real de Moneda. Timber of the finest quality was cut on the eastern slopes of the Andes, in Argentina. Long mule trains marched with this cargo for weeks over precipitous tracks to reach the city; laden with silver ingots and minted money, they left again as soon as possible, for Potosí lies well above the timber line and grazing land was nonexistent. The latest mint, a large complex, was started in the mid-eighteenth century, and construction lasted for about fifty years, costing over a million silver pesos. About that time, however, the mines of central and northern Mexico were surpassing Bolivia in production.

Simon Bolívar's declaration of independence and revolution stopped forever the march, the flood, of silver. The Andean slopes, from which the tall trees had been cut for the mines, began to erode; erosion set into the Spanish empire, also. In the nineteenth century, the Casa de Moneda served as a fortress and, also, as a prison. Today it is a museum displaying many issues of money from the sixteenth century on. In that high altitude, scarce in oxygen, life is slow and dragging. Once, it was the scene of rivalry, intrigue, blackmail, corruption, fratricide, and mass murder. The ghost that wandered around for centuries is not yet completely laid; it raises its frightening head sometimes as a reminder of the very different past of this melancholy land.

The word *reales,* or royal (issue), developed from early Castilian currency, when one real, a silver piece, was about equivalent to a quarter of a silver peso. Later, the *real de ocho* appeared, representing eight times the value of the old silver coin—the "pieces of eight" of romance. British colonials called it a "cob" meaning lump, because of its irregular outline. Up to the mid-eighteenth century, the currency was hand struck, like the piece illustrated about natural size [11.15], which was produced in Potosí in the year 1670, under the rule of Charles II. The four fields between the arms of the cross of Jerusalem contain the heraldic device of the Spanish monarch. Later, the assayer's monogram was included. Currency minted on machinery in other royal mints of Hispanic America, as well as at Potosí, produced an evener shape and milled edges. Coins from Potosí's royal mint circulated all over Peru, south into Chile, Argentina, and as far north as Nicaragua. Traders on the Spanish Main, also, were paid in this coinage by the colonials.

With techniques developed by scuba divers, major treasures are being brought up from Spanish wrecks—notably from the ships of the silver fleet destroyed in hurricanes off the coast of Florida and on the reefs of Bermuda. Some of the silver and gold pieces found have been of a type hitherto unknown. Complete muskets have come to light, cannon barrels, copper and pewter pots and tableware, porcelain from China, buckles and belts, jewelry, crucifixes. Ships' gear and navigation instruments have been recovered, all providing an inventory of the equipment of an eighteenth-century sailing vessel.

In colonial times, miners put up their primitive mills along the Mantaro River, which runs through the central Andean valley, watering many towns and villages. The city of Huancayo, on the east bank of this river, stands on the King's Highway, at an altitude of about eleven thousand feet. Its comfortable inns and seignorial houses received the traveler hospitably, whether he came from Potosí or Cuzco, or was starting the ascent from the Pacific coast. In pre-Columbian times, Huancayo was a main point on the imperial Inca highway, which, like a network of railways, connected the distant points of that vast empire. It was on this road that Pizarro mounted to Cuzco. It was here that the Inca ruler Huayna Capac was carried in a golden litter, surrounded by his richly clad courtiers and preceded by heralds and musicians, when he came to meet the Spaniards. This city became the provisional capital of the republic of Peru.

Today all this is history, and one reads about it in books. But the Indians remain, and on market days, all along the King's Highway, they lay out their fruits and vegetables—oranges, bananas, limes, pineapples, cassava, camote, oca—and their strange idiom recalls a fraction of what life must have been here once. There are displays of intricately woven textiles, of furs of animals from the Andes, of rope and tools, and of plants and herbs, the medicinal value of which the Indians taught the white man. Here also are finely wrought silver jewelry, articles of bone and hide, carved and produced by hand and often still showing the tradition of the ancient arts and crafts.

In Inca times the imperial road was kept up by special employees. It was broad if on open ground and narrow where it had to be hacked out of solid rock. The swift streams would raise havoc at certain seasons. When a river could not be forded, a bridge was provided. Stone piers still exist that the Incas laid wooden beams across. For the suspension bridges used to span some of the streams, quantities of reeds were woven together to make two cables as thick as a man's thigh, which were then made fast to trees or large rocks on each side of the water. A floor of wattlework was constructed. Two other cables, strung above, served as a railing, with more wattlework fixed between the upper and lower ropes. The chronicler reports, "They shake a lot but are secure."

By the seventeenth century, a great number of these bridges had been replaced with structures of stone. Our chronicler of that period, the Carmelite friar Antonio Vázquez de Espinosa mentions them with pride. They were wide enough for a coach to travel across. Many were covered, so that one could take refuge in them in case of need. This writer has seen remnants of abandoned bridges, usually arched very high, with solid balustrades. The ground was knobby with small cobblestones. In the middle ran a narrow channel, and the side walls were pierced to drain off rain water.

Thornton Wilder centers his novel *The Bridge of San Luis Rey* around an accident on a suspension bridge in Peru. He describes a shrine at one end, where the traveler offered a prayer for a safe crossing or thanksgiving before continuing his journey. The story is laid in 1714. Actually, by that time, all the bridges on the King's Highway—that most important link between Lima and Cuzco—were probably built of stone. One such bridge still spans the Mantaro River near Huancayo [11.16]. A chapel is there, at the left, with its tiered tower. The writer's imagination has created a vivid word picture of the colonial scene. The dramatic landscape gives it a backdrop of reality.

[11.1] Triptych. Peru.

[11.2] Silver gilt plaque. Sucre, Bolivia.

[11.3] Viceregal coach. Lima, Peru.

[11.4] Cedar cupboard. Cathedral. Sucre, Bolivia.

[11.5] Carved cupboard. La Paz, Bolivia.

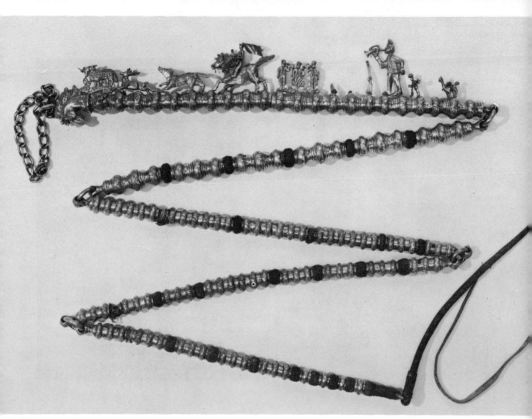

11.6] Silver lead line. Peru.

[11.7] Silver mug. Peru.

[11.8] Silver lobed vase. Peru.

[11.10] Central section of Lenten veil.

[11.12] Detail of embroidered rug, 1783. Mexico.

[11.11] Heraldic tapestry. Peru.

[11.13] Puebla majolica bowl. Mexico.

[11.14] Puebla majolica jar. Mexico.

[11.15] Interior, Casa de Moneda, and silver piece of eight dated 1670. Potosí, Bolivia.

[11.16] Colonial bridge on the King's Highway. Near Huancayo, Peru.

The Philippine Islands

THE WESTWARD COURSE

Historians often end their chapters on the Middle Ages with 1492 and the arrival of Christopher Columbus in the New World. But no historical age can be limited by a single date. Many events prepared the ground for that portentous voyage. The intellectual achievements of Asia and the Near East became disseminated through the Crusaders, who for two hundred years—from the end of the eleventh to the end of the thirteenth century—struggled to recapture and hold the Holy Sepulcher at Jerusalem from the Muslim infidel. Scribes, artists, and other learned persons accompanied the Christian armies, and Europe greatly profited from a knowledge of the technical skill, the vastly more elegant standard of living, and the varied diet of those distant lands lying to the East. A non-Christian and non-European civilization not only stimulated the imagination and intellect of many Europeans but brought immense commercial profits.

The pointed arch, later a characteristic of the Gothic style, was encountered by the Crusaders. It had been in use in Egypt, Syria, Armenia, Persia since the sixth century. The craft of metallurgy was far more advanced in the Near East than in Europe. Silks, brocades, damasks, rugs, jeweled ornaments, were brought by caravans to the eastern shores of the Mediterranean, thence to enter the markets of Europe. At that period, a large part of Spain was in the hands of the Muslim Moors, who lost their last vestiges of power in the Iberian Peninsula the very year that Columbus reached America. In medicine, literature, and mathematics, the Muslim world was ahead of Europe. Many a classic work—such as *Aesop's Fables* —was saved from oblivion by Arab translations found in Spain, whence it spread to other lands in Europe.

Frustration in the face of Turkish might, political dissension, and sheer greed turned Christian against Christian. In 1204, the Crusaders took Constantinople, Pearl of Christendom, capital of the Byzantine empire, while at the rim of the great amphitheater, non-Christian nations watched the weakening of a position that they, also, coveted. It must have been apparent to them that it was not so much for religion as for loot that the

West Europeans were fighting. On the other hand, the European powers did not seem to realize that if the Byzantine empire—which they had so successfully undermined—should fall to the Turks, the next on the list would be Central Europe. Within the same century, Acre was lost, the last Crusade stronghold on the Asian mainland; and in 1453, "the City" as it was known all over the world—the *Polis* of Constantine—fell to the Ottoman Turks, never to be redeemed by any Christian power.

A tremendous and terrifying Ottoman nation became the neighbor —both on water and on land—of Central and Western Europe. From the north and west African shores, along the entire eastern Mediterranean coast, from Serbia through Hungary into Poland and to the gates of Vienna, Turkish power prevailed. The commerce of the Mediterranean and the Adriatic was at its mercy. Heavy bribes and toll fees were demanded for permission to fly any flag but that of the Crescent Moon. The Venetians and Genovese, especially, continued their commercial connections with the Levant. The Turks allowed a certain number of ships to come into their harbors, while Venice created a compound on one of its islands as quarters for Turkish merchants.

Restrictions and intrigues, however, grew more and more complex— and the vastly lucrative trade that brought treasures from the East Mediterranean into West European countries became more and more costly and less and less in volume. Since Marco Polo's return from China in the thirteenth century, the supreme intellectual and artistic achievements of the Chinese empire had been subjects for conjecture and envy. There was no possibility of penetrating that fabulous land over thousands of miles through hostile territory. The nations facing the West with outlets on the North Sea and Atlantic Ocean had to probe beyond the vast mysterious waters to find a new route.

In the wake of Columbus's voyage to the West came the incredible exploit of the Portuguese mariner Vasco da Gama (1497–99). He sailed around the African coast, then northeast into the Indian Ocean and beyond. His was the first European ship to land in the great ports of Asia and to bring back samples of the wealth of those distant empires, hitherto known only in part by trade through many hands. By 1502, he had established Portuguese power in Indian waters and created harbors for rest and repair along the African coast by the usual harsh methods.

As early as 1493, Pope Alexander VI had issued a papal bull dividing the uncharted territory of a new world between Spain and Portugal. Born in Spain in 1431 of parents named Borja, it was Alexander's good fortune to have a cardinal as an uncle. When this relative became pope, under the name of Calixtus III, the path was open to the young Spaniard. Moving to Rome, he changed his name to Borgia, was made a cardinal at the age of fifteen, and moved up in the administration of the papal curia. The year that Columbus landed in the New World, he was elected pope. His regime was notable for its profligacy. Among his illegitimate children, Cesare and Lucrezia Borgia typify for us the intrigue, the military pressures, the bribes, the outright murder that scandalized even that worldly period. This was the man, surrounded by fellow countrymen, who with one flourish of the quill, gave away lands many times larger than the entire continent of Europe.

The Portuguese navigator Fernão Magalhães had accompanied da Gama on his first voyage. Better known as Magellan, he later sailed in the service of Spain through the strait at the southern tip of the South American continent, crossed the Pacific, and landed at a Philippine settlement on the island of Cebu, on April 7, 1521—the same year that Cortés, after earlier defeat, established his seat in Mexico. Magellan lost his life in a skirmish with Philippine natives on Mactan, a tiny island east of Cebu, and a faithless lieutenant—del Cano, a Spaniard—had the honor of bringing home the only ship of the original five to circumnavigate the globe for the first time.

It was more than forty years later that the first permanent Spanish settlement was founded at Cebu in the Philippines. The growing jealousy of the other maritime powers and the resulting activities of privateers in the Atlantic convinced Charles V, the Spanish king, that if effective use was to be made of the Philippine possessions, a better route from Europe than all the way around Cape Horn would have to be found. He, therefore, ordered Hernandez Cortés to dispatch an expedition across the Pacific— this time from Mexico. The feasibility of such a route was established as early as 1528 by Alvaro de Saavedra, whose fleet, however, was unable to make port in the Philippines or to return the way it had come. In 1564, four ships with an escorting frigate—all built on the west coast of Mexico —set sail with over four hundred men from Navidad, a port north of Acapulco. The commander was Miguel López de Legaspi. Of Basque parentage, an experienced mariner at an early age, Legaspi had come to the Mexican capital some eighteen years earlier as chief scribe to the *cabildo,* or city council, there. His recommendation to head the expedition calls him "a worthy and reliable man, resident of the City of Mexico. . . ." Several missionaries accompanied him, and his pilot was the able geographer and mathematician Andrés de Urdaneta, who had been with Saavedra's expedition many years before.

Legaspi's fleet crossed the Pacific without incident, except for the discovery of a number of beautiful coral islands, now known as the Marshalls, where he made a rest stop. He reached the island of Cebu in February of 1565. The Spaniards met some resistance on Luzon, where the natives had artillery, probably furnished by the Portuguese, but the garrison soon surrendered to the Spanish army of three hundred men. Through Legaspi's diplomacy, friendship was also initiated with the Chinese *sangleyes* ("traders") already firmly established there.

This was the real beginning of more than three hundred years of Spanish domination and growing economic connections in the Philippines. Soon the first trade ship, one of Legaspi's vessels, sailed eastward to Mexico. Four months later, the *San Pablo* departed from Mexico with a small amount of merchandise and returned with a very valuable cargo of cinnamon from the southern island of Mindanao—the first vessel to complete the round trip. This route became the regular course of the Manila galleon, which sailed between Acapulco and Manila, as the main harbors.

For the mariners of many lands, the circle was now closed. The facts were known—how Asia could be approached via Africa and via America. Portugal and Spain dominated the seven seas. In Spain, however, which had a broad front on the Mediterranean also, the memory of Muslim occupation was still acute. Infidels were hunted down by the Inquisition. Charles V's campaign in North Africa (in which Cortés played a part) did not change the hegemony of the Crescent Moon. And after the "victory" at Lepanto in 1571, the sultan is said to have remarked that he had lost only a navy but the allies, important islands and harbors.

Danger for Spain lurked on both coasts of the Americas. English, Dutch, and French privateers began to raid the Spanish treasure ships, forcing them to sail under convoy, which slowed the crossings. With freedom to move in the Mediterranean curtailed and with increasing danger from privateer attack in the Atlantic and the Caribbean, Spanish policy placed increased hope in trade with the Philippines.

Privateer activity was held to a bearable scale until Sir Francis Drake appeared on the scene. Born around 1540, Drake, together with the older John Hawkins, became the most daring of sea captains. Even with the share of booty delivered to Queen Elizabeth, these two became rich men. Drake proposed an expedition to circumnavigate the world, the purpose this time, not to explore, but to capture as much treasure as possible. Underwritten by English investors, he started from Plymouth in November 1577. The next year found him past the Strait of Magellan and moving up the Pacific coast, where he brought terror to the coastal cities of Chile and Peru and reaped a rich harvest for his daring. Panic spread as he sailed northward, for until his appearance, these ports had been exempt from privateers and had felt secure. Off Nicaragua, he captured a small ship carrying two pilots bound for the Philippines and took their detailed charts of the route across the Pacific—of far greater value to him than any hoard of gold. Three months later, he came to the Moluccas, then weakly held by the Portuguese, and after further adventures, sailed around Africa, landing in Plymouth harbor in September of 1580—three years after leaving from that same port.

The rumors and alarms in Spain were general on learning that freebooters had reached the Pacific and threatened the treasure ships plying between Acapulco and the Philippines. Orders went out to fortify and strengthen the Pacific coast, measures never fully effective.

Philip II of Spain, who yearned to make the whole world Roman Catholic, turned his attention to Protestant England, the main source of Spain's harassment. Though Spain was bankrupt for the second time under his rule, despite the riches which Potosí and the Mexican mines provided, he had to act against the privateers who had bitten so considerably into his income and to mete out punishment to the island that had so long defied his warnings.

England under Elizabeth tried to avert an open confrontation. But Drake, well informed about Spanish plans for invasion, felt that a surprise visit to the port of Cádiz might clarify matters. He sailed into that Spanish harbor so wonderfully protected by nature, and to the amazement of the Spanish naval authorities, wrought swift havoc on the ships gathered there for the campaign. The stubborn Spanish monarch did not, however, change his plans, although his captains argued about a poorly equipped fleet and noted the vigor with which the English were preparing to defend their homeland. The two navies met in the English Channel (1588), and a series of clashes ensued. Soon it became evident that the English with their lighter and more mobile ships had a marked superiority. Besides, they had an intimate knowledge of the changeable weather. When a gale of unusual force blew apart the formidable Spanish formation, the fate of the Armada was sealed. Some vessels returned to Spain, rich in experience and with the somber realization that the Spanish empire here and overseas faced a growing menace from hostile lands.

The Philippine Archipelago was not, as America was, an isolated continent. In the Philippines was a population that for centuries had maintained commercial and cultural contacts with the Asian mainland, though the fastnesses of the inland mountains were, and still are, inhabited by diverse, comparatively uncivilized tribes. From China's great trading harbor Canton, the voyage is some seven hundred miles—still less from the Chinese mainland to the northernmost of the Philippine Islands. Both Hindu and Arabian boats visited the islands to barter. That the Philippine population profited in its own way from the contact was revealed in recent excavations in the Santa Ana district of Manila. There Chinese porcelain dating from the ninth century to the time of the Spanish Conquest was found in hundreds of pre-Spanish graves, together with tomb furniture and other paraphernalia of Asian tradition. Siamese and Annamese material, also, was discovered.* The quality was often not of the best. Evidently, imperfect pieces, misfired and discolored wares, were being sent to the Philippines,

* Leondro and Cecilia Locsin, *Oriental Ceramics Discovered in the Philippines.* Rutland and Tokyo: Charles E. Tuttle Company, 1967.

especially during the Ming period, while the best products were reserved for the Chinese connoisseur on the mainland.

Written reports of the Chinese, from the twelfth century onward, record commercial dealings with the Philippine people. Some describe in detail the behavior of the natives on the arrival of a Chinese trading group and list the items used in barter.

The Philippine population was cognizant of the religions of India and Arabia through the traders. Islam was already well established in the islands before the Spaniards arrived and continued to remain strong, especially in Mindanao. The newcomers had to face settlements of worshipers of Allah—the faith that for centuries had made their homeland a vassal. Even today, there are considerable areas where the fez is worn or where Buddhism is practiced.

The Spaniards, with their accustomed energy, brought in the religious orders—Augustinian, Dominican, Franciscan, and Jesuit. By the end of the sixteenth century, much of the rich arable land was given over to them, and they performed their mission with great vigor. Despite their efforts, Roman Catholicism did not penetrate there to the same degree as in the Western Hemisphere. Even in the Americas, certain rites of the American Indian and mestizo are so different as to shock and alienate the European Roman Catholic.

The establishment of the Spaniards in the Orient whetted the appetites of the English and Dutch, who had gained footholds in India and the East Indies. Chinese brigandage, also, was rife. And the powerful and in many ways enigmatic Chinese population, residing in Manila and other harbors of the archipelago, was an ever present menace to the Spaniards. The first rebellion of the Chinese under Spanish administration occurred early in the sixteenth century, very soon after commerce with the Americas began to flow.

The Spaniards established their own city of Manila and fortified it. At the center lay the Plaza de Armas with the governor's palace, which grew in size and elaboration until its destruction in 1863. The houses of the Spanish merchants were described by travelers as furnished with great luxury. When the Manila galleon had departed and no foreign invasion was signaled, life was leisurely and sophisticated.

The chief monastic orders erected their buildings in other sections of the walled city, or Intramuros. They built hospitals and schools, even cared for the female population. Outside the walls were the quarters of the Japanese, who were drawn in growing numbers to this center of commerce in the Pacific. The better class of Tagalogs, or native Filipinos of Luzon, had access to the beach beyond the walled city; and a large, well-built, and showy enclave lay across the Pasig River, where the Chinese colony, often numbering fifteen thousand, throve, as one chronicler put it, "still within shot."

Thus, the Spanish population kept itself within the relative safety of its own fortress, the gates of which were closed at dusk to avoid surprises. With so many nationalities and different intellectual capacities at work, it was natural that the articles of commerce should become more and more varied. Silver poured in from the mines of Peru and Mexico, and the Manila galleon returned each year to the New World with its precious cargo of silks, chinaware, and spices. These Manila galleons were often the largest ships afloat, owing to the fact that the Seville Consulado insisted that only two ships a year sail to the Philippines.

Although during the nearly three hundred years of their functioning, the Manila galleons on their annual round trip confronted not only the dangers of the seas but also of swift-sailing marauders, only a few were taken intact. The first Englishman to capture a galleon was Thomas Cavendish (1587). Waylaying the great ship off the coast of Lower California, he found her unarmed and completely unprepared for attack. Her cargo, bound for Mexico, contained some 122,000 pesos in gold, a quantity of Oriental pearls, silks, satins, damasks, musk, conserves of exotic fruits, and fine wines. Having transferred the booty to his own vessels, Cavendish put the crew and passengers ashore, providing them with food and weapons to defend themselves against hostile Indians. Then he ordered the galleon set afire. But skillful handling by the victims saved the hull, which was repaired enough for the party to re-embark and to reach Acapulco some two months later.

In the following century, more and more buccaneers infested the high seas. Though they sometimes carried dubious documents of privilege, they were actually engaged in open piracy, in looting and violence, and were responsible to no authority but their own. Woodes Rogers, however, held a legal commission as privateer and was employed by a group of Bristol merchants. In 1709, he captured and exacted ransom from the city of Guayaquil, Ecuador, one of the great ports of the Pacific coast of South America. A coastwise ship fell into his hands, with an estimated cargo of thirty tons of religious objects. There were five hundred bales of papal bulls, images in wood and stone, holy medals, rosaries and crosses; also, fragments of bones labeled with the names of saints, destined for reliquaries and to serve the tradition that every new church (and there were thousands in that new land) should be founded upon such a sacred memento. Later, Rogers' small company lay in wait off Lower California for two galleons due to return from Manila. They took the smaller one, but the larger beat them off in fierce fighting. For by then, the galleons were equipped with heavy artillery manned by trained soldiers, and the planks of their hulls were sometimes as much as four feet thick, upon which English cannons made little impact.

In 1740, under orders of the British navy, Commodore George Anson set out in the *Enterprise* with a squadron to break the Spanish monopoly of Spanish-American and Asian ports. Though he harried the west coast of South America, he was unable to engage the Manila galleon in combat until the autumn of 1743. Meanwhile, his ships were granted asylum in Macao, on the China coast, where he stayed for five months to recondition them and restore his men. Sailing out with refreshed forces, he detoured around the Philippine Islands, and though Manila had been forewarned by Chinese intelligence, was able to waylay the *Covadonga* from Mexico, carrying 1,313,843 pesos in coined silver and silver bullion to the value of 35,862 ounces. He sold the vessel in Macao and carried home the treasure in his own bottoms.

The previously-mentioned exploits were carried out by ships sailing from England. The last and greatest attack was launched from Madras, India, in 1762, during the Seven Years' War. Thirteen men-of-war were outfitted, for the purpose of expelling the Spaniards from the Philippine archipelago and thus extending Britain's already great Asian colonial empire. The fleet under Admiral Samuel Cornish captured Manila, but the islands' lieutenant governor, Simón de Anda y Salazar, escaped with a small contingent and established himself in a bay less familiar to the British. Meantime, two Spanish treasure galleons were at sea—one having left Manila some time earlier, and one due to arrive from Mexico. De Anda was able to divert the latter, carrying silver as her main cargo, which he used to support his provisional government. The other galleon, the *Santísima Trinidad,* with its Asian treasures had encountered such devastating storms that she was forced to return for refitting and fell prey to the British. She was sailed into Plymouth with a British crew, to the jubilation and admiration of all. The vessel was perhaps the largest the populace had ever seen. She had a tonnage of about two thousand, a gun deck measuring nearly 170 feet, and a poop over 30 feet high, a fact that was especially remarked since centuries earlier, in the interests of speed and maneuverability, the English had changed the form of their vessels to a lower-lying, lighter build.

The Dutch, also, took their share of the Manila trade, operating from their bases in the East Indies, especially Java. Nevertheless, all their exploits do not approach those of the English, whose history on the high seas is unparalleled in courage, endurance, inventiveness, and in the amount of treasure borne home.

Whether exotic merchandise or silver and gold, much that was destined for the Spanish exchequer fell into inimical hands. Besides, many vessels foundered at sea. Though the losses were tremendous, the arrival of each treasure ship caused the market in Europe for goods and precious metal to decline. What had been mined with so much blood and brought home under such hair-raising dangers produced a glut that contributed to the chronic bankruptcy of the Spanish kingdom.

12/A Different Flowering

Mexico became a Spanish colony in 1521; Peru, in 1533; the first Spanish administration in the Philippines, in Luzon, did not begin before 1571. Mexico asserted its independence in 1812; Peru, in 1821; the Philippines remained in Spanish hands until 1898. Thus, a time lag occurred not only in the beginning but also at the end of Spanish hegemony in the Malay Archipelago. The art of the Hispanic period in the Philippines differs in more ways than one from that of the Americas. Though the Americas suffered ruthless destruction of their ancient civilization after the Conquest, there remained an Indian artistic tradition upon which the Spanish-European styles were grafted.

In the Philippines, on the other hand, the fact that various mature arts already existed, emanating from the Asian mainland and even farther, made a similar grafting process impossible. Chinese, Hindu, and Muslim influences had previously played a part there and continued to do so, as the architecture, sculpture, and painting, and even the more fragile archives, bear witness.

The value of the Philippine Islands to Spain lay in trade possibilities, rather than in the exploitation of natural resources. The coastal traders from Asia resented the encroachment, and the Spaniards were forced to fortify the most important harbors and gather their nationals within protective walls. A mid-seventeenth–century map of Manila shows the divisions [12.1]: the Spanish administrative buildings, warehouses, etc., within the fortress; the outlying districts apportioned to other nationals.

The Spaniards regarded manual work as beneath their dignity, and with silver flowing in from the Americas, they strove here also for the life of a hidalgo. Heavy labor and often the arts and crafts were left to the Chinese, who were more intelligent and better informed than the natives, though they resisted conversion to Christianity. The Chinese were occupied with fishing, gardening, carpentry, masonry, the manufacture of lime, brick, and tile. They were the ironmongers, the druggists, candlemakers, tailors, cobblers, pastry cooks, as well as largely the painters, wood carvers, and to two hundred years. Over the round window, skillfully placed and flanked by the volutes of the inner pediment, is a medallion containing the figures of Christ and John the Baptist in glory. The portal has an accumulation of figures above it, representing, perhaps, the "cloud of witnesses" before St. John or the Redeemer. The niches, framed by heavy tropical garlands, are unusual in their strong three-dimensional character.

Over the lateral entrance of this church is a similarly complex sequence [12.8]. At the top, Mary and Elizabeth, the two expectant mothers of the Visitation, can be seen in warm embrace. The two figures at the sides can be identified as the parents of St. John the Baptist: the high priest Zacharias standing before an altar, at the left, and Elizabeth before a prie-dieu, on the other side.

Most churches in the Philippines were built by methods somewhat similar to those used in Hispanic America. A rough sketch of the plan and decoration was produced by the priest or someone who had an approach to some source of design. Then the native and Chinese craftsmen took over. Raw materials were furnished by the population. Master masons and wood carvers were often called in, even from another island, when there were funds to pay for their contribution. An extremely strong binding material was produced in a traditional mixture, consisting of fine lime, molasses, and duck eggs. It was impermeable and solidified into such a monolithic mass that even fortress walls were sometimes constructed with it.

The church of San Vicente Ferrer, Ilocos Sur, also on Luzon, shows a type that could have stood in tropical Spanish America, or even in Brazil [12.9]. It is built of brick with a facing of whitewashed stucco. The roof had to be light, on account of earthquake danger—the repaired buttresses and the newly-added heavier ones testify to this constant threat. There is a stockiness in the side walls, a lack of striving for height. The façade is convex, using classical columns and finials, but has not much ornament as it stands today. The round windows and the oval medallion with its figure of a saint at the peak of the pediment show Rococo influence and set the building's date. The completed twin towers here are a rarity in early Philippine churches.

La Purísima Concepción, Baclayon, Bohol Island, was founded by the Jesuits at the end of the sixteenth century, then passed on to the Augustinians. The present structure was begun in 1727. Within, an amazing display of the wood carvers' art can be observed [12.10]. The main altar (left) shows a buildup of basic classical elements with some early Baroque features; some statues, probably, were added later. The general aspect of the retable in the foreground, with its well-accustomed series of statues, bespeaks its European ancestry. But the central section at the top, in its stocky compactness, is reminiscent of ornaments in Chinese temples. The effect is like two different melodies, which although played parallel, have little to do with each other.

Work in wood was always a major craft of the Pacific peoples. Many islands produced boats of masterly construction, and their ceremonial objects were carved with an assured—although to us, alien—aesthetic sense. The native Philippine lived in huts made of perishable material—wood, reed—often raised on tall piles to avoid the inundations of the rainy season. The pre-Hispanic shrines of the Chinese, Arab, and other nationalities were mainly of wood and other light material. Spanish taste dictated more solid roofing, and as churches began to be built on a larger scale, the vaulting became a special problem. Unfortunately, very little remains of the work in this line from the sixteenth to eighteenth centuries. Earthquakes, together with the bombardment and deliberate destruction in World War II, have left ruins from which all too little can be deduced.

Since the eighteenth century, when taste turned to the Rococo, the shortcoming was often made up with vaulting in wood, which could be effectively decorated with painting, using biblical pictures and other imported iconographical material as models. The Augustinian church of San Miguel Arcangel, at Argao, Cebu Island, is a good example [12.11]. The wooden barrel vault is divided into various fields and filled with lively scenes and symbols. The central medallion presents an apocalyptic vision of the Last Judgment, with St. Michael battling the forces of darkness (to the right of the onlooker) while the dead rise from their graves, Mother and Child hover nearby, and angels blow the last dread trumpets. In contrast to the relatively light and airy ceiling, the retable—which was not subject to the same danger—has a buildup of considerable weight, both as to structure and decoration. One senses the fine grain and the durability of the native wood on which the carver could put his craftsmanship to best use. The pulpit appears to be of a somewhat later period. On its *porta voz,* or sounding board, rich volutes form a crown, topped by a small figure, probably the Holy Child of Cebu, about whom more will be said later.

If ever a construction reveals its Asian character, it is the church at Badoc, Luzon, dedicated to St. John the Baptist [12.12]. Ungainly scrolls ornament the massive brick buttresses, which bespeak a sort of desperation with the recurrent earthquakes. Note the thinness of the colonial brick, in contrast to that manufactured today. Despite its dilapidated condition, its Chinese character and the strength of the binding material, already mentioned, are evident.

The stairway in the eighteenth-century Convent of the Santo Niño, Cebu City [12.13], shows the extraordinary quality that wood carving in the Philippines achieved with the tropical woods of the islands. One intri-

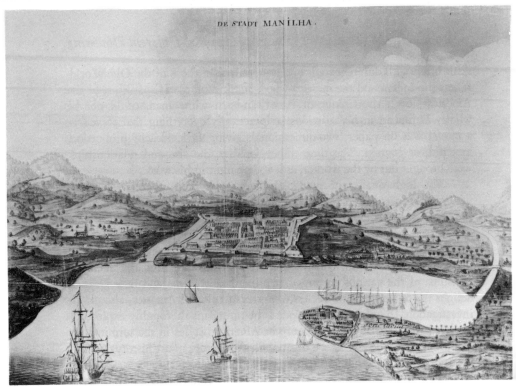

[12.1] Manila in the seventeenth century. Luzon, Philippines.

[12.2] House at Bustos, Luzon.

[12.3] San Gerónimo. Morong, Luzon.

[12.4] Santo Tomás de Villa Nueva. Pardo, Cebu Island.

[12.5] San Lorenzo (now Santiago). Paete, Luzon.

[12.6] Detail of façade.

[12.7] San Juan Bautista. Calumpit, Luzon.

[12.8] Side portal.

[12.9] San Vicente Ferrer. Ilocos Sur, Luzon.

[12.10] La Purísima Concepción. Baclayon, Bohol Island.

[12.11] San Miguel Arcangel. Argao, Cebu Island.

[12.12] Scroll buttresses, San Juan Bautista. Badoc, Luzon.

[12.13] Monastery stairway, Santo Niño. Cebu City, Cebu.

[12.14] Vestry chest. Manila, Luzon.

[12.15] St. John of Nepomuk. Philippines.

[12.17] La Inmaculada. Philippines.

[12.16] El Santo Niño de Cebu. Cebu City.

[12.18] Bodhisattva. China.

Selected Bibliography

In making the small selection of titles for this bibliography, the writer took into consideration that the libraries in the United States, often even in small towns, are excellently up to date in books on our subject and offer their variety to the interested general reader with courtesy.

THE ANCIENT EPOCH

BENNETT, WENDELL C. *Ancient Arts of the Andes.* New York: Museum of Modern Art, 1954.

————, and BIRD, JUNIUS H. *Andean Cultural History.* New York: Doubleday and Company, 1964.

BENSON, ELIZABETH P. *The Maya World.* New York: Thomas Y. Crowell Company, 1967.

BERNAL, IGNACIO. *Mexico Before Cortez: Art, History, and Legend.* Trans. by Willis Barnstone. New York: Doubleday and Company, 1963.

BOYD, E. *Saints and Saint Makers of New Mexico.* Santa Fe: Laboratory of Anthropology, 1946.

CASO, ALFONSO. *The Aztecs: People of the Sun.* Norman, Oklahoma: University of Oklahoma, 1959.

COE, MICHAEL D. *The Jaguar's Children: Pre-Classic Central Mexico.* New York: Museum of Primitive Art, 1965.

COE, WILLIAM R. *Tikal, A Handbook of the Ancient Maya Ruins.* Philadelphia: University of Pennsylvania, 1967.

DOCKSTADER, FREDERICK J. *Indian Art in Middle America.* Greenwich, Conn.: New York Graphic Society, 1964.

————. *Indian Art in South America.* Greenwich, Conn.: New York Graphic Society, 1967.

EASBY, DUDLEY T., JR. "Early Metallurgy in the New World," *Scientific American,* April, 1966.

EASBY, ELIZABETH KENNEDY. *Pre-Columbian Jade from Costa Rica.* New York: Emmerich, 1969.

KELEMEN, PÁL. *Medieval American Art. Masterpieces of the New World before Columbus.* New York: Macmillan, 1943; Dover, 1969.

KIDDER, ALFRED V. *An Introduction to the Study of Southwestern Archaeology* (rev. ed.). New Haven: Yale University, 1962.

MASON, JOHN ALDEN. *The Ancient Civilizations of Peru* (rev. ed.). Harmondsworth, England: Penguin, 1964.

PADDOCK, JOHN, ed. *Ancient Oaxaca.* Palo Alto: Stanford University, 1966.

ROBERTSON, DONALD. *Pre-Columbian Architecture.* New York: Braziller, 1963.

SAWYER, ALAN R. *Mastercraftsmen of Ancient Peru.* Princeton: Princeton University, 1968.

THOMPSON, J. ERIC S. *The Rise and Fall of Maya Civilization.* Norman: University of Oklahoma, 1966.

VON HAGEN, VICTOR W. *The Ancient Sun Kingdoms of the Americas.* New York: World, 1961.

WAUCHOPE, ROBERT. *Lost Tribes and Sunken Continents.* Chicago: University of Chicago, 1962.

WISSLER, CLARK. *Indians of the United States* (rev. ed.). New York: Doubleday and Company, 1966.

Also included should be:

Archaeology, a quarterly published by the Archaeological Institute of America.

Expedition, issued quarterly by the University Museum of the University of Pennsylvania.

THE COLONIAL SCENE

AHLBORN, RICHARD E. "Churches of Luzon," *Philippine Studies,* VIII, 1960; XI, 1963.

ANNIS, VERLE L. *The Architecture of Antigua Guatemala* (bilingual edition). Guatemala: University of San Carlos of Guatemala, 1968.

CASTEDO, LEOPOLDO. *A History of Latin American Art.* New York: Praeger, 1969.

DUNN, DOROTHY. *American Indian Painting of the Southwest and Plains Areas.* Albuquerque: University of New Mexico, 1968.

KELEMEN, PÁL. *Baroque and Rococo in Latin America.* New York: Macmillan, 1951; Dover, 1967.

LEONARD, IRVING A. *Baroque Times in Old Mexico.* Ann Arbor: University of Michigan, 1966.

MEANS, PHILIP A. *The Fall of the Inca Empire and the Spanish Rule in Peru, 1530–1780.* New York: Gordian Press, 1964.

SANFORD, TRENT ELWOOD. *The Architecture of the Southwest.* New York: W. W. Norton and Company, 1950.

SCHURZ, WILLIAM LYTLE. *The Manila Galleon.* New York: E. P. Dutton and Company, 1959.

SIMPSON, LESLEY BYRD. *Many Mexicos.* Berkeley: University of California, 1966.

TOUSSAINT, MANUEL. *Colonial Art in Mexico.* Trans. and ed. by Elizabeth Wilder Weismann. Austin: University of Texas, 1967.

VÁZQUEZ DE ESPINOSA, ANTONIO. *Compendium and Description of the West*

Indies. Trans. by Charles Upson Clark. Washington: Smithsonian Institution, 1942.

WETHEY, HAROLD E. *Colonial Architecture and Sculpture in Peru.* Cambridge: Harvard University, 1949.

———. "Hispanic Colonial Architecture in Bolivia," *Gazette des Beaux-Arts,* November, 1949.

Although this bibliography contains only titles in English, which in the majority of cases are easily accessible, an exception has been made for the following publications:

Anales, del Instituto de Arte Americano e Investigaciones Estéticas. Argentina: University of Buenos Aires.

Anales, del Instituto de Investigaciones Estéticas, Universidad Nacional Autónoma de Mexico.

Boletín, Instituto Nacional de Antropología e Historia, Mexico.

Their decades of pioneering work, dignified in tone and authentic in scholarship, point up the lack of anything similar in the United States.

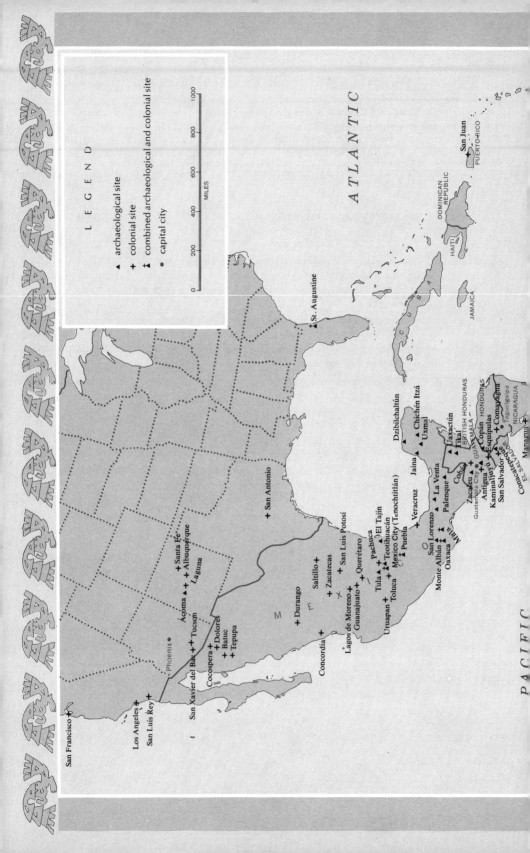

LEGEND

▲ archaeological site
✝ colonial site
⟐ combined archaeological and colonial site
● capital city

0 200 400 600 800 1000
MILES

ATLANTIC

PACIFIC

San Francisco ✝
Los Angeles ✝
San Luis Rey ✝
San Xavier del Bac ✝✝ Tucson
Cocospera ✝
Batuc ✝ Dolores
Tepupa ✝
Phoenix ●
Concordia ✝
Ácoma ▲ ✝ ✝ Santa Fe
Albuquerque
Laguna ▲
Durango ✝
M E X
Lagos de Moreno ✝
Guanajuato ✝
Saltillo ✝
Zacatecas ✝
San Luis Potosí ✝
Querétaro ✝
Pachuca ✝
Tula ▲ El Tajín ▲
Uruapan ▲ ⟐ Teotihuacán
Toluca ✝ Mexico City (Tenochtitlán) ⟐
Puebla ✝
San Antonio ✝
St. Augustine ▲
Veracruz ✝
La Venta ▲
San Lorenzo ▲
Monte Albán ▲
Oaxaca ●
Mitla ▲
Jaina ▲
Dzibilchaltún ▲
Chichén Itzá ▲
Uxmal ▲
Palenque ▲
Yaxactún ▲
Tikal ▲
Cobá ▲
Zaculeu ▲
Guatemala City ●
Kaminaljuyú ▲
Antigua ✝
Copán ▲
Esquipulas ✝
San Salvador ●
Comayagua ✝
Tegucigalpa ●
Conacaste ▲
El Mamanar ▲

BRITISH HONDURAS
GUATEMALA
HONDURAS
EL SALVADOR
NICARAGUA

CUBA
HAITI
JAMAICA
DOMINICAN REPUBLIC
PUERTO RICO
San Juan ✝

Caracas •

V E N E Z U E L A

Ciudad Bolívar •

GUAYANA

Manaus •

C O L O M B I A

+ Tunja

• Bogotá

♱ Popayán   ▲ Tierradentro
          ▲ San Agustín

B   R   A   Z   I   L

PANAMA City

Panama City

▲ Chiriquí ▲ Coclé
▲ Veraguas

ECUADOR
• Quito
♱ Guayaquil

Esmeraldas •

P

E

R

♱ Cajamarca

Lambayeque ▲
Chan-Chan ♱
Trujillo ♱
Cerro Sechín ▲

▲ Chavín de Huántar

✚ Huanuco

U

Lima •
Pachacámac ▲
Paracas ▲
Ocucaje ▲

Wari ▲

▲ Machu Picchu
▲ Pisac
▲ Cuzco
Λ Ayacucho

Nazca ▲

+ Exaltación

▲ Tiahuanaco
Puno ♱ Lake Titicaca
Copacabana   • La Paz

B O L I V I A

✚ Santa Cruz

✚ Sucre
✚ Potosí

✚ Salta

PARAGUAY

Piticlebuy ✚
Asunción •

ARGENTINA

CHILE

CHINA

FORMOSA
(TAIWAN)

LUZON

THE PHILIPPINES

Manila ✚

Legaspi ✚

Cebu ✚

BOHOL

Drawn by Miklos Pinther

Appendix

Art history is a latecomer among the disciplines in the humanities. Although books and albums devoted to some phases of art—frequently the inventories of a collection—were published long before the nineteenth century, it was not until around a hundred years ago that something approaching a system developed. At that time, photography was in its infancy, and illustrations were taken from sketches made *in situ* or from prints often inaccurate. Even in such countries as France and Italy, traveling conditions were only tolerable, and to go to the Near East or beyond meant a real expedition and sometimes considerable physical danger.

As photographic techniques improved, the teaching of art history became more feasible. Projections were still primitive. Large glass black and white slides were put into an apparatus with cold water running continuously through it, to reduce the overheating of the arc light and the danger of scorching the glass plate. The method was universal when the writer attended classes in art history at the universities of Budapest, Munich, and Paris between 1911 and 1914, and it even survived World War I.

In early 1914, I lived in Berlin, and my greatest pleasure was to sit in the Print Room of the Kaiser Friedrich Museum, which was seldom visited by more than two or three people at a time. Occasionally, a military parade marched along Unter den Linden, led by Kaiser Wilhelm II under a silver helmet with flowing white horsehair plume, in a silver cuirass with gold eagle on the breast, a cream-colored cape lined with scarlet, and in the high boots of a medieval knight, and surrounded by his sons in the uniforms of his various armed forces. For the Kaiser no art existed except the Classic and Renaissance; hence, for a director of any state museum to think of buying an El Greco or an Impressionist painting would have been courting dismissal.

After World War I, Germany shrank in territory; the Kaiser went into exile —but the horizon of his intellectuals remained limited. Professors were not greatly stimulated to look in new directions; enough to try to satisfy the authorities who swung from the Spartacus and other Communist revolutions to incipient Nazism. Students and visitors at German universities, while admitting the good qualities in their teaching, were depressed by the atrophy and the overspecialization into which the instruction had deteriorated. As early as 1908, a Hungarian literary critic wrote his very successful *Die Wissenschaft des Nicht-Wissenswerten** (*"The Science of Knowledge Not Worth Knowing"*), about this clinging to limited subjects, this splitting into smaller and smaller fragments, this knowing more and more about less and less. The condition worsened after World War I. T. S. Eliot wrote: "The Germans are like sponges or sea anemones—soaking up foreign influences for a while, then rejecting it all."

With the coming of Nazism, many historians of art had to leave the country. Since Italy was for a while not completely under the heel of Fascist militarism, Florence and Rome, where German art historical institutions existed, became centers for those expatriates, many of whom finally came to the United States. They were not all the cream of art historians—most were young, not more than associate professors in their native country, or curators in some provincial museum, docents, or clerks in a library or in a photographic archive. Arriving in this country, their first great difficulties were the language and the completely different system of education in the few universities and in the many colleges (most of which later attained the status of university) where they found positions. Lacking an understanding of what American education was trying to achieve, they regarded themselves as guardians of the spirit of their native country that had to be transplanted into the soil of this new land. Very few realized that most of the students —who came from the Middle West, the Far West, from the South, and even those with a New England background—did not know Europe. With a war in the making and finally bursting upon us, the scenes so alive in the memory of the refugees were to these young Americans merely words or photographs in a book or on a screen.

The newcomers were inclined to deprecate all forms of artistic expression of the New World. This tendency to regard the emanations of the American spirit as inferior in every respect to those of Europe was already widespread, even among native-born American critics in related fields. Departments of English in most universities of the United States scorned the teaching of American literature and viewed with veiled contempt their colleagues who offered courses in this area of letters. Similarly, where instruction was given in Hispanic literary culture, it invariably dealt exclusively with that of the Iberian Peninsula. In the first decades of this century, its professors, whether Spanish or North American, tended to ridicule any claim of Spanish-American literature to serious attention. These attitudes slowly changed in these New World fields.** No corresponding broadening of approach was observed in the history of art, owing in large measure to the influx of foreign-born scholars into American universities who, by training and a certain European provincialism, were incapable of perceiving aesthetic values other than those they

---

* Ludwig Hatvany, *Die Wissenschaft des Nicht-Wissenswerten*. Leipzig: J. Feiler, 1908; Berlin: Deutsche Verlags Anstalt, 1911. Published, also, in Budapest.

** How much advance has been made in these disciplines in the last decades and how little in the fine arts becomes evident in *Latin American History—Essays on its Study and Teaching, 1898–1965*, Vol. 1, compiled and edited by Howard F. Cline, Austin: University of Texas Press, 1967.

brought with them from overseas. Hence, they were indifferent to the needs of American—particularly Latin American—graduate students seeking to prepare themselves for careers in their inherited cultures and in their own fields of art.

A young Brazilian, on a scholarship at the Institute of Fine Arts of New York University, to train for assuming the directorship of a regional museum in his own country, came to the writer in despair (1943–44). His term paper dealt with the rearrangement of the first three rooms in the Uffizi Gallery of Florence. He and, indeed, most of his American classmates had never been outside their native states. Why was the class not directed to a subject that could be studied as a reality, such as the first three rooms at the Metropolitan Museum of Art across the street?

When the writer made his first visit to the United States in 1932, the teaching of art history as a standard course was limited to four universities: Harvard, Columbia, Princeton, and Chicago. On other campuses, the subject appeared occasionally in the framework of the department of architecture, to familiarize the budding architect with the great styles of Europe. Here again, the Gothic of France and the Renaissance of Italy were paramount on the program. Perhaps, this situation is one reason why so many art historians are still involved with "problems" of architecture, and neglect other manifestations of the artistic and creative talent of mankind. It is interesting that while the American Antiquarian Society was founded in 1812, the Archaeological Institute of America in 1879, the official organization of art historians, the College Art Association, did not come into being until 1912. Despite the small number of members, its two publications, the *Art Bulletin* and *Parnassus*, had a varied program and thus presented to their limited audience a rather broad panorama.

With the coming of the European refugees, a drastic change occurred. Their involvement with the Classic, the Gothic, and the Renaissance left little inclination for less conventional fields; and they deplored the fact that here in the United States the program was loose but elastic. Through the generous attitude of the Americans, many of them obtained remunerative positions, and they soon formed an influential group at meetings where decisions were made. What could be called clinically closed cocoons developed, which kept many American students from continuing in the profession. American subjects were not accepted for dissertations, including the pre-Columbian and Hispanic-American, even when examples were close at hand.

It is not generally realized that the doctoral degree, the Ph.D., in Germany is a sort of union card to certain higher civil service jobs; for, all education is in the hands of the state there, while many American institutions of higher learning are privately supported. The refugee's insistence upon the doctorate here has not raised the standard of scholarship but has limited its vision and circumscribed its scope. To obtain his Ph.D., a Chinese scholar who could make an important contribution by writing on early Chinese scrolls had to select a Renaissance subject from Italy. Deems Taylor, distinguished composer and author, remarked that our age is the age of the pedant run amok.

All too many émigrés regarded the museum as an unworthy place—partly because in America it means contact with the general public as well as visual acquaintance with the objects. As a result, when one asks a graduate student his plans for the future, the reply is all too often a uniform "teaching on college level." There is a growing need for well-educated curators and directors. The American Association of Museums lists 4,595 museums devoted to the arts and sciences. About 300,000,000 persons visit these facilities annually, and Congress recently authorized the development of information centers to help small museums. But from where will informed curators come?

In the rush to produce doctoral degrees, the fact has been overlooked that most museum directors, even in Europe, had not even an M.A. (Neither this degree nor the B.A. exist there.) A talented person could attend classes at a university for a few years and then obtain a position in a museum on the basis of his knowledge, his gifts, and eventual performance. It was a matter of connoisseurship which is visual, not verbal. Verbalization is a disease of our age. Schliemann of Troy fame left school at fourteen, and he had accomplished wonders long before his work was acknowledged by the professors in his native land. English, French, Spanish, and Italian museum directors, art critics, and historians without the Ph.D. became justly famous. The great directors of the Metropolitan Museum in New York, Francis H. Taylor and James J. Rorimer, lacked a Ph.D.—the latter had only a B.A. André Malraux, whom even many Germans admire for his French intellect, did not get a high school diploma.

The distinguished professor of the University of Michigan, Leslie A. White, observing the teaching of anthropology under the late Franz Boas at Columbia University, remarks that a compact group of scholars, principally German-born, were gathered about the leader and virtually controlled this discipline in the United States.* Professor White states that Boas used the material of others outside his own group sparingly and that he tended to disparage the views of "outsiders." He ignored the work of contemporary French anthropologists, and in an address on the history of anthropology, he failed to mention the founding of important American ethnological and anthropological departments and institutions. One can observe a situation not too dissimilar in influence and activity in art history, strongly Teutonic, specializing in one particular subject, concentrated in the narrow segment of the metropolitan Eastern Seaboard.

In *The Visual Arts in Higher Education* (1966), a study prepared by the College Art Association of America, we read, under the heading "The High Mortality Rate of Graduate Students in Art History" (p. 39):

"A high percentage of the graduate students who come to the Eastern universities have not risen from the undergraduate programs of these schools but have come from far away—from the Midwest, the South, the West. They represent a great variety of backgrounds and a wide range of competence. They also may reflect the provincialism of their own original milieu. Poorly oriented, conscious of their inadequacies, torn between remedial undergraduate courses and highly

* Leslie A. White, "The Social Organization of Ethnological Theory," *Rice University Studies,* Vol. 52, No. 4, Houston, 1966.

specialized graduate work . . . they easily become discouraged. Even those who persevere may never acquire a harmonious and coherent education in the history of art but may go on to become one-sided and overspecialized teachers."

At a congress on Byzantine art and archaeology on the Eastern Seaboard, the official language was German, and a short synopsis was furnished for Americans unable to follow the proceeding. At the closing banquet of an art-historical convention, the speaker, a retired German refugee, reflected on teaching in America and the problems confronting the younger art historians. After mentioning a former colleague as a gesture of courtesy, the only authors he quoted were Winckelmann, Nietzsche, Burckhardt, Justi, and Woelfflin—a list not only purely German but to a considerable degree outdated. Is there not one Scandinavian, English, French, Spanish, Italian scholar—to say nothing of American—whose work could have been included toward the illumination and instruction of his American audience?

Laura Fermi, who with her husband, the distinguished atomic physicist, was forced out of Mussolini's Italy, recently published a book that she calls *Illustrious Immigrants.** Its nearly four hundred and fifty pages provide a long list of atomic scientists, psychoanalysts, natural and social scientists, writers, publishers, musicians, and musicologists; and the reader cannot fail to notice how one-sided is her praise. For our purpose, the chapter on art historians is pertinent. Reading through the six laudatory pages of names, one would think there was nobody American who prepared the ground for these refugees. Her list shows, also, how nearly exclusively is the German refugee occupied with the Gothic and Renaissance. As if realizing that her roster suggests that no one has done any work in the field of the arts of the Americas, she closes the chapter by saying: "The art of the western continent was not entirely neglected. In Europe Pál Kelemen, art historian and archaeologist, had been interested in early Christian art, but after coming to the United States in 1932, he turned to pre-Columbian and Colonial art in Latin America, made many survey trips to Latin America, and published books among which is a two volume history of Medieval American art. . . ."—an excerpt from *Who's Who in America*. My inclusion in Mrs. Fermi's book is fallacious from more than one point of view, especially since the names of Henri Foçillon (France), Lionello Venturi (Italy), Henri Gregoire (Belgium), Charles de Tolnay (Hungary)—scholars who have contributed much more than many of those she lists—are omitted.

Strange marriages developed from the various interests in intercampus relationships. At one Ivy League college, where sons of traders and brokers created the hierarchy, money played a role not only in the selection of those accepted as colleagues, but also in how an art work was judged. At another, the *Social Register* was of paramount importance; the poor though talented person who worked himself up to a Ph.D. there and won a teaching position could not obtain tenure. At a third institution, left-wing political orientation sowed its seeds also in the department of art history.

Certain art historians realized that something was basically wrong. Twice since this writer began observing the scene in 1932, round tables were arranged

* Laura Fermi, *Illustrious Immigrants*. Chicago: University of Chicago, 1968.

and questionnaires were sent out to ascertain how to improve the teaching of the subject. But since those questionnaires went to the same people who were responsible for the existing pedantry and atrophy, it was useless to expect constructive and perceptive criticism. The question arises whether the teacher's ability to illuminate his students is ever sampled by one in authority. This writer has sat in the darkened rooms where pedants, obviously full of arrogance, envy, sometimes even hatred, instructed young and impressionable students.

As this narrowness settled on the American academe, fair play and generosity all too often succumbed. When Bernard Berenson died, the brilliant pioneer art historian of world fame, not one line of obituary appeared in either of the official publications of the College Art Association, though less important persons receive glowing tributes. In *Die Meistersänger von Nürnberg,* Richard Wagner created the figure of Beckmesser, the critic motivated by envy and hate. Unhappily, Beckmesserism thrives in many sectors of the American academe. Newspapers and periodicals remark repeatedly on the unethical behavior of critics in the arts, especially in book reviews. Often they fail to appraise the work, using the space to score points at the writer's expense and to prove that they could have done a better job. Scholars in Europe and Latin America complain of the ruthless treatment of their work, against which they have no recourse.

Art on the American campus has nearly always been a touchy subject. The administrations tend to leave it to "the experts." They are glad to accept money for a new football field, an ice skating rink, or a gymnasium. When, however, an alumnus or donor perpetuates his name with millions of dollars for a gallery to house his private collection of material from Europe with which our museums are already loaded, research in art history on the campus is in danger of being more influenced by the art dealer and by snobbery rather than by a desire to enlarge the horizon of the students.

In France, a teacher is a Frenchman, saturated with the *gloire* of his country, familiar with its geography, history, and literature, and he will do his best to emphasize to his students his country's great contribution to culture. The same applies to other European lands and to Latin America. It is only in the United States that we now have teachers by the hundreds coming from an alien background, who lead our students in their most impressionable years. That the Spaniard is unwilling to admit the originality of colonial art here is humanly understandable. That others, who are often parvenus in the americanistic field, but who have not the sentimental thread and could be objective, should base their criticism on such details as the lack of new spatial relations in architecture, is difficult to explain. Sculpture and painting, furniture, textiles, ceramics, even gardens, musical instruments, work in silver and gold, belong to the panorama of the Hispanic-American art world. Collections of all these objects are gathering today, both in Latin America and in the United States. Yet some of the "experts," instead of trying to clarify, denigrate the originality and importance of the subject.* Second-rate art

* Pál Kelemen, "Pre-Columbian Art and Art History," *American Antiquity,* Vol. 11, January, 1946.

that mimics the European is much more highly valued than the bold and authentic American original.

Pedantry has gone so far as to rule out folk art as unworthy of investigation. Folk art is, however, a direct expression of a people whether Mexican or Peruvian or coming from nations of such great folkloristic tradition as Poland, Hungary, Serbia, Spain, and the Scandinavian lands—all *terra incognita* to most art historians in the United States. One is reminded of Aldous Huxley's remark that the difference between the fine arts and folk art is largely snobbery.

One European critic has pointed out that art history is no longer an ivory tower, but a straitjacket in which methodology, footnotes, and quotations from other books are more important than original contributions. A recent Ph.D. candidate was "defrocked" when it was discovered that his dissertation cited over a hundred nonexistent sources.* But the emphasis on such matters had misled him into committing this act. Here the book review should be mentioned which recommended using primary sources only and condoned borrowing them from Latin American and European publications without acknowledgment. Bibliography and footnotes have become a basic ploy of thesis writing. The style has degenerated into a jargon. To read the pretentious pseudoscientific manner in which the art historian all too often expresses himself is like trying to swim through wet sand. Small wonder that color plates are preferred to text.

It must not be forgotten that the first and second generation of American art historians who laid down the base for the epigones, were historians, linguists, litterateurs, classicists, philosophers. The withholding of the achievements of one nation from another's—a process in which the Germans have become masters— caused Béla Bartók to exclaim: "They try to obscure the West for the East and the East for the West." The Pole Josef von Strzygowski, a pioneer in realizing the great importance of the early Christian iconography of Armenia, Syria, Abyssinia, was ridiculed by the Germans. However, the message of his book *Orient or Rome?* (1901) becomes more vindicated from year to year. He was among the first to point out that the art of the migration period and that of the Scandinavian countries would furnish a key to many problems.

Certain Europeans are unable to recognize that the Americas have produced anything original. The umbilical cord holds them so strongly to their university tradition, little changed since 1914. When this writer spoke of pre-Columbian art with German refugees, scarcely five minutes passed before Goethe was quoted, though Goethe admired the classics exclusively and, in his time, nearly nothing was known of ancient America. However, the German had to assert his authority by quoting a name that was for him supreme.

The art of the Americas, as already seen, was deprecated. Just as World War II broke out and it was in the interest of this country to implement the Good Neighbor policy, the *Art Bulletin* solicited an article on pre-Columbian metallurgy,

* John H. Mitchell, *Writing for Professional and Technical Journals*. New York: John Wiley and Sons, 1968.

which was approved by the late George Vaillant, a leading archaeologist. But the article never appeared.

The Austrian sinologist, who knew nothing about ancient American art, suddenly "discovered" trans-Pacific influences. This writer visited him repeatedly in the New York Museum of Natural History, surrounded by books open to old sketches and out-of-date illustrations, together with Chinese works. In his little room, he spun his theory by which he confused not only himself but some Americans impressed by his title and academic rank. In vain did I invite him to go to the objects themselves and compare directly a Chinese libation vessel with a Southern Maya marble vase from the Ulua Valley. Good-naturedly, he asserted that he did not need such a comparison; he had it all on the pages of his books. In vain did I write a letter of recommendation to Alfred M. Tozzer at Harvard, a leader in American archaeology, so that my Viennese friend could talk with one who had spent a lifetime in research and field work.

Similarly, the conclusions of Alfonso Caso, dean of Mexican archaeology, and of generations of solid field work, now supported by carbon-14 tests, were attacked by a shipwrecked German ethnologist in a display of mythological mishmash. Fantastic theories have been promulgated—China, India, Japan, the Near East, and Africa were brought in to cloud the picture.

Unfortunately, Latin America as a world, offering a picturesque and varied landscape, both physically and culturally, was seldom treated in a dignified way by United States newspapers and periodicals. An earthquake, the assassination of a president, are "news." The more sensational a theory about the fantastic origin of the autochthonous civilization, the better its chance of publication. Articles on folklore, music, art, or other subjects of the humanities, when they appear, are usually incidental.

Now that England and France have lost their empires, they have begun to show more interest in Latin America. In the last few years we have seen not only an increase in business news from that part of the world but color articles on the arts. Some critics in Europe affirm with enthusiasm the originality of this art.* It is ironical that such material as is sampled in this book may become generally accepted in the United States because it is receiving the stamp of approval from abroad.

Actually, the art of ancient America has long fascinated connoisseurs, artists, and photographers and such outstanding Americans as Frank Lloyd Wright and Bernard Berenson. Now, with the growing number of museums interested in the material, it is becoming fashionable. That it was not always overlooked is evident in a decree of the trustees of the Metropolitan Museum of Art in New York, dated 1882, to the effect that "with all deliberate speed a department of Ancient American Art should be established."

The immigrant art historians are slowly disappearing from the campus. But their pupils who, because of the teacher's limited background, have specialized

* Paul Guinard, "La Tradition Précolumbienne dans l'Art Colonial Mexicain," *Journal de la Société des Américanistes,* Paris, 1965.

in one small aspect of a limited subject will seldom have the imagination and courage to leave that narrow field in which at least they can speak with authority. Where is the forum where the college student may get acquainted with the arts of Japan, China, Korea, Cambodia, India, Ceylon, Persia, Turkey, and the Arabian countries—even of Egypt, Ethiopia, and the original African cultures, to say nothing of the Latin American ancient and colonial arts—and make his own choice, not his teacher's, in which subject to continue?

In the 1930's, my interest was drawn toward the Philippines, as a part of the idea of comparing this large area of Hispanic colonial art to that of the Americas. When I turned in desperation from commercial archives to the Hispanic Foundation of the Library of Congress, Washington, I found photographs of narrow-gauge railroads, sugar plantations, harbor installations, even of the American Club in Manila—but no colonial buildings, whether mansions, palaces, chapels, or churches. Now, with the ghastly ruins of World War II, only fragments remain; and even these were not available to an ambitious Spanish scholar who took up the subject and had to illustrate her volume from a small number of postal cards and eighteenth-century drawings.*

To the graduate student, a thesis on an unknown painter from the hills of Tuscany, or a side portal in a French cathedral where nearly every head had been chopped off, was more important than to gain knowledge and spread appreciation of a little-known field of art. Of course, the word "appreciation" is taboo to many art historians. They regard it as amateurish, and fail to recognize that they themselves are less than amateurs in vast areas of universal art history. Periodicals do appear devoted to the arts of Asia, but only in Europe. One, concerned with antique glass, is produced in America, but among the fifteen or so contributors in one or another number, not two are American—because there has been no stimulus to enter these fields. There is not one American publication in which general informative articles appear concerning what is going on in the world of art.

We have 320 classes in the Gothic, Renaissance, and related subjects in graduate courses on the American campus—and 12 courses on the art of the Americas, divided among the ancient, colonial, modern, and folk art. Among the very few institutions where the art of the Americas is taught on the graduate level is Yale University. In the recently published *Yale Course Critique* based on the results of a questionnaire circulated among students, we read:

> History of Art No._____is good only for those people specifically interested in Latin America . . . since many of the paintings and buildings covered require a special love if their eccentricities are to be appreciated.**

The professor, it appears, uses his own writings almost exclusively. It is difficult to comprehend how two great epochs of art, reaching over more than two thousand years, can become mere "eccentricities" in a classroom.

* Maria Lourdes Diaz-Trechuelo Spinola, *Arquitectura Española en Filipinas* (*1565–1800*). Seville: Universidad de Sevilla, 1959.
** *Yale Course Critique,* New Haven, 1967.

Paintings, statues, buildings, offer themselves first of all as a visual and emotional experience. If the aesthetic impact is neglected, and analysis and comparisons are preferred, art historians will never really make contact with American life.

The College Art Association, with more than 4,500 professional art historians active in our colleges and universities, issues a placement-bureau listing, where recently 365 persons offered their services. Only two mention an ability to teach the art of the Americas. This illuminates, better than anything else, the situation today. While in anthropology, in Latin American history, languages, and in general Hispanic studies nearly a thousand courses are offered, the art of Hispanic America and of ancient America cannot be taught because no trained teaching staff is available.

The same association, also, recently published a list of doctoral dissertations completed from 1960 to June 1968 and including those in preparation, to a total of 592.* Of this number, 41 are devoted to the arts of Asia, Africa, and the Near East. Seven are concerned with the arts of the Americas, covering only subjects of North America; none deal with Central or South America, either ancient or Hispanic. Yale University, for more than a quarter of a century an arbiter in matters pertaining to the art of the Americas, reports only two papers, one of which partly relates to Spanish art. Both dissertations, incidentally written by women, are concerned with colonial Mexico. There is none about ancient America nor the great achievements of two thousand years in the ancient and Hispanic arts of Central and South America. From the two previous decades, the harvest is similarly poor.

Thus, 544 papers treat the arts of the Gothic and Renaissance and related subjects of Western Europe, and, on reading the titles, one is aghast at the fabricated, tortured, and abstracted subjects. Here moves a broad sluggish stream of dull gray pedantry, based mostly on bookwork in libraries. "This is not the history of art but the autopsy of art."** Little training of visual talent is evinced or consciousness that the art discussed is still alive, even though ancient. Essential are lively teachers and museum curators who can prepare a generation for the realization that the United States has global responsibilities in its educational program, since it has taken on political, economic, and military ones.

Nobody who has been active in the history of art since 1911, as this writer has been, would protest against specialization in any field rich in material. We must take into consideration the fact, however, that the composition of this nation's population has changed in less than a hundred years. Today we have a growing number that go back not only to Central, South, and Eastern Europe, to Ireland, but also to the Near East, Asia and Africa, and include the Portuguese- and Spanish-speaking peoples both of the Old and the New World. Count in also our Negroes and our Indians. Some of the minorities are proud that their civilization is much earlier than that of Western Europe. We have a cultural diversity on the campus

---

* "Doctoral Dissertations," *Art Journal,* Summer 1968, XXVII/4.

** This author's words quoted verbatim by Colin Eisler, *"Kunstgeschichte* American Style," in *The Intellectual Migration, Europe and America, 1930–1960,* D. Fleming and B. Bailyn, eds. Cambridge: Harvard University Press, 1969.

that could be used to broaden the horizon and enlighten the lives of the entire population.

It will probably not be the Ivy League colleges of the Eastern Seaboard that put the art of the Americas into a firm position in the American educational program. It will rather be the accomplishment of institutions in such states as Florida, Louisiana, Texas, New Mexico, Colorado, Arizona, California, where the ancient and Hispanic past still echoes—and there are encouraging signs that they are beginning to recognize this.

Foreign visitors are amazed by the perception and the enthusiasm which many Americans are showing for the arts. We obviously underestimate our potentialities. We have allowed ourselves to be inhibited by those who regard themselves as superior—we suffer from xenophilia and sycophantism. We have too much snobbery in our attitude toward "culture" and art, and very little conviction about what we can show. We have been insensitive to the various periods of art in the Americas in relation to what the other parts of the world have produced. The task today is to convince the great American public that the art of the Americas has much to give —to us and to the entire world.

Acknowledgements

Since 1932, I have made ten intensive research and survey trips to Hispanic America. The present work is drawn from the accumulated experience of those nearly four decades. Throughout this time, I profited by the friendship of a number of outstanding scholars, and the list of my acknowledgments should begin with those already departed: Manuel Toussaint and Manuel Romero de Terreros, Mexico; Julio Tello, Peru; Paul Dony, Argentina; and in the United States, Ralph Linton, Martin S. Soria, and René d'Harnoncourt.

In Mexico, the number of friends is gratifyingly large: Alfonso Caso, Ignacio Bernal, Justino Fernandéz, Francisco de la Maza, Javier Moyssén, Pedro Rojas, Henry Berlin in the capital; Javier M. Castro, Oaxaca; John Paddock, Mitla. Elsewhere abroad: Mario J. Buschiazzo, Buenos Aires; José de Mesa and Teresa Gisbert, La Paz; Luis A. Pardo and staff, Cuzco; Francisco Stastny, Lima; Nicolás Delgado, Quito; Luis Luján Muñoz and staff, Guatemala City; J. Eric S. Thompson, Saffron Walden; Karl Fischer, Zurich; Rudolf Bedö, Budapest.

I am indebted to Jacob Canter, Acting Assistant Secretary of State for Educational and Cultural Affairs, in Washington, and to his staff in Madrid and in Lima; also to Richard B. and Nathalie F. S. Woodbury, George Metcalf, Alan R. Sawyer, Washington; Robert Wauchope, New Orleans; Bertha P. Dutton and E. Boyd, Santa Fe; George Eckhart, Bernard L. Fontana, and Kieran McCarthy, O.F.M., Tucson; Leslie Byrd Simpson, John Barr Tompkins, Berkeley; Robert L. Shalkop, Colorado Springs; Richard E. W. Adams, Minneapolis; Stephen F. Borhegyi, Milwaukee; Beatrice Gilman Proske, Junius B. Bird, Frederick J. Dockstader, Raymond and Anne Ophelia Dowden, New York; J. O. Brew, Cambridge, Massachusetts.

In making the prints for the illustrations of this book, Weiman & Lester Photoservices, New York, have performed excellent work beyond the call of duty, and Marilyn A. Ross, Winter Park, Florida, has not only typed the manuscript, but with her high sense of responsibility, was of great help in various exigencies. Through the generosity of my publisher, ample time was allowed Judith Woracek Barry for the styling of the book and for personal consultation in the arrangement of the illustrations—a task that she performed with talent and efficiency.

For reading chapters on the ancient American epoch, thanks are due to

Acknowledgments

Donald E. Thompson, University of Wisconsin; Dudley E. Easby, Jr. and Elizabeth Easby, Metropolitan Museum of Art; Nora Fisher, Textile Museum, Washington; Richard E. Ahlborn, Smithsonian Institution, not only read the chapter on the Philippines, but also furnished most of the photographs—a number previously unpublished—and invaluable information based on his two surveys of the archipelago. Irving A. Leonard, the distinguished professor emeritus of the University of Michigan, has provided many pointed observations on the Philippine locale—the results of personal experience—and with his fine feeling for writing style, has improved many a paragraph.

My wife, Elisabeth, has been equally unprotesting, whether the night had to be spent in an Indian hut in the Andean highlands of South America or in a touring jeep in a wintry canyon in Mexico. She accompanied me on all my trips and took countless photographs, otherwise unobtainable. Her literary sense has clarified the entire manuscript, and her contribution to this work could be expressed only if she would appear as co-author. As a team, we have proven that, even when partners were born more than five thousand miles apart, the garden of their effort can bring forth rare, rich, and rewarding flowers.

List of Illustrations

The pottery serpent head on the cover, from Conacatepeque, El Salvador, is reproduced by courtesy of the Oscar Meyer Collection, Los Angeles, and appears also in black and white in the illustration 3.29. The List of Illustrations contains credits and some data not included in the text or captions. When the photograph has been furnished by the owner of an object, the name is mentioned only once.

The following abbreviations have been used:

CI   Carnegie Institution of Washington
DO   Dumbarton Oaks, Washington, D.C. (Robert Woods Bliss Collection)
EZK   Elisabeth Z. Kelemen
INAH Instituto Nacional de Antropología e Historia, Mexico
K-E   Kelemen-Eagle Archive
MAI   Museum of American Indian, Heye Foundation, New York
MAM Museo de Antropología, Mexico
TM   The Textile Museum, Washington, D.C.

381

389

Unless otherwise noted, all the photographs below were furnished through the courtesy of Richard E. Ahlborn.

Index